The Undying Flame

The Undying Flame

Olympians Who Perished in the Second World War

Nigel McCrery

Pen & Sword
MILITARY

First published in Great Britain in 2021 by
Pen & Sword Military
An imprint of
Pen & Sword Books Ltd
Yorkshire – Philadelphia

Copyright © Nigel McCrery 2021

ISBN 978 1 52674 062 5

Printed and bound in the UK by CPI Group (UK) Ltd,
Croydon, CR0 4YY.

Pen & Sword Books Limited incorporates the imprints of Atlas, Archaeology,
Aviation, Discovery, Family History, Fiction, History, Maritime, Military,
Military Classics, Politics, Select, Transport, True Crime, Air World,
Frontline Publishing, Leo Cooper, Remember When, Seaforth Publishing,
The Praetorian Press, Wharncliffe Local History, Wharncliffe Transport,
Wharncliffe True Crime and White Owl.

For a complete list of Pen & Sword titles please contact

PEN & SWORD BOOKS LIMITED
47 Church Street, Barnsley, South Yorkshire, S70 2AS, England
E-mail: enquiries@pen-and-sword.co.uk
Website: www.pen-and-sword.co.uk

Or

PEN AND SWORD BOOKS
1950 Lawrence Rd, Havertown, PA 19083, USA
E-mail: Uspen-and-sword@casematepublishers.com
Website: www.penandswordbooks.com

For my beautiful and wonderful granddaughter

Harriet Winifred Sharpe

Born 1 July 2021

Golden slumbers kiss your eyes,
Smiles awake you when you rise.

Contents

Contents

Contents

Acknowledgements

A big thank you to all my family and friends who helped me with this book and finding the photographs for it. In particular to Abigail Cobley for all her help and encouragement. I hope you enjoy it. At Pen & Sword, my thanks go to Charles Hewitt, Barnaby Blacker, Jon Wilkinson, Mat Blurton and Matt Jones – without their professional input and enthusiasm this book would not exist.

The book is a memorial to those who reached peaks of athletic and artistic perfection only to have their lives cut short, often with their families, usually in horrific circumstances. Let they and their achievements be remembered forever.

Introduction

This book contains short biographies of all those who took part in the Olympic Games before the Second World War, whether they won a medal or not. I hope it contributes to honouring these fallen Olympians forever and reminds us of the futility of war.

May their memories always be a blessing

The Holocaust

Olympians who perished in the Holocaust

In memory of
LILLI HENOCH (1899–1942)

Also in memory of all those Jewish athletes who never took part in the Olympic Games because of the Nazis' race laws.

I have included Lilli Henoch here, although she never took part in an Olympic Games. An outstanding all-round athlete, she took ten German national championships in four different disciplines and set four world records, the discus (twice), shot put and 4 × 100 metres relay. Being Jewish she was banned by Hitler from taking part in the 1936 Olympic Games despite being one of Germany's finest athletes. Henoch, together with her mother, was deported from Berlin to the ghetto in Riga. They were removed from there in September 1944 and shot by a Nazi murder squad, their bodies thrown into a mass grave. She was inducted into the International Jewish Sports Hall of Fame in 1990.

Isakas Anolikas (1903–43)
Lithuanian
Cycling
1924 Paris
1928 Amsterdam

Isakas Anolikas was born in 1943 in Siauliai into a Jewish family. A fine cyclist, he joined the Jewish sports club Makabi Siauliai in 1921. His talent quickly came to notice and he was selected to represent Lithuania at the 1924 Paris Olympics, competing in the road race. His cycle malfunctioned and he was unable to complete the course.

He was selected again in 1928 to take part in the Olympics, this time in Amsterdam. Again he took part in the 188 kilometre road race, and once again his cycle malfunctioned and he was unable to finish the course.

In 1925 he became Lithuanian champion in the 10 kilometre race, and in 1926 he won the gold in the team 70 kilometre race. In 1943 he was arrested by the Nazis and imprisoned in the Ninth Fort in Kaunas, where, like many other Jews there, he was shot.

József Barna (Braun) (1901–43)
Hungarian
Football
1924 Paris

József Barna, also known as Braun, was born into a Jewish family on 26 February 1901 in Budapest. He played football in his youth for VAC Budapest. He impressed to such an extent that in 1916 he signed for the Hungarian League side MTK Budapest, where he played mainly as a right back. In 1919 he became Hungarian Player of the Year. Braun won nine Hungarian championships and two Hungarian cups with the club. He retired from Hungarian football in 1925 having suffered numerous injuries during his playing career. Making a comeback, he was offered a contract with the USA soccer team Brooklyn Hakoah. He made seventeen appearances for them before joining Brooklyn Wanderers in 1929. He played a further eleven matches before retiring for the last time in 1930. Turning his talents to coaching, he trained SK Slovan Bratislava for several years.

In a distinguished international career, he won twenty-seven caps and scored eleven goals. Two of the caps were awarded when he played for Hungary at the 1924 Paris Olympics. The team came ninth.

Captured by the Nazis, he was transported to a forced labour camp in Korotych, Kharkiv, Ukraine, where he died in February 1943. I have not been able to discover how he died.

Lorenzo Vitria Barrera (1908–41)
Spanish
Boxing
Paris 1924

Llorenç Vitrià Barrera was born into a Jewish family on 2 February 1908 in Barcelona. A fine boxer, fighting flyweight he competed for the boxing club CAC Barcelona. Coming to notice, he was selected to box for Spain at the 1924 Paris Olympics. Although he fought well he was eliminated in the second round, losing to the Canadian boxer Jock MacGregor. After the Olympics, Vitria turned professional. In 1932 he fought for the bantamweight title of Spain, losing to Carlos Flix.

He ran a shop in Barcelona for many years. During the Spanish Civil War he sided with the Republicans, so when the Nationalists occupied the city in January 1939 he fled the country. He managed to reach a refugee camp in France. He remained there until the Nazis invaded in 1940. As a known Republican he was arrested and deported to the Mauthausen-Gusen concentration camp in Austria. On 18 June 1941 he committed suicide at the camp by throwing himself against the electric fence that surrounded it.

Thierry de Briey (1895–1945)
Belgian
Equestrianism
1920 Antwerp

Thierry Marie Ferdinand Ghislain Comte de Briey, Baron de Landres, was born on 29 December 1895 in Brussels into a noble family, his father being at one time governor of the province of Luxembourg. A fine horseman, Briey was selected to compete in the 1920 Olympics in Antwerp. He took part in the men's individual jumping on his horse *Perfect Gentleman* coming twenty-first.

In 1921 he married Simone Burnell (1900–81) and the relationship produced three children, all girls. Briey served with the reserve of officers in the Regiment des Guides and was awarded the Order of Leopold, the Order of the Crown, and later the Croix de Guerre.

During the German occupation of Belgium, Briey joined the Belgian Resistance becoming a member of the *Armée Belge Reconstituée* (later known as the Secret Army). In July 1941 it merged with the Belgian Legion, which became the largest Resistance movement in Belgium.

In February 1944, on learning that his father was seriously ill, he travelled to Brussels despite knowing how dangerous this was. While there he was arrested. No one seems sure if he was betrayed or was just unlucky. The police might have made an educated guess that he would come to see his ailing father. After spending some time in prison under interrogation, he was shipped from Antwerp to Buchenwald concentration camp on 8 May 1944, together with around 850 other Belgians. From Buchenwald he was moved to Camp Harzungen, an extension of Buchenwald. Due mainly to overcrowding, Harzungen was evacuated by the SS on 4 April 1945 and approximately 4,500 prisoners were force-marched to Bergen-Belsen, many dying along the way. Thierry de Briey survived the march but died at Bergen-Belsen on the 11 April 1945, a month before the war ended.

Józef Broel-Plater (1890–1941)
Polish
Bobsleigh
1928 St Moritz

Józef Jan Andrzej Joachim Broel-Plater was born on 15 November 1890 in Lithuania. He came from a distinguished and ancient Lithuanian family. He was educated in Krakow, graduating from the gymnasium of St Anna. Between 1909 and 1911 he read philosophy at the University of Fribourg. During the First World War he served as a lieutenant with the French army, being awarded the Croix de Guerre. A fine all-round athlete he excelled at fencing, motoring, skiing and shooting. Specialising in winter sports, he become part of the Polish five-man bobsleigh team at the 1928 winter Olympics in St Moritz. They were unfortunately involved in an accident and finally finished seventeenth.

In the Second World War he served in the Polish Blue Army as part of the French army. A gifted linguist, he became an interpreter for the High Command. When Poland was overrun by the German army he was arrested by the Gestapo. Being Jewish he was deported to Dachau where he was murdered on 30 June 1941.

Józef Broel-Plater is believed to be seen here at the front of the bobsleigh.

Josef Charous (1894–1943)
Czechoslovakian
Equestrianism
Paris 1924
Amsterdam 1928

Josef Charous was born on 15 June 1894 in Polepy, Kraj, Czechoslovakia. He was of Jewish descent.

He took part in the equestrian events at two Olympics: Paris in 1924 and Amsterdam in 1928. In Paris he competed in the three-day individual event, coming thirty-second, and the men's three-day team event, in which he failed to win a medal. He was selected again for the Olympics, this time in 1928 in Amsterdam. Again he competed in the men's three-day individual event, improving his position from 1924 and coming sixteenth. He also competed in the three-day team event, again failing to win a medal.

In the war he became involved with the Hague Communist Resistance, distributing the Resistance paper *De Vonk*. Unfortunately, as a result of an intelligence operation ordered by the then Mayor de Monchy, Charous and his group was infiltrated and Charous was arrested on 4 August 1941 by the intelligence officer Johannes Hubertus van Soolingen. He was later imprisoned in Buchenwald before being transferred to Dachau in September 1944. Later he was moved to Mauthausen where he was worked to death, finally dying on 23 February 1945.

Cornelis Compter (1894–1945)
Dutch
Weightlifting
1928 Amsterdam

Cornelis Hendrik Compter was born on 16 July 1894 in The Hague. He was of Jewish descent. He became a plumber by profession, although some records say he was a truck driver (maybe both at different times). A featherweight weightlifter he was selected to take part in the 1928 Amsterdam Olympics. His best lift was 237.50 kilograms, which gave him nineteenth place.

In the Second World War he joined the Communist Resistance in the Hague. He was heavily involved in distributing the Communist Resistance sheet *De Vonk* from October 1940. Betrayed by Johannes Hubertus van Soolingen, who had infiltrated his group, Compter was arrested by the infamous Johannes Hubertus Veefkind of the Hague Police Intelligence Service on 4 August 1941. He was first imprisoned in the Oranjehotel, the Scheveningen prison. The Germans imprisoned over 25,000 people here for interrogation (including torture) and prosecution.

From there he was transferred to Camp Amersfoort and then to Buchenwald. In 1944 he was transferred to the Nacht und Nebelkamp Natzweiler, before being sent in September to Dachau and then Mauthausen. He died in Mauthausen's subcamp of Gusen on 23 February 1945 from exhaustion.

Bronisław 'Bronek' Czech (1908–44)
Polish
Skiing
1928 St Moritz
1932 Lake Placid
1936 Garmisch-Partenkirchen

Bronisław Czech was born on 25 July 1908 in Zakopane, in Austro-Hungarian Galicia. He was initially educated at the School of Timber Industry in his hometown and was meant to be a carpenter. However, his passion was sports and he was later educated at a private gymnasium. He moved to Warsaw to attend the Central Institute of Physical Education. On graduation he became a gymnastics instructor and ski instructor. In 1932 he moved to Kasprowy Wierch to work as a ski instructor and established his own ski school. He also became a pioneer of mountain rescue in the Tatra mountains. In 1934 he wrote *Skiing and Ski Jumping Style*. He also ran a sporting supply shop in Zakopane, riding everywhere on his beloved motorbike. As well as his sporting prowess, he was a talented artist, played several musical instruments, wrote poetry to a high standard, and could pilot a glider.

A talented skier, he became Polish champion in various disciplines on no less than twenty-four occasions. He was selected to represent Poland at the winter Olympics on three occasions. He appeared first aged 19 in 1928 at St Moritz. He competed in the men's normal hill, individual ski jump, coming thirty-seventh, and the men's individual combined Nordic, coming tenth. Four years later he was selected again, for the Games at Lake Placid. This time he came twelfth in the ski jumping, eighteenth in the 18 kilometre cross-country skiing, and seventh in the individual Nordic combined. His final appearance was at Garmisch-Partenkirchen in 1936. He came thirty-third in the ski jump, thirty-third in the 18 kilometre cross-country, sixteenth in the individual Nordic combined, twentieth in the combined Alpine, and seventh in the 4 × 10 kilometre relay.

Czech served with the Polish home underground army in the war, working as a courier between Poland and the Allies. He was arrested by the Gestapo in 1940 and deported to Auschwitz, being one of the first people to be sent there. While there he painted landscapes of the Tatras from memory. He died on 4 June 1944 at the camp.

His sister was informed of his death by the sculptor Xawery Dunikowski (1875–1964) in a letter:

I regret to inform you that your brother, Mr. Bronisław Czech, is dead. I knew him very well. I feel very sorry for him because he was a young, very nice man. We were in the hospital together. He died suddenly while with me from a stroke, without pain. It happened on June 5 at 12 noon. The moment of his death was touching. We sat in the window, a beautiful sunny day, in front of our barrack at the camp square. Gypsies played various happy music pieces. Having heard from us about the sudden death of Mr. Bronisław, they stopped playing. In a moment they played Chopin's funeral march.

Several of his paintings are preserved in the Auschwitz museum.

Alfred Flatow (1869–1942)
German
Gymnastics
1896 Greece (the first modern Olympics)
(three Golds, one Silver)

Alfred Flatow was born on 3 October 1869 in Gdansk, Poland, to Jewish parents. He began his athletics career in 1888, concentrating on gymnastics and weightlifting. His first major international competition was at an Italian gymnastics festival in 1895. He was selected together with his cousin Gustav to compete for Germany in the 1896 Olympics in Greece. There he won gold in the parallel bars and silver in the horizontal bars. He was also a member of the German team that took the gold medal in both the parallel bars and horizontal bar.

In 1903 Flatow, as a gym instructor, helped found *Judische Turnerschaft*, the pioneering Jewish sports organization, and became prominent within it. In 1933 he was forced out of his gymnastics club membership because he was Jewish. Nevertheless, and surprisingly, he was still honoured at the 1936 Olympics. In 1938 due to Nazi persecution Flatow fled Germany and settled in the Netherlands. In May 1940, however, after Germany invaded the Netherlands, Flatow was arrested, and on 3 October 1942 was deported to the Theresienstadt ghetto. Many appeals for his release were made by prominent German sportsmen and officials but to no avail. Flatow died of starvation in the ghetto on 28 December 1942 aged 73. Like thousands of others, his body was never recovered.

Since 1997 the German Gymnastics Federation have awarded the 'Flatow Medal' in memory of both cousins. It is awarded for 'excellent all-round performance'. The following year the German Post Office issued a stamp in their memory, and there is also the Flatow-Sporthalle at Berlin-Kreuzberg, on the side of which is a commemorative plaque remembering them.

Gustav Flatow (1875–1945)
German
Gymnastics
1896 Greece
1900 Paris (two Gold)

Gustav Felix Flatow, cousin of Alfred (above), was born on 7 January 1875 in Berent, West Prussia. He moved to Berlin in 1892. A fine gymnast, he was selected to compete for Germany in the 1896 Olympics in Greece. He took part in the individual parallel bars, horizontal bar, vault, pommelled horse and rings, but failed to win a medal. However, competing with his cousin in the team events, he took two gold medals on the parallel bars and horizontal bar (to be fair the horizontal bar was unchallenged). A keen cyclist, he also served as a pacemaker in some of the track cycling events at the same Olympics.

He competed at gymnastics for Germany at the 1900 Paris Olympics. This time he failed to win a medal in any event. It was to be his last Olympics, and he retired from gymnastics to run a textile company. In 1933, as a Jew he was forced to flee Germany and Nazi persecution, finally settling in the Netherlands. However, after the fall of the Netherlands he was arrested and transported to the Theresienstadt ghetto/concentration camp. A year after arriving at the camp, on 29 January 1945 Gustav succumbed to its privations and starved to death. He was 70 years old.

Interestingly, Gustav's memorial urn was discovered by journalists in 1986 and entombed in Terezín.

János Garay (1889–1945)
Hungarian
Fencing
1924 Paris (Silver and Bronze)
1928 Amsterdam (Gold)

János Garay was born on 23 February 1889 in Budapest to Jewish parents. He fought as an officer with the cavalry in the First World War and was decorated for his bravery. An expert with the sabre, he was considered one of the finest fencers in the world in the 1920s. He became national Hungarian sabre champion in 1923, going on to become European individual sabre champion in both 1925 and 1930. He was also part of the team that won the European gold medal in 1930.

At the 1924 Paris Olympics he took the silver medal in the team sabre and the bronze medal in the individual sabre. At the 1928 Amsterdam Olympics he won a gold medal with the Hungarian sabre team.

Garay married and had two children, Juan and Maria. Juan went on to swim for Argentina at the 1948 London Olympics. János was also father-in-law of the famous photographer Áron Gyenge, who won gold in the 400 metres swimming at the 1952 Helsinki Olympic Games.

As a prominent Hungarian Jew, he was arrested by the Nazis in 1944 after their invasion of Hungary and deported, together with 437,000 other Jewish residents, to various concentration camps. He was imprisoned in Mauthausen where he died on 3 May 1945 aged 56.

Garay was inducted into the International Jewish Sports Hall of Fame in 1990.

Oszkár Gerde (1883–1944)
Hungarian
Fencing
London 1908 (Gold)
Stockholm 1912 (Gold)

Oszkár Gerde was born on 8 July 1883 in Budapest into a Jewish family. A medical doctor, his passion was fencing, in particular the sabre. He competed for MAC, Budapest. Considered one of the finest fencers in Europe, he was selected to compete for Budapest at the 1908 London Olympics. Although he failed to win a medal in the individual event, he took the gold medal in the team event. He was selected once again to compete for Hungary at the 1912 Stockholm Olympics. Again he won a team gold. After these Olympics he retired from active participation and concentrated instead on judging international fencing events.

He was arrested by the Nazis in 1944 and shipped to the concentration camp at Mauthausen-Gusen in Austria. He was murdered there on 8 October 1944 at the age of 61. In 1989 he was inducted into the International Jewish Sports Hall of Fame.

Isidore Goudeket (1883–1943)
Dutch
Gymnastics
London 1908

Isidore Goudeket was born on 1 August 1883 in Amsterdam into a Jewish family, diamond cutters by trade. A fine athlete, his passion was gymnastics, in which he competed both at home and abroad from the age of 17. Shortly after his bar mitzvah, Isidore was admitted to the Amsterdam gymnastics club Spartacus. The dozens of Jews who performed their exercises here were known as 'Muskeljuden'. Isidore was selected to represent the Netherlands in gymnastics at the 1908 London Olympics. He took part in the men's individual all-around, in which he scored 159 points and came 62nd. He also competed in the men's all-around team, coming 7th with 297 points.

Isidore married Esther Weening and they had two children, Elise born in 1908 and Simon in 1910. Both grew up to be fine athletes. In 1929 the family moved to Antwerp.

When the Nazis invaded, Simon was tragically arrested in Belgium and deported to Auschwitz where he disappeared on 3 November 1942. Because Isidore worked in the diamond industry, he was exempt from deportation for a time. This exception didn't last long however, and both Isidore and Esther were arrested in their home. From there they were sent to the transit camp at Westerbork. Two weeks later they were transported to the death camp at Sobibor, arriving on 9 July 1943. They were murdered on the day they arrived. Elise, however, survived the war.

Jur Haak (1890–1945)
Dutch
Football
1908 London

Jur Haak was born on 3 November 1890 in Java, moving with his family to Haarlem in the Netherlands in 1904. Becoming a talented footballer, he played (as did his brothers Jan and Albert) for HFC Haarlem, making his first appearance on 17 November 1912.

He was selected as reserve for the national team at the 1908 London Olympics but did not play. The Netherlands did not win a medal.

Jur did play in two international matches: against Germany in Leipzig (international friendly) on 17 November 1912. They won 3–2 and Jur scored one of the goals in the 54th minute in front of 20,000 spectators; and against Belgium on 9 March 1913 in another international friendly, at the Olympisch Stadium, Antwerp, in front of 12,000 spectators. This time they drew 3–3, Jur scoring in the 44th minute.

As well as a fine footballer, Jur was an outstanding athlete. In September 1916 he broke the Dutch high jump record by 10 cm, moving it up from 1.69 to 1.79 metres.

After his sporting career, Jur taught mathematics and physics in the Dutch East Indies and then in Amsterdam's Lyceum.

In the war he joined the Dutch Resistance. He was arrested (almost certainly betrayed) together with his wife, Jet van Eek, after a raid on their home revealed forged documents. He was first transported to Herzogenbusch concentration camp. From there he was sent to Sachsenhausen, where he was either murdered or died of dysentery on 30 January 1945.

Gyozo Halmos (1889–1945)
Hungarian
Gymnastics
1912 Stockholm (Silver)

Győző Halmos was born Győző Háberfeld on 13 June 1889 in Budapest. A fine gymnast, he competed for the Budapest club Ferencvárosi TC under the name of Haberfeld, later changing his name to Halmos. He quickly came to notice and was selected for the 1912 Stockholm Olympics. Taking part in the all-around team (this event featured on the Olympic programme for the first time in 1912 and would appear only once more, in 1920 at Antwerp), the Hungarian team did well, winning the silver medal. Italy took the gold and Great Britain the bronze. Halmos later opened a photo studio in Újpest, changing his name once again, this time to Békési. He was arrested together with his entire family in 1945 (exact date not known). They were all deported to KZ Mauthausen where they were murdered.

Dr Karel 'Maca' Hartmann (1885–1944)
Czechoslovak
Ice hockey
1920 Antwerp (Bronze)

Karel Hartmann was born into a rich Jewish family on 6 July 1885 in the Bohemian town of Pabram, the son of Maximillian and Emma. The family later moved to Prague. He grew up to become an attorney and later worked as a sports journalist. Although born a Jew, he never practised the religion, becoming a catholic, and, having a fine voice, singing in the church choir. A fine skater, he began playing ice hockey, playing rover (the position is now defunct) for Česká Sportovní in Bohemia.

He was selected to play ice hockey for Czechoslovakia at the 1920 Antwerp Olympics and was part of the team that took the bronze medal beating Sweden 1–0 (the USA took the silver having beaten Czechoslovakia 16–0, and Canada the gold). In 1922 he became vice-president of the International Ice Hockey Federation. In 1923 he won a bronze medal at the European Championships. He married Edita Kaufmann and they had two children.

When the Nazis occupied Czechoslovakia, Karl, despite having converted to Catholicism, was arrested together with his entire family and transported to Theresienstadt concentration camp in July 1942. On 16 October 1944 he and his wife were transported to Auschwitz where they were murdered shortly after arrival. Their two sons managed to survive the war and later migrated to the USA.

Oskar Hekš (1908–44)
Czechoslovak
Distance running
Los Angeles 1932

Oskar Hekš was born into a Jewish family on 10 April 1908 in Czechoslovakia. He was selected to take part in the marathon at the 1932 Los Angeles Olympic Games. He ran well, and despite not winning a medal came in a very creditable eighth with a time of two hours forty-one minutes. Hekš later told a newspaper that he could have finished sixth without the stomach problems which had been caused by unsuitable refreshments, as well as timid tactics. He said, 'Before the start I thought I would finish around fifteenth. Perhaps I should have trusted myself more.' He was selected to take part in the Berlin Games of 1936, but he was prevented from attending because he was Jewish, and missed the 'Nazi Games'. A man of great character and not one to give up easily, he was one of the organisers of the 'People's Olympaid'. These games were first planned to be held in Barcelona, but were later moved to Prague due to the Spanish Civil War and held between 19 and 26 July 1936. There he won the 15,000 metres on the day of the Berlin marathon. Hitler and the Nazis would remember.

Shortly after the occupation of Czechoslovakia by the Nazis, Oskar, a marked man, was arrested and deported to the concentration camp at Terezín Fortress with one of the first transports. In October 1941, the Reich Protector Heydrich decided to build a Jewish ghetto in the Terezín Fortress. Among the 342 men assigned to the task was the brave Oskar Hekš. Even before the war had begun, the German *Selbstschutz* in Pomerania had created lists of people to be arrested as soon as they occupied the country. Hekš was transported to Auschwitz on 6 September 1943. He was murdered there on 8 March 1944 by gassing.

Otto Herschmann (1877–1942)
Austrian
Swimming and fencing
1896 Greece (Silver)
1906 Greece
1912 Stockholm (Silver)

Otto Herschmann was born into a Jewish family on 4 January 1877 in Vienna. Although a lawyer by profession, he was also a first-class all-round sportsman, excelling in every sport he competed in. He represented both the 1.W.A.S.C. and Wiener AC, both based in Vienna. A fine swimmer, at the age of 19 he was selected to participate in the 1896 Olympic Games in Greece, taking part in the men's 100 metres freestyle. The event then was held in open water. The competitors were taken by boat into the Bay of Piraeus where from a fixed starting point they had to swim between two buoys, through a course marked by floating hollow pumpkins, to a red-flagged finishing line. Herschmann finished second, only seconds behind the winner Alfred Hajos who took the gold.

After this he concentrated on a different discipline – fencing. He specialized in the sabre. He was selected to represent Austria in the men's individual sabre in the 1906 Games in Greece. Although he gave a fine account of himself, he failed to reach the final. In 1912 he was selected to represent Austria again, this time in the men's team sabre in Stockholm. The team took the silver medal, Hungary taking the gold. To win two Olympic medals in two different sports was rare then, and still is. Interestingly, at the time he won his fencing medal, he was serving as President of the Austrian Olympic committee. He is the only person ever to win an Olympic medal while still serving as president of a National Olympic Committee. He was also President of the Austrian Swimming Federation. He travelled extensively, including in the USA where his achievements were widely celebrated and where he expressed his admiration for the American system of training.

As a Jew he was persecuted in the Nazi occupation of Austria. He was eventually arrested and deported to the Izbica concentration camp on 14 January 1942. On the way to the camp his transport was diverted to Sobibor death camp in German-occupied Poland. He was murdered there by gassing on 17 June 1942.

In 1989 Herschmann was inducted into the International Jewish Sports Hall of Fame. In 2001 Vienna named a road after him: Otto Herschmann-Gasse.

Felix Hess (1878–1943)
Dutch
Art
1928 Amsterdam

Felix Isidoor Hess was born into a Jewish family on 20 June 1878 in Amsterdam. He received his artistic education at the Rijksakademie van Beeldende Kunsten 1901–5, his principal teacher being the celebrated painter Pieter Dupont (1870–1911). In 1910 he became a member of the prestigious Kunstenaarsvereniging Sint Lucas, and the following year the equally prestigious Maatschappij Arti et Amicitiae. He specialised in etchings, lithography, illustrations and book cover design. After the German occupation Felix had to leave both associations. Felix Hess was famously published in the magazines *de Groene Amsterdammer* and the comic strip *Uit het clipping van Jantje*. He became famous for his political comments observed from the point of view of a child. His drawings were so popular they were exhibited in the Kunstzaal van Lier in Amsterdam in 1934/35.

Hess took part in the Amsterdam Olympics of 1928, producing both watercolours and drawings, but he failed to win a medal. Later he worked with the author Leonard Roggeveen on comic strips such as *De Wonderlijke Reis van Jan Klaassen* which appeared in *Algemeen Handelsblad and Nieuwsblad van het Noorden*, and he illustrated the children's classic *De ongelooflijke avonturen van Bram Vingerling*. From 1940 he often worked under the pseudonym Jantje.

Felix Hess was arrested with his wife Eliza Binger and deported to Sobibor extermination camp. They were both murdered there on 9 April 1943.

De Rattenvanger van London naar het Beloofde Land (The Pied Piper from London to the Promised Land) by Felix Hess.

Julius Hirsch (1892–1944)
German
Football
1912 Stockholm

Julius Hirsch was born on 7 April 1892 in Baden. He was the seventh child of a Jewish merchant. A natural left winger, his talent for football was spotted early: at the age of 10 he was playing for Karlsruher FV. Nine years later he was representing Germany internationally, being only the second Jewish player to do so. He made seven international appearances, and formed part of the famous line up called the 'Juller', consisting of himself, Fritz Förderer and Gottfried Fuchs, who became famous for their attacking style. He was part of the team that won the South German Championship for Karlsruher FV in 1910. In 1913 he joined SpVgg Fürth and won a championship with them in 1914. He later returned to KFV, retiring after the war in 1923, however he remained at the club as the youth coach. In 1912 he represented Germany in football at the Stockholm Olympic Games, but they failed to reach the final or win a medal.

Karlsruher FV in 1910. Hirsch can be seen seated, second from the right.

In the First World War Hirsch served with the German infantry for four years, being decorated with the Iron Cross. His brother Leopold was killed in action in 1916.

Hirsch learned in April 1933 that all Southern German clubs were to ban all their Jewish members. As a result he left KFV of his own accord before he could be dismissed and after a thirty-year association with the club. He later expressed his feelings in a letter to the club: 'The Jews have become the whipping boys of the nation. It should not be forgotten that many gave their life blood for the German nation and were true patriots, as shown by their deeds and words.'

Seeing the coming horror, Hirsch divorced his wife in 1939 to try to protect her from the Nazis, and, despite his service to Germany, was deported to Auschwitz on 1 March 1943. He managed to send his daughter Esther a 16th birthday card from Dortmund, one of the stops on the way to Auschwitz. It read, 'My dearest! I arrived safely and everything is well. I am in Upper-Silesia which is still in Germany. Heartfelt greetings, kisses, your Juller.'

After this nothing more was heard from him. Both his children were later arrested as being half-Jews and deported to Terezan concentration camp but both survived. His murder was assumed to have taken place by gassing on 8 May 1945 by the Amtsgericht (District Court) Karlsruhe in 1950. In 2005 the German Football Federation founded the Julius Hirsch prize for exceptional effort, tolerance and human dignity, against extremism, hatred of foreigners and anti-Semitism.

Endre Kabos (1906–44)
Hungarian
Fencing
1932 Los Angeles (one Gold and one Bronze)
1936 Berlin (two Golds)

Endre Kabos was born into a Jewish family on 5 November 1906 in Nagyvárad, Hungary. A practiced fencer, he really came to notice after winning the Slovakian Championship in 1928. He then went on to win no less than six gold medals and one silver in European Championships between 1930 and 1935, specialising in the sabre. Not a rich man, he was forced to retire from fencing, and opened a grocery store in 1934. However, losing such a talent from the Hungarian team bothered many people, and sponsors were found to keep him in.

In the middle of all this he was selected to represent Hungary at the 1932 Olympics in Los Angeles. He won a bronze in the men's individual sabre and a gold in the team sabre. He was also selected to compete in the 1936 Olympics in Berlin. This time he took the gold in the individual sabre and another in the men's team sabre.

As a Jew, Kabos was interned in a labour camp in Vax, Hungary, for five months of the Second World War. He also worked at a labour camp for Jews, teaching officers the sabre in the village of Felsohsangony. However, he was recognised by a prison guard as the Olympic champion and it was arranged for him to go to Budapest. While there he was employed by the army transporting food and provisions to several camps within the district in which he was working. On 4 November 1944, the day before his 38th birthday, Kabos was driving a munitions truck across the Margaret Bridge connecting Buda and Pest when the bridge was destroyed by an explosion from a pipe bomb that had been planted by the Arrow Cross Party (a far right Hungarist party which formed a government in Hungary in 1944/5). During its short rule, ten to fifteen thousand civilians (many Jews and Romani) were murdered and around 80,000 deported to various concentration camps in Austria. Kabos was killed in the explosion along with many others. In 2011 the bridge was extended and the remains of many of the victims were discovered. Kabos was inducted into the International Jewish Sports Hall of Fame in 1986.

Roman Kantor (1912–43)
Polish
Fencing
1936 Berlin

Roman Józef Kantor was born on 15 March 1912 in Łódź into a Jewish family. His parents were Elchanan and Barbara (née Bekier). Moving to Paris, he began his athletics career playing football (he captained his team) and tennis. He also started to train as a fencer and it was clear from the start that he had a natural aptitude for it. He came third at the Academic Championship of Paris and sixth at the Open Championship of Paris. He went on to train in England and Germany. Returning to Łódź in 1934, he joined the fencing section of the Army Sports Club and won the team title of the city championship. In 1935 he came second in the Lvov Open Championship.

He was selected to be part of the Polish fencing team that took part in the 1936 Olympics in Berlin. Despite fencing well and defeating several former champions, he failed to reach the final.

In December 1936 he moved to Łódzki Klub Sportowy. While there he won several championships, including the Nordic Countries and was twice champion of the city in both the individual and team events. He came second in the Polish championship of 1939, the final championship before the outbreak of war.

After Poland was occupied by the Nazis, Kantor, as a celebrated sportsman and Jew, was arrested. Extraordinarily, he was freed by Reinhard Heydrich. The general was a sports fan and enjoyed fencing himself. On his order, Kantor was released with fake documents and money. Making for Lvov in 1940, he managed to win the Soviet Championship along the way.

When the Nazis occupied Lvov, he was arrested again (Heydrich was assassinated in 1942 and with his death Kantor lost his protector) and was transported to Majdanek concentration camp. It is known from records that he was still alive in 1943, but after that there is no mention of him and his exact date of death is not known.

Ernst (also known as Arnošt) Königsgarten (1880–1942)
Austrian
Fencing
1906 Greece

Ernst Königsgarten was born on 14 July 1880 into a wealthy Jewish family in Brno, Czechoslovakia (then part of the Austro-Hungarian Empire). He had four sisters and three brothers. A keen fencer despite having a serious eye infection, he fought left-handed with the foil and épée and right-handed with his favourite weapon the sabre. Such became his reputation that he was selected to represent Austria in the 1906 Olympics in Greece. At 25 he was the youngest member of the team. He competed in the men's individual foil, individual épée, individual sabre, and team sabre. His best result was sixth. In 1907 he co-founded the Vienna Fencing Club, and sat on the board of the Austrian Fencing Association and the Wiener AC. Training hard, he took part in numerous tournaments all over Europe: Marienbad in 1905, Prague, Milan and Trieste in 1906, Carlsbad and Ostend in 1907 and Baden-Baden in 1909. In 1908 he was also part of the Vienna team that was invited to perform in front of King Edward VII in Marienbad.

On 12 March 1938 German troops rolled into Austria and the next day Austria was officially annexed into the German Reich. Seeing the danger Ernst fled Austria on 20 November 1938 and made for Czechoslovakia, moving back into the family home in Brno where he hoped to be safe. He was finally arrested by the Nazis and deported to Theresienstadt on 5 December 1941. He died there a few weeks later on 15 January 1942 at the age of 61. The same transport carried his brother-in-law Leopold Schnürer, his sister Frieda, and their two daughters; all were later murdered at Auschwitz. Ernest's older brother Ludwig was deported to Theresienstadt in April 1942. He was put in charge of building the railway line into the camp which kept him safe for a while. However, once that project was completed in December 1943, he was transported to Auschwitz where he was murdered, probably on the day he arrived.

Memorial plaque to Ernst in Altaussee reads: 'He chose Altaussee as his final resting place, but he died in Theresienstadt in 1942.' (*Michael Garton, Wikimedia*)

Józef Krudowski (1881–1943)
Polish
Mixed music
1932 Los Angeles

Józef Krudowski was born on 18 January 1881 in Poland. He joined the Polish army and became a bandmaster in the 4th Field Artillery Regiment. He composed over thirty songs and marches, including the popular *Rusałka* (the Rusałka is a female water demon) which he wrote as a part song. Probably his best-known work was the *Bochniak Cantata*. He became conductor of the Cracow Academic Choir of the Jagiellonian University and taught singing and geography at the Tadeusz Reytan Boy's High School in Warsaw.

He was selected to take part in the 1932 Olympics in the mixed music section, but he failed to win a medal.

When the Nazis invaded, Józef was arrested and deported to Auschwitz where he was murdered on 7 August 1943, aged 62. Two of his brothers, Jan and Stefan, were murdered in the Katyn massacre. His third brother, Marian, survived the war, dying in Warsaw in 1953.

Roman Kramsztyk (1885–1942)
Polish
Art
1928 Amsterdam

Roman Kramsztyk was born on 6 August 1942 in Warsaw, the son of physician Julian Kramsztyk (1851–1925). His abilities as an artist were clear from an early age. A realist painter, he studied art at the Krakow Academy of Fine Arts under Józef Mehoffer and later in Warsaw under Adolf Eduard Herstein. In 1904 he went to the Munich Academy of Fine Arts to study under Johann Casper Herterich. Moving to Paris in 1910, he became a member of the Society of Polish Artists and the Polish Artistic and Literary Society. He remained in Paris until the outbreak of the First World War when he returned to Warsaw, continuing his studies under Herstein. From 1915 to 1924 he lived in Warsaw where in 1922 he co-founded the Rytm Association of Polish Artists, one of the leading artistic groups of the 1920s.

After the war he returned to Paris and painted portraits, nudes, still life, and genre paintings undoubtedly influenced by Cézanne.

On the outbreak of the Second World War he was caught in Warsaw and as a Jew forced into the Warsaw ghetto where he drew the horrors of day-to-day life there. Some of his pictures survived the war and stand as monuments to the evils of the Holocaust. He was shot dead on 6 August 1942 in the deportation of Jews from the Warsaw ghetto to the Treblinka death camp. His death was later described by an eyewitness: 'The man carried out of the apartment was not walking down the stairs fast enough and a German just shot him in the back of his head. Because in the ghetto there was a rule that you had to move quickly, even to your own death.'

Janusz Kusocinski (1907–40)
Polish
Athletics
Los Angeles 1932 (Gold)

Janusz Tadeusz Kusociński was born in Warsaw on 15 January 1907. He was a keen footballer as a boy and played for several local clubs, picking up the nickname 'Kusy'. He became a gardener by profession but had a remarkable turn of speed, and in his mid-twenties he turned to athletics, joining the sporting club 'Sparta' where he was trained by the famous Estonian decathlete Aleksander Klumberk (1899–1958), world record holder and bronze medal winner of the 1924 Olympics, twelve years prisoner of the Russian gulag system.

Kusociński won the Polish championship titles in the 1,500 metres and the 5,000 metres, in cross-country in 1930 and 1931, and in the 800 metres in 1932. In 1932 he ran a world record time in the 3,000 metres. In the same year he was selected to run for Poland at the Olympics and won gold in the 10,000 metres with a world season's best time of 30:11.4. The following year, 1934, he came second in the 5,000 metres at the European Championships in Turin. Retiring from athletics, he did make one small comeback, taking the Polish 10,000 metres title in 1939.

He joined the Polish army in the war and was wounded twice. On recovering he joined the Polish Resistance. Betrayed (as many were), he was arrested by the Gestapo on 26 March 1940 and taken to the Mokotow internment camp. On 21 March 1940 he became a victim of the Palmiry massacre, when between December 1939 and July 1941 more than 1,700 Poles and Jews were murdered near the village of Palmiry in the Kaminos Forest north-west of Warsaw. On 12 August 2009 he was posthumously awarded the Commander's Cross with Star of the Order of Polonia Restituta 'for outstanding contribution to the independence of the Polish Republic, for sporting achievements in the field of athletics'. There is an annual athletics event held in his honour: the 'Kusociński memorial'.

Eugène Maës (1890–1945)
French
Football
1912 Stockholm

Eugène Maës was born on 15 September 1890 in Paris. He became one of France's first great footballers, mostly playing centre forward. In 1905 he joined the Patronage Olier and won a number of championships and trophies with them. At 19 he was recruited by Red Star Amical Club, one of France's best teams. He won the Football Association League championship with them in 1912 and came second in 1913–14. In his short two-year international career he was selected to play for France on eleven occasions and scored fifteen goals. His most noted achievement was a hat-trick scored on 17 March 1912 in Turin against Italy. France won 4–3; it was the first time ever that France had beaten Italy at football.

He was selected to play for France in the 1912 Olympics in Stockholm but the team pulled out just before the games began.

In the First World War he was wounded in the chest on 29 August 1914 and awarded the Croix de Guerre for his bravery.

After the war he played as an amateur for SM Caen until 1930. In 1933 he received a gold medal from the French Football Association for his services to the game. He later became a swimming coach and opened a dance hall.

In the Second World War Maës was denounced by Marie-Clotilde de Combiens, the mistress of Harald Heyns, the head of the Gestapo in Caen, for speaking out against the German occupation. He was arrested on 21 June 1943 and deported to Dora-Mittelbau concentration camp where he died on 30 March 1945.

After the war, de Combiens was arrested and tried. She was sentenced to death, but this was commuted to life imprisonment and then to twenty years. She was released on parole in 1954.

Elias Hijman Melkman (1903–1942)
Dutch
Gymnastics
1928 Amsterdam

Elias Hijman Melkman was one of six children born into a Jewish family on 24 May 1903 in Amsterdam. His parents were Salomon Hijman and Rosina Melkman. He grew up to work in the diamond industry. He married twice and had four children. A fine athlete and gymnast, he competed for UDI 1896 Sports Club Arnhem and the Plato Gymnastics Club Amsterdam.

He was selected to take part in the 1928 Amsterdam Olympics when he was 24. He took part in seven events: the men's individual all-around (56th), the team all-around (8th), the horse vault, the parallel bars, the horizontal bar, the rings and the pommelled horse. The Dutch team achieved eighth place overall.

Melkman was arrested with thousands of other Dutch Jews after the Nazi invasion of the Netherlands. He was later transported to Auschwitz where he was murdered on 3 January 1942.

Lion van Minden (1880–1944)
Dutch
Fencing
1908 London

Lion van Minden was born into a Jewish family on 10 June 1880 in Amsterdam. He was one of four children born to Abraham and Branca (née Ziekenoppasser). A talented fencer, he represented the Koninklijke Officiers Schermbond in The Hague. Although he enjoyed the épée, he finally specialised in the sabre, progressing quickly until he was selected to compete at the 1908 London Olympics. He was eliminated in the first round and failed to take a medal, having won two of his bouts but lost three. The following year he became the first Dutch champion in the foil.

He later married Esther Mina Schlossberg. They had one daughter, Gertrude. As a Jew, Minden was arrested by the Nazis after their invasion and transported to Auschwitz where he was murdered on 6 September 1944 aged 64. Esther was murdered in Bergen Belsen on 31 May 1945. Gertrude was murdered in Auschwitz in 1945.

Abraham Mok (1888–1944)
Dutch
Gymnastics
1908 London

Abraham Mok was born into a Jewish family on 15 May 1888 in Amsterdam. He was one of seven children born to Samuel and Mietje Lakmaker. A fine gymnast, he represented Club Plato, Amsterdam. At the age of 19 he was selected to represent the Netherlands at the 1908 London Olympics. He took part in the men's individual all-round, coming 78th, and the men's team all-round, coming 7th. He married Henriette Levve in 1911 and they had two children, Samuel and Carolina, and both survived the war.

When the Nazis invaded the Netherlands, Mok and his wife were arrested and deported to Auschwitz. His wife was murdered there on 30 September 1942 (some records have the date as 5 October 1942) and Abraham on 29 February 1944.

Jacob van Moppes (1876–1943)
Dutch
Wrestling
1908 London

Jacob van Moppes was born into a Jewish family on 18 August 1876 in Amsterdam. He grew up to become a butcher, and gained an interest in power sports. He joined the Amsterdam-based athletics club 'Strength through Exercise', a Jewish-founded club formed by wrestlers and weightlifters. He would later become the club's chairman, a position he would hold for fifty years. He also helped found Nederlandse Krachtsportbond in Café de Sport on the Hoge Zand in The Hague. He went on to win over twenty awards in various Greco-Roman wrestling matches.

In 1908 he was selected to represent the Netherlands at the London Olympics. He wrestled in the light-weight Greco-Roman events. Unfortunately because the style adopted by the Olympics wasn't one he had trained for, he was knocked out in the early stages. Moppes retired from wrestling shortly before the First World War and became a driver, but continued to judge wrestling competitions.

In 1943, Jacob and his wife Mietje (née Haringman, married 1931) were arrested as Jews. On 18 March 1943 the couple arrived at Westerbork transit camp. From here they were shipped to Sobibor, where they were murdered together on 26 March 1943.

Henrik Nádler (1901–1944)
Hungarian
Football
1924 Paris

Henrik Nádler was born on 19 March 1901 into a Jewish family in Budapest, son of Izsák, a suitcase maker, and Roza Acht. He had six siblings, Bertalan, Emma, Gizella, Illés, Renée, and Rozalia. A talented footballer, he normally played left-midfield. He played for MTK Budapest between 1919 and 1930 and won the Hungarian championship on seven occasions with them. He also won the Hungarian cup twice, in 1923 and 1925. He played in 107 matches, scored six goals and won seven caps for the national team. He was selected to play for Hungary at the 1924 Olympics in Paris but wasn't selected to play in any of the games.

He was arrested by the Gestapo in the war as a Jew and was transported to Buchenwald concentration camp where he died of exhaustion on 12 May 1944.

Vojtech Neményi (1899–1945)
Czechoslovakian
Water polo
1924 Paris

Vojtech Neményi (also known as Bacla) was born into a Jewish family on 1 August 1899 in Kosice, Slovakia. Becoming a fine swimmer, he was selected for the Czechoslovakia water polo team at the 1924 Paris Olympics. The team reached the semi-finals before being beaten 5–1 by Belgium and coming sixth, narrowly missing out on a medal. France took the gold, Belgium the silver and the USA bronze.

Vojtech Neményi was arrested by the Nazis and deported to the Engerau concentration camp. Engerau is a little-known camp, established in December 1944 as a labour camp. Around 1,700 Jewish men were forced to work there (mostly Hungarian). Most starved to death, died of hypothermia or were murdered. Vojtech was murdered there on 7 April 1945. Today no trace of the camp remains due to a large-scale construction project in Petržalka carried out by the communist government when the former village was transformed into the largest housing complex in Central Europe.

Józef Noji (1909–43)
Polish
Athletics
Berlin 1936

Józef Noji was born on 8 September 1909 in Pęckowo, the youngest of four brothers. His family lived in poor conditions and when he grew up he became a carpenter. Also, representing Syreny Athletics Club of Warsaw, he was one of the finest runners in Poland of the 1930s. He won the national 5,000 metre championship five years in a row (1935–39), the cross-country championship four years in a row (1936–39), and won the 10 kilometre title in 1936. In the same year, he travelled to England and won the six-mile run, taking the title. Two years later he was back in England again, this time taking the three-mile title. He came second in 1936 in the list of the Ten Best Athletes in Poland, and tenth in 1937.

In 1936 he was selected to take part in the Berlin Olympics. He ran in the men's 5,000 metres coming fifth and the 10,000 metres coming fourteenth.

At the 1938 European Championships he came fifth in the 5,000 metres.

After the Nazi invasion of Poland, Noji refused to join the 'Volksliste' (a list of local people with ties to Germany who could be used to suppress disobedience). Instead he joined the Polish Resistance. Betrayed, he was arrested on 18 February 1940 and transported to the infamous prison at Pawiak in Warsaw. Over 37,000 people were murdered at this prison and a further 60,000 transported to death camps. After a year Noji was shipped to Auschwitz. He was murdered there on 15 February 1943 for trying to smuggle a letter out of the camp. According to witnesses he was shot in the back of the neck by an SS guard.

Noji was posthumously awarded the Cross of Valour. Several schools in Poland are named after him, and there is a municipal stadium named Nojiego Cross.

Simon Okker (1881–1944)
Dutch
Fencing
Greece 1906
London 1908

Simon was born into a Jewish family on 1 June 1881 in Amsterdam to Hartog Okker and Clara (née Schenkkan), one of seven children. He grew up to become a well-known fencer, taking part in both the 1906 Olympics in Greece, where he came fifth in the individual men's foil, and the 1908 Olympics in London, where he competed in the épée. He failed to win a medal in either Olympics. A diamond trader by profession, he married Keetje Kloots in 1909 and they had three daughters. She died in 1938.

On the invasion of the Netherlands by the Nazis, Simon Okker was arrested and deported to Auschwitz-Birkenau where he was murdered on 6 March 1944. Two of his three daughters were also murdered there, as were most of his siblings.

Abraham d'Oliveira (1880–1944)
Dutch
Gymnastics
London 1908

Abraham Elia Jessurun d'Oliveira was born on 4 May 1880 in Amsterdam. He was part of the Dutch gymnastics team in the 1908 London Olympics. He took part in the men's team all-around event and came seventh. He married Simcha Lopes Cardozo with whom he had two children, Jacob and Elsa. Their Portuguese ancestry seemed to protect Abraham and his family for a while, but on 1 February 1944 that protection ended and they were all arrested. They were first taken to Camp Westerbork, a transit camp in Drenthe province (over 98,000 Jews were deported from Westerbork to various death camps, mainly Auschwitz). Three weeks later they were assessed as being *Rassisches Untermenschentum* (racially sub-human) and deported to Theresienstadt. From there they were shipped to Auschwitz where all but one of them were murdered, probably on the day they arrived. The one exception was Elsa, who, after an ingenious rescue operation by a neighbour of her fiancé, lawyer Nino Kotting, was allowed to return home a few weeks later. There seems a little confusion as to when Abraham died and at which camp. Some records have him being murdered at Sobibor on 26 March 1944, while others have him being murdered together with his wife Simcha (and many other Portuguese Jews) in Auschwitz on 21 October 1944. I feel the latter date and location are the more likely and that he was murdered together with his wife on that day.

František Pechácek (1896–1944)
Czechoslovakian
Gymnastics
1920 Antwerp

František Pecháček was born on 15 February 1896 in Záhornice. He moved to Nová Paka in his youth and later joined the Czechoslovakian army. He became a non-commissioned officer and was put in charge of the school of physical education. On leaving the army he became a physical training instructor with a local school in Sokol. In 1920 he was selected to represent Czechoslovakia in the 1920 Antwerp Olympics where the team came fourth in the men's team, narrowly missing out on a medal. He wrote several books on physical education.

After the German invasion of Bohemia, Moravia and Silesia, he joined the Resistance as a provincial commander. After the assassination of Heydrich he was arrested together with his wife Emilia and his brother's family. He was interrogated, and then transported, with his wife, to Mauthausen-Gusen concentration camp. Emilia was murdered on 26 January 1943.

Pecháček was later murdered in a grotesque manner. The camp commander was the particularly evil George Bachmayer. A former inmate (Gerhard Kanthack, a former German government official and political prisoner at Mauthausen) later wrote, 'His speciality was to set two mastiff-like bloodhounds on inmates, which would literally rip them apart. This was known in camp jargon as "dying from the dog's kiss". The real cause of death, from a medical point of view, was usually sepsis, if the inmate didn't die immediately of heart failure.' Bachmayer allowed his dogs to attack and rip at Pecháček's body until he felt he couldn't recover. He was sent to the camp hospital where he surprisingly did recover, only to be shot on 3 February 1944.

On 7 March 2019 he was appointed an honorary citizen of Prague. Pecháček was exceptionally good-looking and was a model for several artists.

Attila Petschauer (1904–43)
Hungarian
Fencing
1928 Amsterdam (Gold and Silver)
1932 Los Angeles (Gold)

Attila Petschauer was born into a Jewish family on 14 December 1904 in Budapest. He fenced from the age of 8, firstly under the instruction of the master Károly Fodor, then when he reached 20 with the Nemzeti Vivó Club established by the lawyer Marcell Hajdu. He went on to win four Hungarian national youth championships. He was selected to represent Hungary twice at the Olympics, firstly in 1928 in Amsterdam where he competed in the men's individual sabre, taking a silver, and in the team sabre taking a gold. During this championship he won an extraordinary twenty out of twenty matches. At the 1932 Los Angeles Games, although he only managed fifth in the individual sabre, he was once again part of the team that took the gold in the sabre team. He went on to win gold medals at the World Championships in 1930 and 1931 in the team events, as well as individual silver medals at the Worlds in 1926 and 1930, and bronze in 1925, 1929, and 1931.

In 1938 Petschauer, as a famed Hungarian athlete, was exempted from having to work in the 'Labour Corps'. However in 1943 this exemption seemed to run out and he was arrested and deported to a labour camp in Davidovka, Ukraine. The story goes that at some point during his incarceration Petschauer recognised a fellow Olympian, Kalman Czéh, who had taken part in the equestrian events at the 1928 Games, and that he thought he had found a friend; but it wasn't to turn out like that. Olympian wrestler Károly Kárpáti witnessed what happened next. According to his statement Petschauer called out to Czéh, who noticing him called out to one of the guards telling him to 'make things hot for the Jew'. The guards shouted: 'You, Olympic fencing medal winner… let's see how you can climb trees.' Karpati recalled: 'It was midwinter and bitter cold, but they ordered him to undress, then climb a tree. The amused guards ordered him to crow like a rooster, and sprayed him with water. Frozen from the water, he died shortly after,' on 20 January 1943. However, recent research by historians Csaba B. Stenge and Krisztián Ungváry shows that Petschauer most likely died of typhus in a Soviet PoW camp.

His story was made into a film in 1999, *Sunshine*, starring Ralph Fiennes. The Attila Petschauer fencing competition was named in his honour. His friend and fellow fencer János Garay was murdered at Mauthausen in 1945.

Marcel Pourchier (1897–1944)
French
Military patrol
1928 St Moritz

André Eugène Marcel Pourchier was born on 1 June 1897 in Beuil in the French Alps. He was commissioned into the French army and served in the First World War in which he was gassed. After the war he served in the French mandated territory of Syria between 1920 and 1924. Returning to France he was stationed at his home town of Beuil and became head of the military skiing school there. In 1924 he was selected to represent France at the 1928 Olympic games in St Moritz in the military patrol, still a demonstration event at the time. The team alas finished last.

In 1930 he had the distinction of designing the first ski jumping hill in Beuil. In 1932 he was made the first commander of the newly founded mountain warfare school, École de Haute Montagne in Chamonix, whose purpose was to train French troops in ski reconnaissance patrols. He was also responsible for establishing new tactics and designing better winter clothing.

At the outbreak of the Second World War he left the school and began to work on the logistics of the Norwegian campaign. After the Franco-German armistice he was demobilized. The following year he joined the Resistance and became a logistics officer with the *République du Vercors*. On 4 January 1944 he was captured in a Gestapo ambush and shipped to the Natzweiler-Struthof concentration camp in Alsace. Here, together with 471 others, he was executed on 1/2 September 1944.

He had been awarded the Croix de Guerre in both world wars, had been made a member of the Légion d'Honneur, and had been awarded the Medaille de la Resistance. The French army posthumously appointed him lieutenant colonel. He is commemorated on the war memorial in Beuil and a street is named after him, *Boulevard Marcel Pourchier*.

Two of his cousins, both officers, also fought with the Resistance. One, Captain Albert Pourchier, died in Neuengamme concentration camp.

Gino Ravenna (1889–1944)
Italian
Gymnastics
1908 London

Gino Ravenna was born into a Jewish family on 30 August 1889 in Ferrara to Tullio Ravenna and Eugenia (Pardo). He ran a successful food warehouse in Ferrara and his passion was sport. He excelled at tennis and gymnastics. At the age of 18 he was selected to take part in the 1908 London Olympics as a gymnast. He competed in the men's all-round team event, the team eventually coming sixth, missing out on a medal by a whisker. Sweden took the gold, Norway the silver and Finland the bronze.

Gino Ravenna married Letizia Rossi Ravenna and they had three children, Eugenio, Marcello and Franca. After Italy's surrender on 8 September 1943, the Nazis began to arrest Italian Jews. Gino tried to get his family out of the country and headed for Switzerland. Unfortunately in December 1943 the Nazis caught and arrested them all in Domodossola. The family were first deported to Fossoli and then to Auschwitz. Letizia was murdered on 22 February 1944, Franca was murdered in January 1945, Marcello was murdered on 22 February 1944, Gino was murdered on 19 April 1944. Eugenio survived the holocaust and finally died in February 1977.

Paolo Salvi (1891–1945)
Italian
Gymnastics
1912 Stockholm (Gold)
1920 Antwerp (Gold)

Luigi Paolo Salvi was born on 22 November 1891 in Brescia. A fine athlete, he competed for the Forza e Costanza gymnastics club of Brescia. During the 1911 World Championships, Salvi won the silver medal in the pommelled horse, and the bronze medal in the parallel bars and the team all-around events. He was also a member of the Italian gymnastics team that won a bronze medal in the team all-around event at the 1913 World Championships.

Salvi represented Italy twice at the Olympic Games. In 1912 in Stockholm he competed in the men's all-round team event taking the gold medal. In 1920 in Antwerp he again competed in the men's all-around, again taking the gold.

He later served as a judge.

In November 1944 Salvi was arrested for distributing anti-fascist leaflets and later shipped to Mauthausen-Gusen concentration camp, where the authorities alleged he was killed in an air raid on 12 January 1945.

Martial van Schelle (1899–1943)
Belgian
Swimming and bobsleigh
1920 Antwerp
1924 Paris
1928 Amsterdam
1936 Garmisch-Partenkirchen

Martial van Schelle was born into a Jewish family on 6 July 1899 in Merksplas. He had a Belgian father, Albert Jozef Karel van Schelle, and an American mother, Annie-Marwin Fowler-Protvoth. He spent much of his youth in the United States, mainly in Chicago. His mother, sailing on the *Lusitania* on 7 May 1915 while returning to Europe shortly after the outbreak of war, was torpedoed by the Germans. Although she survived the original sinking, she died shortly afterwards from injuries sustained in the attack.

Martial van Schelle joined the US army in 1917 and travelled with the first draft to France where he remained throughout the war. After the war he decided to remain in Europe and returned to his family home. In 1919 he finally settled in Brussels, devoting himself to various sports. Specialising in swimming, he became Belgian champion in the 100 metres freestyle for an extraordinary ten consecutive years.

He was to compete in the Olympics for Belgium on four occasions. Three times in the 1920 Antwerp Olympics, swimming in the 100 metres freestyle; in the 1924 Paris Olympics, this time in the men's 4 × 200 metres freestyle; at the Amsterdam Olympics where he competed in the 100 metres and 4 × 200 metres freestyle; and in 1936 – by which time he had changed his sport from swimming to bobsleigh – at the winter Olympics in Garmisch-Partenkirchen. He came ninth in the two-man bobsleigh and fifth in the four-man bobsleigh.

As well as running a sporting shop and earning the patent for a tennis racket in 1935, this very remarkable man built swimming pools and ice rinks all over Belgium, including one in the Royal Palace of King Leopold II, and helped to revive the sport of ice-skating in the country. He was also a keen aviator and took part twice in the Gordon Bennett Cup, the oldest gas balloon race in the world.

In the Second World War, Martial van Schelle joined the Resistance and began spying for the Allies, arranging for refugees to escape to Great Britain. He was betrayed and on 15 January 1943, arrested by the Gestapo and taken to the transit camp at Fort Breendonk. Tortured for weeks, he was eventually shot on 15 March 1943. He is buried today at the honorary park of the executed.

Richard Schoemaker (1886–1942)
Dutch
Fencing
1908 London

Richard Leonard Arnold Schoemaker was born on 5 October 1886 in Roermond, Limburg. He became a cadet at the Royal Netherlands Military Academy in 1905. He later joined the Army of the Netherlands, East Indies, to serve with the engineers. A keen sportsman, he fenced, rowed and shot. He became so accomplished with the sabre that at the age of 21 he was selected to take part in the 1908 London Olympics as part of the Netherlands fencing team. In the men's individual sabre event he was eliminated in the second round and failed to win a medal.

After the games he was promoted to second lieutenant and returned to the Dutch East Indies. He became a lieutenant in 1910 and a captain in 1915. Leaving the army after the First World War (although remaining with the reserve with the rank of major) he became a professor of constructional engineering at the Technical Academy in Bandoeng. Returning to the Netherlands he took up a position as professor of architecture, specialising in structural engineering, at the Technical University in Delft. Shortly after the outbreak of the Second World War he joined the Dutch underground, becoming part of the Ordedienst (OD), a fusion of several underground groups. He was betrayed and on 2 May 1941 was arrested by the Nazis. He was firstly imprisoned in Scheveningen (in the so-called Oranjehotel). He was then transported to Sachsenhausen concentration camp. Here he was murdered on 3 May 1942 aged 55 (he was murdered together with the Dutch bronze-winning Olympian Pierre Versteegh).

After the war a street was named after Schoemaker just outside Delft University. He was also one of ninety-five Resistance fighters to receive the Dutch Cross of Resistance after the war.

Werner Seelenbinder (1904–44)
German
Wrestling
1936 Berlin

Werner Seelenbinder was born on 2 August 1904 in Szczecin. He grew up to become a joiner by trade, but his passion was wrestling, especially the Greco-Roman style, at which he excelled. He wrestled for Sportvereinigung Ost Berlin, winning German titles in 1933, 1935–38 and 1940. In 1937 and 1938 he finished third at the European Championships. His success would have been greater had he not bravely refused to give the 'Hitler salute' in the 1933 German Games. For this insult to the master race he was banned from his sport for eighteen months.

He had always had an interest in Marxism and had connections with the young people's workers while still young. His interest and affiliations to left and communist groups led to him being expelled from his sporting club in 1928. He represented Germany in the first Spartakiad games in 1928 held in Moscow (the Spartakiad was an international sporting event sponsored by the Soviet Union; five were held between 1928 and 1937). He eventually joined the Communist Party of Germany, as a result of which he was arrested several times and held in prison for short periods.

Surprisingly, he was selected to represent Germany at the 1936 Berlin Olympic Games. He fought in the men's individual light-heavy weight Greco-Roman style. Injured in the competition, he only managed fourth. This was particularly disappointing for him because he again wanted to refuse to give Hitler his salute.

Working as a courier, Seelenbinder joined the Uhrig Group, a communist underground Resistance group named after Robert Uhrig (1903–44, also murdered by the Nazis) who organized it. He was arrested along with dozens of other members of the group on 4 February 1942. He was tortured for eight days before being moved from camp to camp over the next two years. He was finally murdered for treason on 24 October 1944 at the Brandenburg-Görden prison by being beheaded with an axe. He wrote a last letter to his father from prison: 'The time has now come for me to say goodbye. In the time of my imprisonment I must have gone through every type of torture a man can possibly endure. Ill health and physical and mental agony, I have been spared nothing.

I would have liked to have experienced the delights and comforts of life, which I now appreciate twice as much, with you all, with my friends and fellow sportsmen, after the war. The times I had with you were great, and I lived on them during my incarceration, and wished back that wonderful time. Sadly fate has now decided differently, after a long time of suffering. But I know that I have found a place in all your hearts and in the hearts of many sports followers, a place where I will always hold my ground. This knowledge makes me proud and strong and will not let me be weak in my last moments.'

After the war he had many streets and stadiums named after him. In 1963 the East German Post published a stamp with his portrait, and in 2008 he was inducted into the Hall of Fame of German Sport.

Antal Vágó (1891–1944)
Hungarian
Football
1912 Stockholm

Antal Vágó was born into a Jewish family on 9 August 1891 in Pásztó. A good all-round athlete who specialised in football, he first played mid-field for Fővárosi TC (later Terézvárosi Torna Club). His talent quickly came to note and in 1908 he moved to MTK Budapest (Magyar Testgyakorlók Köre), the most successful club in Hungary. He remained with them until 1923 winning eight championships and the Hungarian Cup five times. He also won seventeen international caps between 1908 and 1917. In 1912 he was selected to play for Hungary at the 1912 Stockholm Olympics. They lost their first game to Great Britain 7–0, but picked themselves up going on to beat Germany 3–1 and Austria 3–0. They failed to reach the finals or win a medal however, finishing fifth. Antal captained the team twice in the Olympics. He was 20 years old. The historian Andrew Handler in his book *From the Ghetto to the Games: Jewish Athletes in Hungary* wrote about him: 'He had a flawless ball control... the ability to be in the right place at the right time, and displayed an astonishing array of defensive skills.'

As a Jew he was arrested by the Nazis and his fate was sealed. Records of his death vary. Some claim he was shot and his body dumped in the Danube in late 1944 with thousands of other Jews from Budapest. Others have him being murdered in a concentration camp on 21 March 1944.

Vago, standing centre, with the Hungary national team.

Pierre Versteegh (1888–1942)
Dutch
Equestrianism
1928 Amsterdam (Bronze)
1936 Berlin

Pierre Marie Robert Versteegh was born on 6 June 1888 in Indonesia. After completing his education in 1906 he joined the army, training at the military academy in Breda. In June 1909 he qualified as a second lieutenant and joined the Third Division in Ede. He became an active equestrian, winning several local competitions. He was promoted to captain in 1925 and then major in 1936. He was awarded the Order of Orange-Nassau with Swords in 1931. He married Sophia Oudshoorn, who was Jewish, and they had one child.

He was selected to compete for the Netherlands at the 1928 Olympics. He competed in the dressage individual, coming ninth, and the dressage team coming third and taking a bronze medal on his horse *Excellence*. In 1936 he was selected again. In Berlin he finished eighth in the dressage individual and fifth in the dressage team.

After the German army invaded, Versteegh joined the Dutch Resistance working with the Ordedienst. Betrayed, he was arrested on 2 May 1941 together with ninety-four other members of his group. He was incarcerated in the 'Oranjehotel' in Scheveningen, tried in March 1942, and sentenced to death. On 1 May 1942 he and the Olympic fencer Richard Schoemaker were transported to Sachsenhausen where the two great Olympians were shot by firing squad on 3 May 1942.

After the war they were awarded posthumous Dutch Crosses of Resistance, and on 3 May 1946 they were commemorated on a plaque dedicated to the members of the Dutch Resistance who lost their lives in the war. His wife survived the war.

'Hans' van Walsem (1916–43)
Dutch
Rowing
1936 Berlin

Johan Frans van Walsem was born on 14 December 1916 in Jakarta. He became a chemist and later taught chemistry at the local university. A keen athlete, his passion was rowing, but as a man of small stature, he was best suited to be cox. In 1936, as cox he became Dutch champion in the men's coxed pairs, qualifying him for the Olympic Games. At the 1936 Olympics his pair was Karel Hardeman (1914–2010) and Ernst de Jonge (1914–44). The latter was a victim of the Holocaust; he died of tuberculosis at Mauthausen-Gusen aged 26. The rowing competitions were held at the regatta course at Grunau. The course was 2,000 metres long and wide enough to allow six boats to start simultaneously. Although the Dutch qualified for the semi-finals, they advanced no further and failed to take a medal.

Changing his interest to fencing and competing for the Leiden Student Fencing Association, he became the 'academic fencing champion' of the Netherlands. While teaching at the university he helped found the Leiden Resistance newspaper. The paper, distributed in secret, gave advice on resistance against the Nazi occupiers. Betrayed, he was arrested by the Gestapo and transported to the Neuengamme concentration camp where he died on 2 January 1943.

Dr Ernst Weiss (1882–1940)
German
Art (literature)
1928 Amsterdam (Silver)

Ernst Weiss was born into a Jewish family on 28 August 1882 in Brünn, Moravia (now Brno in the Czech Republic). After his father's death, when he was 4, it was his mother who stimulated his interest in art. Despite this he went on to study medicine in Prague and Vienna, becoming a surgeon in 1908. While practising he contracted TB, as a result of which he became a ship's doctor, travelling to India and Japan in the hope that the change of climate would help his condition. In 1913 he met the dancer, actress and novelist Rahel Sanzara. They remained together, mostly living in Berlin, until she died of cancer in 1936 aged 41. Weiss also became friendly with Franz Kafka, as well as many members of the Prague Circle, including Franz Werfel, Max Brod and Johannes Urzidil.

In the First World War he served on the Eastern Front being awarded the Gold Cross for bravery. After the war he gave up his career as a doctor and went to live in Prague. In 1921 he moved to Berlin and began writing, at the rate of one novel per year. In 1928 he was selected to take part in the Amsterdam Olympics. He won the silver medal in the Epic Works section. In 1933 he returned to Prague to care for his ailing mother. As a Jew he was unable to return to Nazi Germany, so settled in Paris in 1934. Only able to survive thanks to friends, he wrote his final novel, *The Eyewitness*, in 1938. It told the story of a veteran of the First World War, called AH, struggling to survive with conversion disorder (then known as hysterical blindness). Hitler had been treated for conversion disorder after the war while hospitalized at Pasewalk.

On the invasion of Paris by the Nazis, Weiss committed suicide by poison, dying in a Paris hospital on 14 June 1940 rather than being forced to go to a prison camp.

Árpád Weisz (1896–1944)
Hungarian
Football
1924 Paris

Árpád Weisz was born on 16 April 1896 into a Jewish family in the Hungarian town of Solt, near the border with Austria. A talented football player, he turned out for several European clubs, mostly playing on the left. In Hungary he played for Torekves SE, in Czechoslovakia he played for Makabi Brno, and in Italy he played for Alessandria and Internazionale. Between 1922 and 1923 he won seven caps for Hungary and turned out for them at the 1924 Olympics. They beat Poland in the first round 5–0 but were knocked out in the next round 3–0 by Egypt. Uruguay took the gold by beating Switzerland 3–0 in the final. Sweden took the bronze (the captain of the team was another legendary Jewish footballer, Bela Guttman). Continuing with his football career, Weisz first went to South America, visiting Argentina and Uruguay and learning much about their style, tactics and motivations. On his return he became an assistant coach at Alessandria before moving to FC Internazionale Milano. He managed them in 1926–28, 1929–31 and 1932–34. He won the championship with them at the 1929/30 season. He also coached the Italian teams Bari, Novara and Bologna with whom he won two league titles in 1936/7. During the 1937/8 season he was considered to be the best manager in Europe. In 1938 Bologna beat Chelsea 4–1 in Paris to win the equivalent of today's Champions League. After this surprise victory, the European press woke up and hailed both Weisz and the team, saying they would 'make the world tremble'. That same year, Mussolini passed a number of anti-Semitic laws and ordered that all Jews be expelled from the country. Weisz, despite his fame, was forced to flee, together

Weisz can be seen here on the far right.

with his wife and two children. They fled to Paris, living there for three months, before moving to the Netherlands where Weisz found a coaching job with the small provincial club of Dordrecht. It was far from what he was used to, but it was a job, and in football, so he was grateful. Shortly after war broke out, the Netherlands were occupied and the round-up of Jews began. In August 1942 the Gestapo arrested Weisz and his family. They were transported to the Dutch labour camp of Westerbork from where a few months later they were shipped to Auschwitz. On arrival Weisz was separated from his wife and children, Elena, Roberto and Clara. They were sent to the death camp at Birkenau where they were murdered almost at once. Weisz survived for a further eighteen months as forced labour. He died in the camp in January 1944.

In January 2020, Chelsea FC unveiled a mural by Solomon Souza on an outside wall of the West Stand at Stamford Bridge. It was a part of the club's 'Say No to Antisemitism' campaign funded by its owner Roman Abramovich. Included within the mural are depictions of the footballers Arpad Weisz, Julius Hirsch (1894–1945), who was murdered at Auschwitz, and Ron Jones who was known as the 'Goalkeeper of Auschwitz'.

Gerardus van der Wel (1895–1945)
Dutch
Athletics
1920 Antwerp

Gerardus Johannes van der Wel was born on 5 January 1895 in The Hague. He became a gardener by profession and was also a gifted athlete. His main disciplines were medium- and long-distance running. He competed for the club Vlug en Lenig. Wel was Dutch champion on five occasions in different distances: twice in the 1,500 metres (1918 and 1921) and three times in the 5,000 metres (1919–21). In 1920 he set a new Dutch record in the 3,000 metres with a time of 9.17.6, a record he held for six years. In 1920 he was part of the Dutch Olympic team and took part in the 5,000 metres, but failed to win a medal.

Wel died at Bergen-Belsen concentration camp on 31 May 1945.

Israel Wijnschenk (1895–1947)
Dutch
Gymnastics
1928 Amsterdam

Israel Wijnschenk was born into a Jewish family on the 24 November 1895 in Amsterdam. Becoming a fine gymnast, he competed for BATO Athletics Club Amsterdam. He was selected for the 1928 Olympics where he took part in the men's individual all-round (64th), the team all-around (8th), the horse vault (74th), the parallel bars (71st), the horizontal bar (65th), the rings (72nd) and pommelled horse (54th).

After the Nazi invasion, Israel, as a Jew, was arrested and deported to Auschwitz, where he was murdered on 31 January 1943.

Paul Wormser (1905–1944)
French
Fencing
1936 Berlin (Bronze)

Paul Albert Wormser was born on 11 June 1905 in Sainte-Radegonde, Aveyron, into a Jewish family. He studied at the University of Strasbourg and after qualifying became a dentist in Colmar. A fine fencer, he won the French national épée championship for university students in 1927, coming third the following year. In 1927 at the Student World Championships in Rome he won the individual gold medal and was also a member of the silver-medal-winning French team. In 1928 he was a member of the French fencing team that came second. In 1929 he was on the Mulhouse team that won the Alsace championships and in 1932 he won the silver medal at the French National Championships.

As a Jew he was obliged to hide in a commune in Aveyron after the German invasion of France and the anti-Semitic laws passed by the Vichy government. On 19 July 1944 he became involved in a firefight between a German patrol and a group of Resistance fighters. While helping a wounded man he was captured and imprisoned in Rodez. On 17 August 1944, with the Germans losing the war and the Allies closing in on Rodez, the camp was evacuated. However, before doing so thirty members of the Resistance were taken out, including the brave Wormser, and shot. Their bodies were dumped in a ditch. The murders later became known as the 'Le massacre de Sainte-Radegonde'.

The Aveyron council erected a memorial to all those murdered in the massacre. The list of the Aveyronnais 'righteous among the nations' was added, for the selfless help given to the many Jews who had taken refuge in the department but were mercilessly hunted down by the Vichy government and the Germans.

THE DUTCH WOMEN'S GYMNASTICS TEAM

Amsterdam have only hosted the Olympic Games once, in 1928. The Dutch did very well, winning a total of nineteen medals: six gold, nine silver and four bronze. The women's gymnastics team did especially well, winning the gold medal in the women's team all-round. The team consisted of twelve gymnasts. Five were Jewish. Of these only one was to survive the war. The other four were murdered in either Auschwitz or Sobibor. Their coach, Gerrit Kleerekoper, who was also Jewish, was also murdered by the Nazis.

Estella 'Stella' Agsteribbe (1909–43)
Dutch
Gymnastics
1928 Amsterdam (Gold)

Estella Agsteribbe was born on 6 April 1909 in Amsterdam. A fine athlete, she took part in the ninth modern Olympics in the summer of 1928 in Amsterdam. A total of sixty women took part, forming five teams of twelve. Together with her team, she took the gold medal in the women's team all-around event. Scores were determined by adding drill, apparatus, and vault components, the team with the most winning.

It was the first time a women's gymnastics team had taken part in the Olympic Games (although not the first time women had been allowed to compete at the Olympics, which was in 1900 in Paris). It would not be repeated until the 1936 Games. The lack of women's participation was largely due to the attitude and influence of one of the movement's founders, Pierre de Frédy, Baron de Coubertin, who was against women participating in the Olympics. It wasn't until after he had left the scene that things improved for female athletes. It was also the first time the Olympic torch had been used (although not the torch relay – that would have to wait for the 1936 Berlin Olympics). Another first for the games was the standard sixteen days for the event. Only five teams competed in the women's gymnastics event. The Dutch team took the gold with 316.75 points, the Italians the silver with 289.00, and Great Britain the Bronze with 258.25. Hungary and France came fourth and fifth.

Being Jewish, Estella was arrested by the Nazis in 1943, together with her husband Samuel Blits, their 6-year-old daughter Nanny and their 2-year-old son Alfred. They were shipped to Auschwitz. Estella and her children were murdered there on 17 September 1943. Samuel died at Auschwitz seven months later, having lived with the knowledge that his beloved wife and children had been murdered before him.

Anna 'Ans' Dresden-Polak (1906–43)
Dutch
Gymnastics
1928 Amsterdam (Gold)

Anna Dresden-Polak was born on 24 November 1906 in Amsterdam. She was part of the twelve-strong women's gymnastics team that won the gold at the 1928 Olympic Games. When the Germans invaded Holland, Anna, with her husband Barend Dresden and 6-year-old daughter Eva, was arrested. They were first shipped to Westerbork concentration camp. Anna and Eva were then deported to Sobibor where they were murdered on 23 July 1943. Barend died in 1944 in Auschwitz. She was later inducted into the International Jewish Sports Hall of Fame.

Gerrit Kleerekoper (1897–1943)
Dutch
Gymnastics coach
1928 Amsterdam (Gold)

Gerrit Kleerekoper was born on 15 February 1897 in Amsterdam. He grew up to work as a diamond cutter. He married and had two children, Elizabeth and Leendert. Kleerekoper had always had a passion for gymnastics and was selected to train the Dutch gymnastics team. His talent and strict training regime were largely responsible for creating the most successful gymnastics team in Dutch sporting history. But it was still to everyone's surprise that the team won the gold at the 1928 Olympics.

Years later Alida van den Bos said in an interview: 'The training for the Olympics always took place at indoor gymnasiums, even though the Olympics that year took place at an outdoor stadium. A few months before the Olympics, Kleerekoper made us only practice outdoors because he said that you never know how the weather will be the day of the Olympics and that we must be prepared for hot weather or any weather. The practice outside was very good, because we noticed that you have a lot more energy outdoors than needed.'

Arrested when the Nazis invaded Holland, Kleerekoper was deported, together with his wife Kaatje, 14-year-old Elisabeth and 21-year-old Leendert, to concentration camps. Gerrit, his wife and daughter were murdered on 2 July 1943 at Sobibor. Leendert died of exhaustion at Auschwitz in July 1944.

Helena 'Lea' Kloot-Nordheim (1903–43)
Dutch
Gymnastics
1928 Amsterdam (Gold)

Helena Nordheim was born on 1 August 1903 in Amsterdam. A hairdresser by profession, she was part of the Dutch women's Olympic gymnastics team of 1928. She later married Abraham Kloot and they had one daughter, Rebecca. After the Nazi invasion of Holland, she was arrested together with Abraham and 10-year-old Rebecca. The family were first deported to Westerbork concentration camp, before being shipped to Sobibor, where Helena and her entire family were murdered on 2 July 1943.

Biographies

(by year of first Olympics attended)

1908

Georges 'Géo' André (1889–1943)
French
Athletics
1908 London (Silver)
1912 Stockholm
1920 Antwerp (Bronze)
1924 Paris

Georges Yvan André was born on 13 August 1889 in Paris. He was educated at the École Supérieure d'Électricité and the École Supérieure de l'Aéronautique. He taught physical education, specialising in boxing, swimming, wrestling and tennis. He also got his gliding certificate.

Gaining the nickname Le Bison, André became one of France's finest all-round athletes. He won French titles in the hurdles, the high jump and the standing high jump, and held national records in the 110 and 400 metres hurdles, the high jump and the 4 × 400 metres relay.

A fine rugby union player, he represented Racing Club de France, Paris, and represented France on seven occasions in the 1913/14 season, playing left wing against South Africa, England, Wales and Ireland. Alas France lost all these matches, but it was early days for French rugby as they developed as an international team.

Remarkably he represented France in four Olympic Games. In the 1908 London Games he took silver in the high jump and came fifth in the standing high jump. In 1912 in Stockholm he took part in the 110 metres hurdles, the high jump, the standing high jump, the standing long jump, the pentathlon and the decathlon.

Then he joined the army, the 103rd Infantry Regiment, and played centre forward for their football team.

The French army mobilized on 2 August 1914 and on 2 September he was promoted to sergeant. He was taken prisoner, and despite being seriously wounded he attempted to escape six times, successfully on the final occasion. On recovery, having passed his aviator pilot's licence before the war he joined the Flying Corps, flying with the Stork Squadron and winning the Military Medal with them. He was shot and wounded in the ankle, which grounded him.

But he fully recovered and returned to athletics to represent France in the 1920 Olympics in Antwerp. There he competed in the 400 metres, the 400 metres hurdles coming fourth, and the 4 × 400m relay winning a team bronze.

Four years later he was back at the Olympics, this time in Paris, where he was the French flag bearer. He only took part in one event: the 400 metres hurdles. He just missed out on a medal, coming fourth. He was 18 when he competed in his first Olympics, 34 in his last.

After retiring from competition, he worked as a sports journalist for several French newspapers: *La Vie Au Grand Air, The Sports Mirror* (in which he was head of the athletics section), *L'Excelsior* and *L'Intransigeant*. He also wrote the book *La Course à Pied* in 1936.

In the Second World War he enlisted into the African Free Corps. He became a fighter ace credited with sixteen victories, and was finally shot down and killed on 4 May 1943 in Mateur, Bizerte, Tunisia. He was 53 and married with two children.

One of his sons, Jacques, was French champion in the 110 metres hurdles in 1938.

There is a commemorative plaque outside his former home at 9, Rue Marguerin, in Paris. Many stadiums are also named after him.

(Some records have him being shot by the SS as a member of the French Resistance in Tunisia, but I can't find any confirmation of this.)

K DIVISION (METROPOLITAN POLICE) TUG-OF-WAR TEAM.

Thomas Homewood (1881–1945)
British
Tug-of-war
1908 London (Bronze)

Thomas Homewood was born on 25 September 1881 in East Peckham. He joined the Metropolitan Police. A keen member of the tug-of-war team, he was selected to take part in the 1908 Olympics as part of the K Division Metropolitan team 3. Seven countries originally entered the competition but Germany and Greece withdrew. Interestingly, three teams of British policemen then competed against teams from the United States and Sweden. In the first round the police team from Liverpool pulled the US team over the line almost immediately. However, the Americans launched a protest: they alleged that the Liverpool police team were wearing illegal boots. This was denied and the Liverpool team offered to pull again, barefoot if they wanted. The American team refused this offer and withdrew from the competition. The complaint was later disallowed. The Liverpool team then defeated the Swedish team in the semi-finals but were defeated by the London City Police team in the final. The London City Police took the Gold, the Liverpool Police the Silver, and K Division Metropolitan Police the Bronze.

Homewood was killed together with his family when a V2 rocket hit his home at 50 Barnby Street, Stratford, in the early hours of Thursday, 1 February 1945. His family consisted of Beatrice 23, Ellen 15, Victor 25, and Matilda 54. They are all remembered with honour in the West Ham County Borough memorial. They were hit by a rocket named Big Ben 645; a total of thirty people were killed in the attack.

John Wodehouse, 3rd Earl of Kimberley, CBE MC JP (1883–1941)
British
Polo
1908 London (Silver)
1920 Antwerp (Gold)

John Wodehouse was born on 11 November 1883 in Witton, Norfolk, eldest son of John Wodehouse, 2nd Earl of Kimberley. He was educated at Eton, and Trinity Hall, Cambridge, where he began playing polo. He was on the losing side in the annual match against Oxford in 1903, but made up for that when he captained the winning Cambridge team for the next two years.

In 1906 he was elected MP for Mid-Norfolk as a Liberal. Being only 22, he became the Baby of the House of Commons.

In 1908 he was selected to represent Great Britain at polo at the London Olympics. Competing with the Hurlingham team he took the silver medal. Only three teams entered, two from England and one from Ireland, meaning that only two matches were played. The English teams entered under the names of their clubs, the Roehampton and the Hurlingham. The Irish Club seems to have been called just that. The Irish team never played Hurlingham and qualified for the final by drawing a bye in the first round. The winning Roehampton team was awarded the Hurlingham Trophy in addition to their gold medals. Hurlingham and the Irish Club shared the silver.

Wodehouse also played in three Westchester Cup matches and was a member of the team which won the Champion Cup six times between 1908 and 1914.

In 1911 Wodehouse was commissioned into the Norfolk Yeomanry as a lieutenant, serving with them at the outbreak of war. Later he served as a captain with the 16th Lancers, and was wounded twice and twice mentioned in despatches. He served on the Western Front in 1914–17 and in Italy 1917–18. He won the Military Cross (*LG* 3 June 1918), the Croix de Guerre, and the Italian War Merit Cross.

After the war he remained with the reserve of officers and worked as assistant private secretary to the then colonial secretary, Winston Churchill. He was awarded a CBE in 1925, and succeeded to his father's titles in 1932.

He was selected to play polo again at the 1920 Antwerp Olympics. This time the British team took the gold, defeating Spain 13–11 in the final. The USA took the bronze.

On 16 April 1941 John Wodehouse was killed by a German parachute mine at 48 Jermyn Street, Westminster, while visiting London. His remains were returned to Norfolk and buried in the churchyard of St Peter's, Kimberley. He is also commemorated on the Wymondham World War Two Memorial to victims of the Blitz. He was succeeded by his son John. John's godfather was P.G. Wodehouse who based his character Bertie Wooster on him.

1912

Luigi Barbesino (1894–1941)
Italian
Football
1912 Stockholm

Luigi Barbesino was born on 1 May 1894 in Casale Monferrato. Becoming a fine footballer, he played mid-field for AS Casale Calcio, Casale Monferrato. He spent all his eight playing seasons with them, being part of the team that won their only Italian football championship. He played 83 league matches scoring 11 goals between 1912 and 1920.

He was selected to play for Italy at the 1912 Stockholm Olympics. He made his international debut on 1 July 1912 in a 1–0 away win over Sweden. Italy later lost to Austria 5–1. Italy was knocked out in the rounds and failed to win a medal.

Barbesino was awarded five international caps and went on to coach Roma between 1934 and 1938.

At the beginning of the Second World War he joined the Italian Air Force as a major observer, serving with the 193rd Bomber Squadron flying out of Sicily. On 20 April 1941 he was flying in a reconnaissance aircraft as an observer with five others over the Sicily Channel. An hour after take-off they experienced bad weather and the aircraft reported it was turning back to base. It was the last anyone heard of Barbesino or his aircraft. To this day he and the entire crew of six are still posted as missing.

Barbesino seen here standing third from the right.

Sergey Filippov (1893–1942)
Russian
Football
1912 Stockholm

Sergey Pavlovich Filippov was born on 2 July 1893 in St Petersburg. A fine footballer he represented several St. Petersburg/Leningrad teams between 1909 and 1927.

He was champion of Russia in 1912 and was selected to represent the Russian football team at the 1912 Stockholm Olympics. In their first game, against Finland on 30 June 1912, they were beaten in a close game 2–1. They next took on Germany on 1 July 1912 and despite high hopes were crushed 16–0. Germany were captained by Gottfried Fuchs who scored ten of their goals, equalling the Olympic record which had been set by Denmark's Sofus Nielsen in 1908. With this defeat they were eliminated from the Games. Great Britain took the gold, Denmark the silver and the Netherlands the bronze.

He was killed in the German blockade of Leningrad some time in 1942, exact date unknown.

1920

Antonio Bonilla Sanmartín (1882–1937)
Spanish
Shooting
1920 Antwerp

Antonio Bonilla Sanmartín was born on 6 December 1882 in Guadalajara, Mexico. He was later selected to represent Spain at the 1920 Antwerp Olympics. He took part in the following events:

Team: 30 metre military pistol (6th); 300 metre military rifle prone (7th); 50 metre small bore rifle (9th); free rifle (11th); 50 metre free pistol (12th); 300 and 600 metre military rifle prone (12th); 600 metre military rifle prone (13th); 300 metre military rifle standing (14th).

Individual: 300 metre free rifle three positions (result unknown), 50 metre small bore rifle (result unknown).

Bonilla was killed in action in the Spanish Civil War on 9 November 1937.

Shooting team at the 1920 games.

Erminio Dones (1887–1945)
Italian
Rowing
1920 Antwerp (Silver)

Erminio Dones was born on 14 April 1887 in Venice. Becoming a keen and talented athlete, he divided his sporting time between rowing and mountain climbing, at both of which he excelled. He won his first medal, a bronze, rowing with the eight at the 1905 European Championships in Ghent. At the 1907 Championships in Strasbourg he took bronze in the single sculls and gold in the double sculls with Emilio Sacchini. He was both singles and doubles champion in Strasbourg in 1907. At the 1908 European Championships in Lucerne he took silver in the doubles, again with Emilio Sacchini. In the 1908 Championships, this time on Lake Geneva, he won gold in the doubles, this time with Pietro Annoni.

He was selected to represent Italy in the rowing events at the 1920 Antwerp Olympics. With Pietro Annoni he picked up a silver in the doubles, being pipped to the gold by the USA.

At the European Championships in Barcelona in 1922 he won another silver, with his partner Lorenzo Salvini. Finally, in 1923, again at the Europeans, on Lake Como, he took bronze in the double sculls with Salvini.

Dones was also an accomplished mountain and rock climber. He was among the first to ascend the Southern Grigna (Grignetta). He dedicated many of his climbs to lost friends and family, the most memorable being in 1924 when he erected a cross in memory of Angelo Vassalli who died in the First World War (Monte Pertica, December 1917). On the Cigar, which he finally conquered on 8 August 1915 with his friends Eugenio Fasana and Angelo Vassalli after several attempts, he dedicated one of his harder climbs to his sister.

He was commissioned into the Italian Infantry in the war and was killed in action as a captain on 25 April 1945.

Robert Feyerick (1892–1940)
Belgian
Fencing
1920 Antwerp
1924 Paris

Robert Feyerick was born on 18 January 1892 in Ghent, son of Ferdinand Feyerick (1865–1920) who won a team bronze in the épée at the 1908 Olympics. Following in his father's footsteps, Robert took up fencing, specialising in the sabre, becoming a member of St. Michael's Guild, which, founded over 400 years ago, is the oldest fencing club in the world.

Robert participated in two Olympic Games. In 1920 in Antwerp he took part in the individual and the team sabre; his best position was fourth in the team event. At the 1924 Games in Paris he took part in the same events but again failed to take a medal.

In the Second World War he served as a major with the infantry, becoming commanding officer with the 22nd Line Regiment. He was seriously wounded at Eeklo on 25 May 1940 in the eighteen day campaign. He died from his wounds on 18 June at the military hospital in Sint-Andries Abbey.

Julien Lehouck (1896–1944)
Belgian
Athletics
1920 Antwerp

Julien Lehouck was born on 14 August 1896 in Egem. A natural athlete, he competed for ASSA Ronse. He was selected to compete in the athletics competition at the 1920 Antwerp Olympics, where he ran in the men's 100 metres, the 4 × 400 metres relay and the long jump. He failed to win a medal in any event.

In the following year he married Simonne Gerbehaye, daughter of the wealthy mayor of Senzeille. On his death she inherited his metal construction company and became mayor in his stead.

In the war both Lehouck and his wife joined the local Resistance. From 1941 the couple began to hide Jews to protect them from the Nazis, around the castle in which they lived. They were betrayed and on 11 February 1944 the Gestapo surrounded the castle and arrested everyone inside. Lehouck was charged with espionage and assisting the Allies. He was deported to Fort Breendonk where he was hanged on 25 February 1944. His wife survived the war.

Charley Paddock (1900–43)
USA
Athletics
1920 Antwerp
1924 Paris
1928 Amsterdam
2 x Gold 2 x Silver

Charles William Paddock was born on 11 August 1900 in Gainesville, Texas, to Charles H. and Lulu (née Robinson). The family moved to Pasadena when Charles was a child. Towards the end of the First World War, Charley was commissioned as a lieutenant into the field artillery in the US Marines. After the war he studied at the University of Southern California. Although he had been Californian sprint champion for the previous three years, it was at the Inter-Allied Games (the Allied nations competing against each other in a friendly game) that he really came to notice, winning both the 100 and the 200 metre sprints. One newspaper named him 'The Fastest Man Alive'. He became the most famous track athlete of the twenties being noted for his bouncing stride, high knee action and a famous 'jump finish' in which he leapt across the finish line at the end of the race. He always wore silk when he ran and, being a successful journalist, was his own and very successful publicity manager. He also appeared in several movies – usually playing himself.

In 1920 Charley was selected to represent America at the 1920 Antwerp Olympics. At the age of 19 he took the gold in the 100 metres, silver in the 200 and gold in the 4 × 100 metres relay – not a bad haul for his first Olympics.

In 1924 Paddock was selected to represent America at the Paris Olympics. In the men's 100 metres he came 5th. Harold Abrahams took the gold, an achievement made famous in the film *Chariots of Fire*. Paddock took the silver in the 200 metres, Jackson Scholz took the gold and Eric Liddell the bronze. Liddle went on to take the gold in the 400 metres which also featured in *Chariots of Fire*.

Paddock was also selected to take part in the 1928 Games in Amsterdam, but failed to take a medal in the 200 metres.

The 'fastest man alive' died in a plane crash near Sitka, Alaska, on 21 July 1943 while serving as a captain in the Marines. He is buried in the Sitka National Cemetery. He was inducted into the National Track and Field Hall of Fame in 1976.

Juan Muguerza (1900–37)
Spanish
Athletics
1920 Antwerp

Juan Muguerza Sasieta was born on 6 May 1900 in Elgoibar in the Basque country. At the age of 17 he became Spanish champion in both the 1,500 and 5,000 metres, and retained the titles for five years, finally losing them in 1922. He also won the Spanish Championship in the 800 metres and the 110 metres hurdles and was a member of the Gipuzkoa relay team that took the Spanish championship. In 1921 he won four titles in the Spanish championships held in Galicia: standing long jump, shot put, discus and javelin. In 1920 he was selected to compete for Spain in the Antwerp Olympics. He took part in the 1,500 and 5,000 metres but failed to win a medal in either event.

He was killed in the Spanish Civil War on 5 May 1937 in the bombing near Mungia, Vizcaya, fighting for the Republicans. The Juan Muguerza Cross-Country Race, also known as the Elgoibar Cross-Country Race, takes place every January in Elgoibar in memory of Muguerza.

Josip Šolc (1898–1945)
Yugoslavian
Football
1920 Antwerp

Josip Šolc was born on 30 January 1898 in Zagreb. A talented and skilful footballer, he played in the midfield for HSK Concordia (a Zagreb club founded in 1906) between 1917 and 1928. He was selected to play for Yugoslavia at the 1920 Antwerp Olympics. The team was defeated in its opening match 7–0 by Czechoslovakia (who were later disqualified in their match against Belgium for walking off the pitch in protest at the decisions of the match officials). They only played in one more match – a friendly against Egypt which they lost 4–2. They finished twelfth out of thirteen teams. Belgium took the gold, Spain the silver and the Netherlands the bronze.

Šolc joined the Yugoslav Royal Army, serving with it from 1919 to 1940. During this time he also became a fencer, becoming a member of a small Yugoslavian team that took part in an international competition in Bucharest in 1938.

In the Second World War he became commander of the Zagreb garrison of the Nazi-backed Croatian Home Guard, remaining in that post until 1944. During this time he was awarded the Military Order of the Iron Trefoil 4th Class with Oak Wreath. In December 1944 he was promoted to general. In 1944 he was given command of the 1st Storm Division. In May 1945 he was captured by Yugoslav partisans and in June imprisoned in the military prison in Belgrade. He was tried, sentenced to death, and on 19 September 1945 was executed by firing squad.

Frans Tempel (1898–1944)
Dutch
Football
1920 Antwerp

Franciscus Jacobus Ludwig Tempel was born on 20 March 1898 in Hilversum and grew up to become a talented goalkeeper for HVV Tubantia.

He was selected to represent the Dutch national team at the 1920 Antwerp Olympics. Controversy dogged the team from the start: Tempel, together with team mates Jan de Natris, Jaap Bulder and Evert van Lingehe, were unhappy with their accommodation. The players were housed in small houseboats. Unable to resolve the matter with the Dutch Football Union, they were banned from taking any further part in the tournament. When Tempel then threatened to lead the team out on strike, he was suspended. However, the Dutch team declared their solidarity with them, the officials changed their minds, and they were allowed to stay. But neither Tempel nor Bulder were picked to play in any further games. The team went on to take the bronze medal, their third in a row.

Tempel was also a keen jazz pianist.

In the war Tempel joined the Dutch Resistance group based around Twente, collecting intelligence on the German occupiers. His group was betrayed and arrested by the Gestapo on 25 August 1943. In 1944 he was taken to the infamous prison camp Oranjehotel, Scheveningen. Tempel was eventually shot, together with five other Resistance fighters, on 25 July 1944 at Fort Rijnauwen in Bunnik, Utrecht.

Sigurd Wathne (1898–1942)
Norwegian
Football
1920 Antwerp

Sigurd Wathne was born on 12 February 1898 in Copenhagen. Becoming a talented goalkeeper, he played for SK Brann, representing Denmark on fourteen occasions.

He was selected to represent Norway in the 1920 Antwerp Olympics. They beat Great Britain 3–1 in the first round, were beaten by Italy 2–1 in the next round, and beaten by Czechoslovakia 4–0 in the next. They eventually finished fifth.

In the war Wathne served with the Norwegian merchant navy. He was chief engineer on the SS *Risøy* when it left Southampton loaded with scrap iron. She was escorted by one destroyer and three armed trawlers. Between eight and nine o'clock on Friday 20 March 1942, while the convoy was a little to the north of Trevose Head Lighthouse, she was attacked by several German bombers. One of the bombs exploded in *Risøy*'s number three hold. The order to abandon ship was given ten minutes later and the crew took to the lifeboats. Five minutes later, *Risøy* sank.

L'équipe Norvégienne

At first Wathne couldn't be found, but he was eventually discovered in the water, wounded. He was taken to Swansea General Hospital with a broken leg and other serious injuries. He died six days later. He was buried in Swansea's Danygraig Cemetery, grave 318.

Frederick Habberfield (1895–1943)
British
Cycling
1924 Paris

Frederick Henry Habberfield was born on 5 February 1895 in Kentish Town. Son of Francis and Kate, he had five siblings: Thomas, Dorothy, Winifred, Elsie and Eva. In 1925 Frederick married Irene Mowbray Wilkinson and they had one child.

A keen and talented cyclist, he competed for the Polytechnic Cycling Club in Westminster. In 1924 he was selected to take part in the Paris Olympics. He competed in the men's 2,000 metre tandem sprint with Thomas Harvey (who had competed in the 1920 Games). The pair came fourth, just missing out on a medal. Habberfield also took part in the men's team pursuit 4,000 metres, coming seventh. Despite not winning a medal he gave a very good account of himself.

Habberfield joined the Royal Navy and served as a canteen manager on the type three destroyer HMS *Holcombe* (named after the Holcombe Hunt in Lancashire). On 12 December 1943 *Holcombe* formed part of an escort deployed to protect convoy KMS34. The convoy was being stalked by U-593 commanded by Kapitänleutnant Gerd Kelbling. He sank HMS *Tynedale* off Jijel, Algeria, with the loss of seven officers and seventy-three men. The other escort ships then went in search of the U-boat, firing depth charges. Unfortunately during this search the U-boat managed to fire a torpedo at HMS *Holcombe* and sink her with the loss of eighty-one officers and men, including Habberfield. He is commemorated on the Chatham Naval Memorial.

U-593 surrendered the following day and was then sunk by USS *Wainwright* and HMS *Calpe*. Of the 164 ships in the convoy only eighty survived.

Robert Hilliard (1904–37)
Irish
Boxing
1924 Paris

Robert Martin Hilliard was born on 7 April 1904 in Moyeightragh, County Kerry, into a prosperous shop-owning family. He was educated at the Cork Grammar School followed by the Mountjoy School, Dublin. In 1921, having won a sizarship scholarship, he attended Trinity College, Dublin. While there he became a strong republican, cofounded the Thomas Davis society, and later became involved in the Irish Civil War.

Hilliard was also a fine sportsman. He was a founding member of the university's hurling club, and in 1923 became amateur Irish Boxing Association champion as well as the British and Irish Universities champion. He was selected to represent Ireland at the 1924 Paris Olympics, boxing bantamweight, but was knocked out in the second round by the Argentinian boxer Benjamín Pertuzzo.

Hilliard left Trinity in 1925 without a degree (although he did return in 1931 and got his BA). He married Edith Rosemary Robins and they had four children. Moving to Hindhead in Surrey, Hilliard worked as a journalist and in advertising. During this time he became deeply interested in the Oxford Group of evangelical Christians. He was ordained as a priest into the Church of Ireland in 1931 and then worked at St Anne's Cathedral Belfast in the mission for the poor.

He later joined the Communist Party of Great Britain, abandoning his family and his mission in Belfast. Moving to London, he worked as a journalist again. His personal views changed remarkably during this time: he became an atheist. He also joined the Communist Party of Ireland.

Outraged at what was happening in Spain, he joined the International Brigade and fought for the Second Spanish Republic with the Connolly Column of Irish Volunteers. He was selected as one of fourteen men left behind to cover the retreat of the Republicans after the Battle of Jarama. All were killed or later died of their wounds. Hilliard was seriously wounded and died five days later on 22 February 1937 in a makeshift military hospital in Castellon de la Plana. Before dying he managed to send a letter to his wife:

My dear, Five minutes ago I got your letter ... Teach the kids to stand for democracy ... Do not worry too much about me, I expect I shall be quite safe. I think I am going to make quite a good soldier ... I still hate fighting but this time it has to be done, unless fascism is beaten in Spain & in the world it means war and hell for our kids. All the time when I am thinking of you & the children I am glad I have come. Give my love to Tim, Deirdre, Davnet & Kit. Write when you can, it will help – love to you, Robert (24/1/37)

Christy Moore sang about him in *Viva la Quinta Brigada*:

> Bob Hilliard was a Church of Ireland pastor,
> From Killarney across the Pyrenees he came.
> From Derry came a brave young Christian Brother,
> Side by side they fought and died in Spain.

He was also commemorated in Blánaid Salkeld's poem *Casualties*:

> Who would think the Spanish War
> Flared like new tenure of a star
> The way our rhymes and writings are.
> That Hilliard spilled his boxer's blood
> Through Albacete's snow and mud
> And smiled to Comrade Death: Salud!
> That Charlie Donnelly small and frail
> And flushed with youth was rendered pale
> But not with fear, in what queer squalor
> Was smashed up his so-ordered valour.
> That rhythm that steady earnestness
> That peace of poetry to bless
> Discordant thoughts of divers men
> Blue gaze that burned lie and stem
> Put out by death.

Thomas Hitchcock Jr (1900–44)
USA
Polo
Paris 1924 (Silver)

Thomas Hitchcock Jr was born on 11 February 1900 in Aiken, South Carolina. He came from a very sporting family; his parents, Louise and Thomas Sr, were steeped in racing and polo. His father was inducted into the US Racing Hall of Fame as a horse trainer. He founded the Meadowbrook Polo Club on Long Island, New York, and captained the American team in the inaugural 1886 International Polo Club.

Thomas Jr played in his first polo tournament at the age of 13 and became a member of the Meadowbrook Polo Club that won the 1916 US Junior Championship.

He was educated at St Paul's, New Hampshire, where he played hockey, football and rowed.

In the First World War he served with the famous Lafayette Flying Circus. He was shot down and captured, spending many months in hospital and prison camps. However, as he was being moved from one camp to another he managed to escape by jumping from a train as it crossed a river. He made for Switzerland, and despite still being wounded, walked over a hundred miles in eight days, mainly at night. He was awarded the Croix de Guerre.

After the war he attended Harvard and then Oxford universities. Keeping up his interest in polo, he captained the US team to victory at the 1921 International Polo Cup, and also at the US National Open Championships in 1923, 1927, 1935 and 1936.

In 1933 he received a serious injury and most thought his career was over, but he was not one to give up easily and he made a full and remarkable comeback, being fit enough to play on the Greentree side that beat Aurora 6–5 to win the US Open in 1935.

Such was his fame that F. Scott Fitzgerald used his character for both Tom Buchanan in the *Great Gatsby* and Tommy Barban in *Tender is the Night*.

In 1928 Hitchcock married Margaret Mellon who came from one of the wealthiest families in America. They had four children.

Hitchcock worked for investment bankers Lehman Brothers. Flying to work each day, he would park his sea-plane in New York harbour close to Wall Street.

In 1924 he was selected to represent the USA at the Paris Olympics. Competing in the men's polo, he took a team silver. During the final the USA took an early lead, but Argentina fought back and managed to tie the match in the final moments. It was left to the Argentine player Juan Miles to score the winning goal in the final chukka, taking the match 6–5 and the gold medal. Great Britain took the bronze.

In the Second World War Hitchcock served as a lieutenant colonel with the US Army Air Force, assigned as an assistant air attaché to the US Embassy in London. He was important in the development of the P-51 fighter, especially with replacing the original Allison engine

with the Packard-built Rolls-Royce Merlin. He was killed in a flying accident on 19 April 1944 while piloting a P-51 on a test flight near Salisbury, Wiltshire, when he was unable to pull out of a steep dive shortly after leaving the 9th Air Force fighter station. He is buried in the Cambridge American Cemetery, plot A, row 6, grave 21.

Considered by many to have been America's greatest ever polo player, he was later inducted into the Museum of Polo and Hall of Fame.

Edward D'Arcy McCrea (1895–1940)
Irish
Tennis
1924 Paris

Edward D'Arcy McCrea was born on 7 February 1896 in Altona, Stillorgan, to Harris and Jeannette (née Seale). He graduated in medicine from Trinity, Dublin, and earned an MCh in 1922. He became a fellow of the Royal College of Surgeons in Ireland in 1922, after which he became an assistant surgeon at Sir Patrick Dun's Hospital. Moving to Manchester, he specialized in Urology at the Salford Royal Hospital, and in 1926 became a fellow of the Royal College of Surgeons. He was elected assistant surgeon to the hospital in June 1927 and surgeon in February 1935. He published a number of papers in the 1930s on his specialty, nerves of the stomach, for the *British Journal of Surgery*, and 'Pre-sacral sympathectomy and the urinary bladder' and 'Epididymal cysts, their aetiology and treatment' both for the *British Journal of Urology*. He built up a successful practice in Victoria Park, Manchester, and lectured on physiology at Manchester University.

McCrea married Edith Willock, also a doctor, who worked in obstetrics. They lived at The Cottage on Barton Road in Salford (where they moved to be safer from German bombs) and had two children.

McCrea was an excellent amateur tennis player, and in 1924 was selected to play for Ireland at the Paris Olympics. He reached the quarter-finals in the mixed doubles with Hilda Wallis (1900–79) who was Irish champion in 1924, 26, 30 and 33, and played at Wimbledon twice. McCrea also played in the singles and men's doubles, but failed to gain a medal.

Although he never played at Wimbledon, he did win a number of other tournaments over the years, including the 1922/3 Derbyshire and the 1927 Manchester Northern Championship. He also played for Ireland in the Davis Cups of 1923 and 1924.

On 22 December 1940 the McCreas were hosting a party at their home in Salford when a German parachute mine struck the house and totally destroyed it. McCrea, his wife, the children aged 9 and 12, the maid and all their guests were killed.

Tomasz Stankiewicz (1902–40)
Polish
Cycling
1924 Paris (Silver)

Tomasz Stankiewicz was born on 28 December 1902 in Warsaw.

In 1923 he became Polish bicycle sprint champion. He also gained attention for beating some of the best cyclists in Europe, including the Italians Boiocchi and Bossi and the Frenchman Galvaing. He won numerous awards, as well as winning several races in Norway, France and Africa, which in 1925 culminated in his receiving the Great Oran Award.

In 1924 he was selected to represent Poland at the 1924 Paris Olympics. With Franciszek Szymczyk (1892–1976), Jan Lazarsski (1892–1968) and Józef Lange (1897–1972) he took the silver medal in the men's 4,000 metres pursuit. The final was between Italy and Poland. It was close for six laps but the Italians pulled away in the final two laps and took the gold by 100 metres. Belgium took the bronze by beating France. It was Poland's first ever Olympic cycling medal.

The following year Stankiewicz gave up cycling to take up a career with the American company Chrysler in Warsaw. In the war he was instructed to remove as many cars as he could from the capital Warsaw. After this task was complete, he was stopped and searched in a random check and found to be carrying pamphlets issued by the Polish underground. He was interrogated and shipped to Palmiry on 20 June 1940 where he was shot by a Nazi firing squad, one of the 1,700 victims of the Palmiry massacres. He died with other well-known cyclists and friends, Janusz Kusociński, Feliks Żuber (see page 244) and Tadeusz Bartodziejski.

Eddie Webster (1902–45)
British
Athletics
1924 Paris

Joseph Edward Webster was born on 15 June 1902 in Rowley Regis. He worked as a school caretaker in Wolverhampton. He started his athletics career as a cross-country runner in 1923. He won the national cross-country running championship in 1926 and 1928 and the international competition in 1925. He also excelled in track events, taking the AAA championships. He won the four miles title in 1926 and the ten miles in 1925 and 1928. He was also the Midland Counties champion in the four miles on three occasions, 1925, 1926 and 1929, and in the ten miles in 1924. His best event however was the steeplechase, in which he won the AAA championship on four successive occasions, 1925–28. He took the English AAA title in 1924–25. He took the Midlands championship eleven out of twelve times between 1925 and 1936 (he failed to take it in 1931 because of a suspension).

He was selected to take part in the 1924 Paris Olympics. He competed in the men's 10,000 metres, the cross-country individual and the cross-country team, but he didn't win a medal.

After winning his fourth consecutive AAA steeplechase title he was considered a certainty for the 1928 Olympics. However, before he had a chance to take part he was suspended for a very minor infringement of the rules involving the promotion of a patent medicine. In February 1931 he was suspended again for irregularities concerning travel and accommodation expenses while competing in Glasgow. Harsh treatment indeed.

Eddie married Lizzie Matilda Webster of Penn, Wolverhampton, and they had a son and a daughter.

In the war he joined the Royal Artillery, becoming Gunner 11256592 Webster. After training he was shipped to Italy where he was involved in several engagements against the German occupiers. After the war was over, he was looking forward to returning home when he was killed in a road traffic accident involving military and civilian vehicles on 22 August 1945. He only had a month left before he was due to be demobbed. He is buried in the Salerno War Cemetery, VII. A. 34.

1928

Kestutis Bulota (1896–1941/2)
Lithuanian
Speed skating
1928 Saint Moritz

Kęstutis Bulota was born on 23 October 1896 in Tallinn. He became an engineer by trade, having studied in Berlin. However his passion was athletics and he was probably his country's finest all-round athlete. He participated in several sports at a very high level. He played football for LFLS Kaunas, winning national titles with them in 1922 and 1923. He was also Lithuanian champion in triple jump, race walking, relay sprint, speed skating, cycling, hammer throwing and ice hockey. He helped LFLS win the national ice hockey league in 1926, 1931 and 1934.

In 1928 he was selected to represent Lithuania at speed skating in the 1928 winter Olympics in Saint Moritz. He raced in the 500 metres coming 28th, the 1,500 metres coming 25th, the 5,000 metres coming 25th, and the 10,000 metres coming 5th. In attending the Games, Bulota became Lithuania's first winter Olympian. Besides the 1928 Olympics, he also contested the 1928 World Championships, which were held a week before the Games in Davos; he came 21st.

On 14 June 1941 he was arrested by the NKVD and together with thousands of other Lithuanians deported to Siberia and imprisoned in a gulag labour camp. According to Soviet sources, he was shot while trying to escape in late 1941 or early 1942.

Frank Cuhel (1904–43)
USA
Athletics
1928 Amsterdam (Silver)

Frank Cuhel was born on 28 September 1904 in Cedar Rapids, Iowa. He was educated at the University of Iowa where he played football and athletics, specializing in track events. In 1928 he won the 220 metre hurdles at the NCAA (National Collegiate Athletics Association) championships, besting the event record in so doing. He won the 400 metres hurdles at the Midwestern Olympic trials, coming second to Morgan Taylor (1903–75) who won an Olympic gold and two bronze medals. At the final trials for the 1928 Olympics Taylor came first in a world record time of 52.0. Cuhel came a close second with a time of 52.1. Both men ran in the 400 metres at the 1928 Olympics in Amsterdam. Frank coming second took the silver and Morgan Taylor the bronze. David, Lord Burghley, running for Great Britain, won the gold.

On graduating, Cuhel was employed as an envoy for a number of Dutch firms doing business mostly in the USA. He was later sent to Java, where he was when war broke out. As the man on the spot, Cuhel was hired by Mutual Broadcasting Systems as a war correspondent, issuing radio reports on the war and its progress. Alas most were of defeats and Japanese advances. When Java fell, he and several other war correspondents made a daring last minute escape out of the country.

Cuhel was killed in a Boeing 314 seaplane called the *Yankee Clipper* when it crashed into the Tagus River just outside Lisbon, Portugal, on 22 February 1943. Of 39 on board, 24 were killed. Interestingly, the popular singer Jane Froman (*With a Song in my Heart*) was seriously injured in it; she never made a full recovery. It wasn't until three weeks later that his body was recovered. That December, a freighter was christened the *Frank J. Cuhel* after him. He was elected to the University of Iowa Athletics Hall of Fame in 1993.

Emile Duson (1904–42)
Dutch
Hockey
1928 Amsterdam (Silver)

Emile Paul Joseph Duson was born on 1 December 1904 in Semarang, Dutch East Indies. He became a very fine hockey player and represented AH&BC Club, Amsterdam. He was selected to play for the Netherlands at the 1928 Olympics. He played half-back in all four matches: against Spain drawing 1–1; Germany winning 2–1; France winning 5–0; and losing in the final to India 3–0 and taking the silver medal.

In the war he served with the KNLI, the Royal Dutch East Indies Army, becoming a member of the city guard at Tiga Roenggoe. Part of the work done by this unit during the Japanese landings on the east coast of Sumatra was to destroy a series of bridges and slow or stop the Japanese advance. They knew that the Japanese murdered anyone involved in these activities. The Japanese landed on 12 March 1942 at Laboean Roekoe. They quickly surrounded the city guard in Tiga Roenggoe and took them prisoner. Twenty-one members of the guard were then tied up, forced to kneel, and shot in the back of the head on 14/15 March 1942, including the brave Emile Duson. The bodies were buried by villagers the following day on the orders of the Japanese.

In 1947 the remains of the city guards were discovered and examined by the forensic physicians Dr T.H. Become and P.J. Boortman. Among those identified was Emile Duson. It was discovered that the man who had given the orders for the murders was Major Junzaburo Nakamura. After a brief search it was discovered he had been killed in New Caledonia, so alas would never face justice.

Emile was later buried with dignity in the Field of Honour 'Ancol' in Jarkarta row V grave 17.

Heywood Lane Edwards (1905–41)
USA
Wrestling
1928 Amsterdam

Heywood Lane Edwards was born on 9 November 1905 in San Saba, Texas, son of Winston C. and Louise (Smith). He was educated at San Saba High School and the US Naval Academy in Annapolis. As a midshipman he wrestled, played football and boxed. He graduated, becoming ensign, in 1926, and was sent on a short course in aviation before joining the USS *Florida*. He rose through the ranks to become lieutenant commander in 1940.

Of the many sports he was involved in, wrestling was his passion. In 1928 he represented the USA in the Amsterdam Olympics, fighting light-heavyweight. He finished fourth, just missing out on a medal.

Returning to duty, he served on the cruiser USS *Reno*, before joining the destroyers *Kennedy* and *William B. Preston*. He also served on several submarines, including *Bonita*, *Bass* and *Barracuda*. In 1935 he joined the destroyer *Detroit*, flagship of the Battle Force. On 6 June 1940 he was posted to command the destroyer *USS Reuben James*, but on 30/31 October 1941 west of Iceland she was torpedoed and sunk by U-boat 552 commanded by Kapitänleutnant Erich Topp (Topp sank thirty-five ships in the war, and after the war worked for NATO). She was the first ship to be sunk in the battle for the Atlantic. Edwards and ninety-nine members of the crew died in the attack, forty-six were later rescued from the sea.

Lieutenant Commander Edwards was posthumously awarded the Purple Heart. In 1943 the USS *Heywood L. Edwards* was named in his honour. He was one of the first American casualties of the Second World War, being killed more than a month before Pearl Harbor.

Billy Fiske (1911–40)
USA
Bobsleigh
1928 Saint Moritz (Gold)
1932 Lake Placid (Gold)

William Meade Lindsley Fiske III was born on 4 June 1911 in Chicago, son of William Fiske, a New England banker, and Beulah. He was educated in Chicago, and France where he discovered and began to participate in bobsleigh events. In 1928 he went up to Trinity Cambridge where he read Economics and History, afterwards working at the London office of Dillon, Reed & Co, the New York bankers. On 8 September 1938 he married Rose Bingham, Countess of Warwickshire (1913–72), thereby becoming part of the British nobility.

In 1928 he was selected to represent the USA at the St Moritz winter Olympics; he was 16 years old. He competed in the five man bobsled and took the gold. He was the youngest

Billy Fiske seen here driving the bobsleigh at the 1932 Olympics.

person ever to win a gold medal at the Olympics (retaining this record until 1992 when Toni Nieminen, the Finnish skier, surpassed him at the age of 16 years and 261 days). The others in the team were Geoffrey Mason (d.1987), Nion Tocker (d.1950), Clifford Gray (d.1968) and Richard Parke (d.1950).

Billy was selected again in 1932 for the Lake Placid Olympics, where he was given the honour of carrying the American flag at the opening ceremony. At these Olympics the bobsled changed from a five- to a four-man bob. Clifford Gray was again in the team, as well as Eddie Eagan (d.1967), the only man to win Olympic golds in both the winter and summer Olympics, and Jay O'Brien (died of a heart attack in 1940). The team won the gold medal.

Fiske was asked to take part in the 1936 Games in Garmisch-Partenkirchen, but declined, strongly disagreeing with Nazi politics.

He was also a Cresta champion, as well as being famous for his jumps from the Badrutt's Palace Hotel bar chandelier in St Moritz (still there today).

In 1936 Fiske became involved with Thomas Fortune Ryan in a project that turned Aspen, Colorado, an old and exhausted mining town, into America's most important winter sports venue, which it still is to this day.

Shortly before the war Fiske was recalled to New York. But he returned to England in August 1939, pretending to be a Canadian (the US was neutral). He was accepted into the RAFVR, becoming a pilot officer in March 1940, joining 601 Squadron (County of London). Pledging his loyalty to England and King George VI, he later wrote, 'I believe I can lay claim to being the first U.S. citizen to join the RAF in England after the outbreak of hostilities.'

On 15 August 1940 his squadron was scrambled from RAF Tangmere to intercept a flight of Stukas. They shot down eight of them, but unfortunately one of the Stukas put a bullet in the fuel tank of Billy's Hurricane. The aircraft caught fire and his hands and ankles were burnt. He remained with his plane instead of baling out and managed to get it home, despite being in great pain. He was carried out of his aircraft badly hurt. Shortly after, it exploded. Fiske was rushed to the Chichester Hospital but alas died two days later. He was the first American to die in the Second World War.

He was buried at Boxgrove Priory Church on 20 August with both the Union Jack and the Stars and Stripes covering his coffin. His flight commander, Sir Archibald Philip Hope, later wrote of him:

'Unquestionably Billy Fiske was the best pilot I've ever known. It was unbelievable how good he was. He picked up so fast it wasn't true. He'd flown a bit before, but he was a natural as a fighter pilot. He was also terribly nice and extraordinarily modest, and fitted into the squadron very well.'

The inscription on his gravestone reads simply: 'He died for England.' Among the many memorials to this extraordinary and brave man is a stained glass window at Boxgrove Priory, dedicated to him on 17 September 2008.

Walter Flinsch (1903–43)
German
Rowing
1928 Amsterdam
1932 Los Angeles (Silver)

Walter Flinsch was born on 7 February 1903 in New York into the Frankfurt branch of a paper industrialists' family. However, instead of joining the family firm, he became a pilot with Lufthansa.

His passion was rowing. He rowed for Frankfurter Ruderverein von 1865, until 1929, before moving to Mannheimer Ruderverein Amicitia 1876. He was German champion of 1923–4 and 1926–28 in the single sculls. In 1924 he was champion in the double sculls. In 1930 he was champion in both the eights and coxed fours, and 1931 in the eights and coxless fours.

He was selected to represent Germany at the 1928 Amsterdam Olympics, but alas was knocked out in the first repêchage of the single sculls. He was selected for the 1932 Los Angeles Olympics where he competed in the coxless fours and the eights. In the coxless fours he was part of the team that took the silver medal. Great Britain took the gold and Italy the bronze. The German eight failed to take a medal.

In the war, as a trained pilot he joined the German air force. He became a test pilot and was killed on 3 February 1943 when he lost control of his Heinkel HE 177 bomber. Although he did manage to get out of the aircraft, he was not high enough for his parachute to deploy properly and he was killed.

Hans Fokker (1900–43)
Dutch
Sailing
1928 Amsterdam

Hendrik Gustaaf Fokker was born on 18 February 1900 in Rotterdam. He worked for Koopman & Co of Bandung, Java. He married Everdina Brand. They had one daughter, Everdina Johanna.

A fine sailor, he was selected to represent the Netherlands at the 1928 Amsterdam Olympics as a member of the crew of the 6-metre *Kemphaan*. The 6-metre event is decided by an initial seven races, with the first four preliminary. After four races, yachts are eliminated that have not been placed in the top three in any of the four preliminary races. Final placements are determined by a majority system. He just missed out on a medal, coming fourth. Norway took the gold, Denmark the silver and Estonia the bronze. His crew was made up of helmsman Hans Pluijgers (d.1974), Carl Hulsken (d.1987), Wim Schouten (d.1941) and Roeffie Vermeulen (d.1963).

In the war he was captured and imprisoned by the Japanese in Burma. He died in Thanbyuzayat on 2 July 1943 of exhaustion and disease. He is buried in the Three Pagoda Pass in the Tenasserim Hills.

Jan Gajdoš (1903–45)
Czechoslovakian
Gymnastics
1928 Amsterdam (Silver)
1936 Berlin

Jan Gajdoš was born on 27 December 1903 in Brno. Czechoslovakia's finest pre-war gymnast, he took three gold medals in the team events at the World Championships in 1926–1930 and 1938. He also took silver in 1934. He took two silver medals in the individual events in 1926 and in 1930, where he also took the overall silver medal, being pipped to the gold by Josip Primozic (d.1985) a Yugoslavian who took part in three Olympics and won both a silver and bronze medal at the 1928 Olympics.

Gajdoš was also an excellent athlete, competing in football, diving, figure skating, handball, and skiing.

He competed in two Olympic Games, first in 1928 in Amsterdam where he was part of the gymnastics team that took the silver medal. He failed to take a medal in the individual competition. The second was the 1936 Berlin Olympics. Here he failed to win a medal, coming fourth in the team event and twenty-seventh in the individual.

In the war Gajdoš became a senior member of the Sokol Resistance group. He was betrayed and arrested in 1943, tried and sentenced to death

The grave of Jan Gajdoš in Brno. (*OISV via Wikimedia*)

by the Nazi occupiers. However, as the Allies broke through and began to get closer to his concentration camp, the Nazis forced the inmates on a march to the labour camp at Zwickau. Although he survived the march, his health broke down. He never recovered and died shortly after the war ended, on 19 November 1945.

In November 2008 an international gymnastics event was arranged in his memory in Brno; the Jan Gajdoš Memorial 2008.

Robert Huber (1906–42)
German
Rowing
1928 Amsterdam

Robert Huber was born on 10 November 1906 in Hessen. He grew up to row for the Mannheimer RV Amicitia, winning the German national titles with them in 1928 and 1931. He was selected to represent Germany at the 1928 Amsterdam Olympics, being eliminated in the quarter-finals of the eights.

Huber fought on the Russian Front with the German infantry in the war and was reported missing presumed killed on 1 July 1942 (some records have the date as 18 August 1942).

John Lander (1907–42)
British
Rowing
1928 Amsterdam (Gold)

John Gerard Heath Lander was born on 7 September 1907 in Liverpool, the son of the Right Reverend Gerald Heath Lander DD. He was educated at Shrewsbury, and while there was a keen rower, winning the Ladies' Challenge Plate at Henley Regatta in 1924. He then went up to Trinity, Cambridge, where he rowed for the First Trinity Boat Club.

In 1928 he was selected for the men's coxless fours at the 1928 Olympics in Amsterdam. Rowing stroke, his crew was made up of Edward Vaughan Bevan (d.1988), Richard Beesly (d.1965) and Michael Warriner (d.1986). The British crew beat the American four by one second to take the gold. Italy won the bronze.

In 1929 Lander was expected to be included in the eight for the Boat Race, but Richard Beesly, the Cambridge president, decided to select Tom Brocklebank instead. Cambridge won by seven lengths.

In 1929 Lander took a job in Hong Kong with the Asiatic Petroleum Company. He continued to row, and became captain of the Royal Hong Kong Yacht Club team at Middle Island.

In 1941 Lander joined the Hong Kong Volunteer Defence Corps as a gunner. After some very basic training he was posted to One Battery at Stanley Fort. He was killed in the battle for Hong Kong on 25 December 1941 near the gate of St Stephen's College. He was the only British gold medallist to be killed in the Second World War. He was buried in the Sai Wan War Cemetery, M.4.

David Lindsay (1906–43)
New Zealand
Swimming
1928 Amsterdam

David Powell Lindsay was born on 12 November 1906 in Wellington. He had one brother, John Douglas. He later moved to Christchurch. One of New Zealand's finest swimmers, he won the national titles for both the 440 yards and 880 yards freestyle on five occasions between 1927 and 1934. He married Mabel Elizabeth of Napier and they settled down at 14 Lawrence Street, Wellington, and had two children, Michael and Neil.

He was selected to represent New Zealand at the 1928 Amsterdam Olympics. He took part in the 400 metres and 1,500 metres freestyle but failed to take a medal in either.

In the war he was commissioned into the 26th Battalion New Zealand Infantry. He was killed at the battle for Orsogna in southern Italy on 12 December 1943 when a shell fired from an Allied 25-pounder fell short of its target and hit his position killing Lindsay and seven other men in his platoon.

He is commemorated in the Sangro River War Cemetery, grave reference XVI.C.23.

Rudolf Lippert (1900–45)
German
Equestrianism
1928 Amsterdam
1936 Berlin (Gold)

Rudolf Lippert was born on 29 October 1900 in Leipzig. Deciding on a career in the army and being one of the country's finest horse riders, he was stationed to the Cavalry School in Hannover. In 1928, by then a lieutenant, he was selected to take part in the Amsterdam Olympics. Riding his horse *Fasan* in the three-day eventing competition, he finished tenth. The German team were obliged to withdraw from the Games after fellow rider Walter Feyerabend was unable to finish the cross-country section and had to withdraw.

He was selected to ride for Germany again at the 1936 Games held in Berlin. Now a captain, he again rode *Fasan*. This time he took a gold medal in the team event. He finished sixth in the individual competition.

In the war he was promoted to major general and put in command of the 5th Panzer Division. His outstanding leadership qualities and bravery won him many honours, including the *Ritterkreuz* on 9 June 1944. He died of wounds received fighting American forces at Bielefeld on 1 April 1945.

Hendrik (Bob) Mangelaar Meertens (1908–44)
Dutch
Field hockey
1928 Amsterdam (Silver)

Hendrik Mangelaar Meertens was born on 30 September 1908 in Semarang, Indonesia. Becoming a talented hockey player, he played for the club HLC and was selected for the Dutch national side at the 1928 Olympics in Amsterdam. But although selected, he was never picked for the side. He was never to win an international cap.

Settling in the Dutch East Indies, he continued to play hockey for various local clubs. He had a lucky escape when on 20 October 1936 his ship the SS *Van der Wijck* capsized in a storm near Tanjung Pakis. Thirty-four people lost their lives, but Meertens was plucked from the sea in time.

In the war Meertens decided to enlist in the Dutch East Indies Army. He was captured by the Japanese in 1942. After enduring a prison camp for two years he was transported on the 'hell ship' *Junyo Maru* to work on the railway being built between Pakan Baru and Muaro in Sumatra. The *Junyo Maru* was torpedoed by the British submarine HMS *Tradewind* on 18 September 1944, killing 5,620 of the people on board. They consisted of 1,377 Dutch (including Bob Meertens), 64 British and Australian, 8 Americans and 4,200 Javanese slave labourers. There were 680 survivors, many of whom died later working on the railway. It was the world's greatest ever sea disaster at the time.

The *Junyo Maru*, on which Meertens was transported as a PoW.

Jack Murdoch (1908–44)
Canadian
Rowing
1928 Amsterdam (Bronze)

John Lawrence Cosgrave Murdoch was born on 18 July 1908 in Toronto, one of five children. He was educated at De La Salle College and St Michael's. He rowed in the Argonaut eight and at Henley. After school he worked for the Gair Company of Canada which produced munitions.

A fine rower, he was selected to go to the 1928 Amsterdam Olympics. Canada fielded a strong eight and took the bronze medal, the US taking the gold and Great Britain the silver.

In 1939 he joined the reserve, becoming attached to the 19th Field Company, Royal Canadian Artillery, as an officer, rising to the rank of captain. He landed with them in Normandy on D-Day and was killed in action on 10 October 1944 in Holland. He was buried in the Adegem Canadian War Cemetery VIII. A. 7.

Jules Noël (1903–40)
French
Athletics
1928 Amsterdam
1932 Los Angeles
1936 Berlin

Jules Joseph Noël was born on 27 January 1903 in Norrent-Fontes in the Pas-de-Calais. He grew up to become one of France's most outstanding and popular athletes. In the French athletics championships he won no less than nineteen medals in twelve years, including thirteen golds.

Noël appeared in three Olympic Games. In 1928 in Amsterdam he took part in the men's discus but was knocked out in the heats.

In the 1932 Los Angeles Olympics he was the French flag bearer, proudly leading the French team into the Olympic stadium. He came tenth in the shot put and fourth in the discus throw. Amusingly, the French team convinced the Olympic committee that red wine was an essential part of their diet – despite the nationwide prohibition – and received an exemption from the law. There was serious controversy after one of Noël's discus

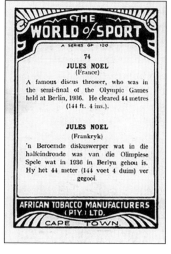

throws – which beat even the gold-winning throw – was disallowed because the officials hadn't been concentrating and couldn't find the landing mark. He had already broken the record at the French trials throwing a distance of 49.44 metres. He was allowed an additional throw but was unable to match his previous one. To be fair, the American, Anderson, went on to improve his distance to 49.49 metres and break the Olympic record.

Four years later he travelled to Berlin for the Olympics and once again was selected as the French flag bearer, but he failed to qualify for the shot put and came twelfth in the discus throw.

In 1938 Noël competed in the European Championships in Paris. He finished seventh in the discus and ninth in the shot put, improving on his positions at the 1934 championships in Turin.

Noël refused a job at the Joinville School, deciding instead to join the army, rising quickly to the rank of sergeant. He was seriously wounded outside Escaudoeuvres in the German invasion, and died from his wounds on 19 May 1940.

Peter Reynolds (1912–44)
USA
Lacrosse
1928 Amsterdam
1932 Los Angeles

Peter William Reynolds was born on 21 January 1912 in Baltimore, Maryland. He grew up working in his father's grocery store. He was educated at the Mount Saint Joseph High School in Baltimore before attending Johns Hopkins University where he studied engineering. There he excelled at American football and lacrosse. It was at lacrosse however that he was to shine.

He was selected to represent the US team at the 1928 Olympics in Amsterdam. Three countries took part, Canada, USA and Great Britain. In 1928 it was only a demonstration sport and the three teams played round-robin matches on 5–7 August 1928. Each ended the tournament with a record of 1 win and 1 loss.

Reynolds was selected again to go to the Games in 1932 in Los Angeles. It was once again a demonstration game, this time with only Canada and the USA taking part. The USA came out on top, winning two games out of the three.

In the war Reynolds served with the Marine Corps, rising to the rank of captain. When Japan invaded the Philippines, despite being badly armed and equipped the American and Filipino troops held on for four months. However, as the fighting continued, casualties became high and the defenders were running out of food and ammunition, eventually forcing General Edward King to surrender. Reynolds was taken prisoner and managed to survive the Bataan Death March. During this time Reynolds was able to get a few postcards sent to his family via the Red Cross.

In 1944, with 1,800 other American prisoners of war, Reynolds boarded the *Arisan Maru*. Unfortunately, on 24 October 1944 the ship was attacked and sunk by the American submarine *Shark* (which was later destroyed by the Japanese) in the Bashi Straits, about 250 kilometres south-west of Formosa. The submarine's captain had been unaware that there were Americans on board. Only nine Americans survived the sinking, as the Japanese vessels in the area refused to help them. Of the nine, five managed to reach China, the other four were recaptured and died in Japanese hands. Reynolds did not survive the sinking.

Many years later, in 1997, he would be voted into the Sports Hall of Fame at his old school.

Farid Simaika (1907–43)
Egyptian
Diving
1928 Amsterdam (Silver and Bronze)

Farid Simaika was born on 12 June 1907 in Alexandria. His family were one of the oldest Coptic families in Egypt and very influential.

He became Egyptian diving champion before leaving for the USA in the 1920s. He joined the Ambassador Swimming Club in Los Angeles in 1927 before winning the Amateur Athletics Union low board championship. He then came second in the American national fancy high diving competition, and won it in 1930 to 1932. Simaika's performance in the 1932 American diving championship was noticed by some Japanese, who invited him to compete in the Japanese high diving competition in Tokyo in 1932. He did so, and won easily.

He was selected to dive for Egypt at the 1928 Amsterdam Olympics and took part in the men's springboard, winning the bronze, and the men's platform, winning the silver. There was some controversy about his silver as it was originally thought he had taken the gold. The *Charleston Gazette* explains: 'The finals in the men's diving saw one of the most curious incidents of the Olympiad. Simaika, the California-trained Egyptian plunger, finished with top points at 99.58, and the Egyptian flag was hoisted and the Egyptian national anthem sung for the first time of the meeting. But soon afterwards it was announced that a majority of the judges by a vote of 5 to 4 had decided that Desjardins of Miami was the winner, with the best general average of points for the eight dives.' Simaika's gold was withdrawn and he was given the silver.

He went on to perform in several World's Fair 'water shows' and toured the world giving diving displays. His high-diving act included a blindfolded tandem dive, which he also performed in the film *Double Diving* (1939). He also performed in *Seas Beneath* directed by John Ford (1931) and *Water Sports* (1941) by Del Frazier, and did two-a-day 66-foot tower dives at the Canadian National Exhibition in Toronto.

In 1935, Simaika married Betty J. Wilson (his second marriage) but it was a close call: when he filed his intention-to-wed notice, the marriage licence bureau in California turned it down over issues concerning his ethnicity. Was Simaika an Egyptian or a Caucasian? California law at the time prevented Caucasians from marrying people of a different race. However it was finally ruled that Egyptians were after all Caucasian and the marriage went ahead. In March 1942 Simaika finally received American citizenship.

In August 1942, further keen to establish himself as an American, Simaika enlisted in the US army. After training as an intelligence officer for a bombardment group, he was commissioned as a second lieutenant and served with 530th Bomber Squadron, 380th Bomber (Heavy). He took off with a crew of eleven in his B-24D Liberator from Fenton

Airfield, Northern Territory, Australia, on a strike mission over Makassar, Sulawesi, on 11 September 1943. It is believed that his Liberator was shot down by ground anti-aircraft fire over Makassar. The entire crew was lost. At the time he was only posted as missing. There were rumours that he had been captured by either the Japanese or local tribesmen after escaping from his plane, but they were never substantiated. His death was finally confirmed on 10 December 1945.

He was awarded the DFC and a Purple Heart. In 1982 he was inducted into the International Swimming Hall of Fame. A major road in Cairo is named after him, and he is commemorated at the Manila American Cemetery in the Philippines.

Harry Simmons (1911–44)
British
Athletics
1928 Amsterdam

Henry Augustus Simmons was born on 21 February 1911 in Southampton, son to Francis and Catherine Fanny. He was educated at Taunton School, Southampton. As a fine young athlete, he represented the school in the high jump at the 1928 Public Schools Championship at Stamford Bridge. He won it with a new championship record of 5′ 10½″ (1.79 metres), a record that held until after the Second World War. In the same year he set the UK junior record of 6′ 1″ (1.86 metres) at the AAA Championships.

At 17 he was selected to represent Great Britain at the 1928 Amsterdam Olympics. He qualified for the final, but only finished 11th. Still, a fine result for one so young.

He was commissioned into the RAF as a pilot officer (29049), representing them on numerous occasions in the high jump. He won the Inter-Services Championship in 1930–33 and 1935.

Wing Commander Harry Simmons was posted to RAF Sywell. Sywell was used for training RAF crews; over 2,500 RAF, Commonwealth and Allied pilots were trained there. He was killed in a flying accident on 23 April 1944 when the Wellington bomber he was piloting suddenly stalled and crashed to the ground two miles from the airfield. He and all his crew of five were killed.

He is commemorated in the Oxford (Botley) Cemetery, plot 1/2 grave 185. The inscription on his headstone reads 'In very proud and tender Memory', put there at the request of his parents.

1932

Lewis Clive (1910–38)
British
Rowing
1932 Los Angeles (Gold)

Lewis Clive was born on 8 September 1910 in Tooting. He was a son of Lieutenant Colonel Percy Clive, who was the Liberal Unionist MP for Ross, killed in action in 1918 with the Grenadier Guards.

At Eton Lewis became Captain of Boats. He then went up to Christ Church, Oxford, where he rowed in the Boat Race in 1930 and 1931 (though he was in the losing boat on both occasions). However, in 1931 and 1932, partnered with Hugh Edwards, he won the Silver Goblets at Henley.

In 1932 they were selected to go to the Los Angeles Olympics. In the coxless pairs they won the gold medal in the final at Long Beach, California.

The same year, Clive was commissioned into his father's old regiment, the Grenadier Guards, but he resigned his commission in 1937. Like his father, he had a keen interest in politics. He was a member of the Fabian Society (socialist reformers) and was elected as a Labour councillor for Kensington.

THE OXFORD UNIVERSITY CREW 1931

Feeling passionately about the civil war in Spain, he joined the International Brigade, becoming a company commander in the British Battalion. He was killed in action at Hill 481 near Gandesa on 2 August 1938 at the Battle of Ebro. Ebro was one of the most savage battles of the Spanish Civil War, with tens of thousands killed, and disastrous for the Second Spanish Republic.

He is commemorated on the memorial in the foothills of Ebro mountains (restored in 2000 by the local population). He is also commemorated in Wormbridge Church, Herefordshire, with other members of his family.

His *The People's Army* was published in 1938 by Victor Gollancz with a foreword by Clement Attlee. Clive had asked the author Mary Wesley (1912–2002) to marry him and she later featured him in *The Camomile Lawn* as the character Oliver (later portrayed by Toby Jones in the ITV adaptation).

His brother Major Meysey George Dallas Clive was killed serving with the Grenadier Guards in North Africa on 1 May 1943. Both died fighting fascism.

George Cooke (1906–41)
New Zealand
Rower
1932 Los Angeles

George Campbell Cooke was born on 17 March 1906 in Wellington. He was the son of John George and Elizabeth Jane Cooke, of 154 Moxam Avenue, Wellington, New Zealand. He became a clerk by profession. His passion was rowing and he competed for the Star Boating Club of Wellington. His talent didn't go unnoticed and he was selected to row stroke for the eight at the 1932 Olympics in Los Angeles. The games were held between 30 June and 14 July at the height of a worldwide depression, but New Zealand fielded twenty-one athletes at these Games, including Cooke. However, the New Zealand eight were knocked out in the heats and failed to take a medal. The US took the gold, Italy the silver and Canada the bronze. Interestingly, it was at the 1932 Games that the New Zealand team first used the Haka.

On the outbreak of war Cooke enlisted into the ranks of the 19th Battalion, New Zealand Expeditionary Forces, and saw action, appropriately, near Mount Olympus in Greece. He was promoted to corporal. The Allies lost the battle for Greece and the surviving troops were evacuated to Crete. On 20 May 1941, Corporal Cooke was commanding a ten-man unit guarding a British howitzer unit. At approximately 11 am on 20 May 1941 they were attacked by German paratroopers and Cooke was seriously wounded in the action that followed. Captured, he was sent to the German prisoner of war hospital near Galatos. He was well cared for, and even treated by a German doctor who had competed in the Olympics. Despite his best efforts however, Cooke died of his wounds on 23 May 1941.

Cooke is commemorated on the Athens Memorial, Phaleron War Cemetery, face thirteen.

George Cooke can be seen here in the middle of the group.

Frank Courtney (1906–44)
Canadian
Rowing
1932 Los Angeles

Frank Courtney was born in Reading on 13 July 1906. His father, bandmaster with the 3rd Royal Berkshire Regiment, died when he was two and the family moved to Halifax, Nova Scotia.

After leaving school Frank worked on the staff of the Old Queen Hotel before joining the Nova Scotia Liquor Company. He married Jean Coyle and they had one son.

While still a young man Frank took a keen interest in rowing, joining the Jubilee Amateur Rowing Club. He was also a member of the Mic Mac Aquatic Club. His ability was recognised and in 1932 he was selected to go to the Los Angeles Olympics, rowing in the coxless fours along with Fraser Herman (d.1972), Russell Gammon (d.1968) and Henry Pelham (d.1978); but they failed to reach the finals or win a medal.

He served before the war as a captain with Princess Louise Fusiliers of the Non-Permanent Active Militia. On the outbreak of the war he transferred to the West Nova Scotia Regiment. In 1942, while training in the UK, he dived into the Thames and rescued several drowning soldiers, for which he received a commendation for bravery. Promoted to major he was involved in training before becoming second in command of the Canadian Commando Corps. After being involved in several fierce actions he was killed in France on 28 August 1944 in the Canadians' advance along the 'Rocket Coast'.

Frank Courtney can be seen here at the very back of the boat.

Janis Dimza (1906–42)
Latvian
Athletics
1932 Los Angeles
1936 Berlin

Jānis Dimza was born on 1 November 1906 in Ipiķi parish. He became a police officer and worked in Kemeri. A fine athlete, competing for sports clubs SSS, ASK, and RPDSK, he specialised in the decathlon. In total he was Latvian champion thirty-six times in a wide variety of events and held Latvia's record in eleven track and field disciplines.

He first came to international notice at the 1930 International University Games in Darmstadt where he came second in the pentathlon, and was selected to go to Los Angeles for the 1932 Olympics competing in the decathlon (the pentathlon had been discontinued as an Olympic event in 1924). He did well in the early events, getting himself into the silver medal position. However he injured himself in the pole vault, landing awkwardly, and was unable to continue.

In 1934, after recovering from his injuries, he came fourth at the European Championships held in Turin, and in 1936 he was selected to go to the Berlin Olympics. Once again injuring himself, he was forced to retire, and the USA took gold, silver and bronze. In 1932 Dimza was awarded the Order of the Three Stars (V-Class).

He was arrested by the NKVD in August 1940 and on 24 June 1941 was transported to a Soviet concentration camp. He died there on 24 June 1942.

Hans Eller (1910–43)
German
Rowing
1932 Los Angeles (Gold)

Hans Eller was born on 14 August 1910 in Gdańsk Oliwa. His father was a naval captain. Hans decided to become a lawyer and read law at Grenoble. Later he gained a law degree from Berlin. He went to work for Wirtschaftsgruppe Elektroindustrie. At the time they were exploiting the forced labour of deported people in extermination camps and owned a plant in Auschwitz.

He married a long-time friend Hildegard Kluge in Dresden on 23 December 1939 and they had one son, Hans-Peter, born in 1943.

A member of the Berliner Ruder Club he took part in the coxed fours at the Henley Regatta. In 1930 he finished second in the coxed fours at the German championships. In 1932 he rowed in the coxed fours at the Los Angeles Olympics. The team won the gold medal, pipping the Italians to the post by 0.2 seconds. Poland took the bronze. He also finished third in the eights at the 1934 German championships.

Commissioned into the German army in the war, he became a lieutenant, and was wounded in France in 1940. On recovery he was sent to the Russian front, where in 1943 he was reported missing in action. It was later discovered that he had died in a Soviet prison camp near Starobielsk on 4 April 1943.

His name is engraved on a stone memorial at the German war cemetery near Kursk-Besedino.

David Haig-Thomas (1908–44)
British
Rowing
Los Angeles 1932

David Haig-Thomas was born on 1 December 1908 in London. He was educated at Eton and St John's, Cambridge. He was a keen rower at both. At Cambridge he was a member of the Lady Margaret Hall Boat Club, the St John's rowing club named after Lady Margaret Beaufort, the college's founder. He rowed bow in the Oxford v Cambridge boat races. In 1930 Cambridge won by two lengths, their seventh consecutive victory. In 1931 Cambridge won by two and a half lengths, their eighth consecutive victory. In 1932 Cambridge won again, their ninth consecutive victory. This was the first time Cambridge had equalled the winning streaks of Oxford in 1861–69 and 1890–98.

In 1932 Haig-Thomas was selected to row bow for the British eight at the 1932 Olympics. The eight missed a medal by a whisker. The USA took gold, Italy silver, and Canada took the bronze with a time of 6.40.4; England's time was 6.40.8.

He married Nancy Catherine Bury, daughter of Major Lindsay Edward Bury.

In 1933 he travelled to Abyssinia to find the source of the Awash River with Wilfred Thesiger, with whom he had gone to school.

In 1934 he became the ornithologist on the Oxford University Ellesmere Land Expedition, organised by Shackleton to explore the north of Ellesmere Island and map its coastline.

In 1936 Haig-Thomas led an ornithological expedition to Iceland and in 1937 led an expedition in north-west Greenland and Ellesmere Island. His collection of medals from Greenland and northern Canada was later donated to the British Museum. Haig-Thomas Island was named after him.

On 2 March 1940 Haig-Thomas was commissioned as a second lieutenant into the Royal Army Service Corps. He operated in Iceland and East Greenland before joining the Special Commando Boating Group (No 14 Commando), serving with, among others, Sir Peter Scott, the ornithologist. A speciality of the group was limpet mine attacks using canoes.

While serving with C Troop, No 4 Commando, he landed on D-Day with the 6th Airborne Division. He came down in marshy ground near the River Dives some distance from his intended landing zone. He was ambushed with his group and killed.

He is buried in the churchyard in the village of Bavent, Calvados.

Jeffrey MacDougall DFC (1911–42)
British
Modern pentathlon
1932 Los Angeles
1936 Berlin

Jeffrey MacDougall was born on 16 September 1911 in Buenos Aires. His family came to England when he was 8 and settled in Newbury, Berks. He was educated at Malvern College, where he became a prefect and boxed featherweight for the school. Going up to Sandhurst, he continued boxing, representing Sandhurst and captaining the team. In 1932 he was commissioned into the Duke of Cornwall's Light Infantry.

MacDougall began to specialise in the modern pentathlon, which included riding, fencing, shooting, swimming and running. Excelling in the event, he was selected to represent Great Britain at the 1932 Olympics in Los Angeles. He came fifteenth overall, his best positions being second in the running and fourth in the swimming. He became British modern pentathlon champion before being selected again to take part in the Olympics, this time in Berlin. Here he came thirteenth, his best position being sixth in the running.

In the same year, 1936, he joined 110 Squadron RAF as a pilot. In 1939 the squadron was posted to Wattisham and on 4 September 1939 Nos. 110 and 107 Squadron led the first RAF raid of the war against Wilhelmshaven. The squadron, flying Blenheim bombers, was mainly involved in anti-shipping strikes in the early part of the war, and was then posted to India in March 1942. He was promoted to squadron leader and received the DFC for gallantry: 'One night in November, 1940, Squadron Leader McDougall was the pilot and Sergeant Gray the air gunner of an aircraft detailed to carry out harassing attacks on enemy aerodromes. At 0300 hours Amiens-Glisy aerodrome was identified and found to be illuminated for night-flying. A large four-engined enemy aircraft was seen in the air and Squadron Leader McDougall decided to attack it before bombing the aerodrome. He rapidly overhauled the enemy and from close range Sergeant Gray opened fire. His first burst entered one of the port engines which immediately emitted smoke. He then fired two long bursts into the fuselage. The aircraft was seen to fall, out of control, and eventually it hit the ground and exploded. Squadron Leader McDougall then returned to Amiens-Glisy and bombed the aerodrome in the face of intense and accurate anti-aircraft fire.'

MacDougall completed twenty-two operations before being killed on 11 December 1942. Some mystery surrounds his death. CWGC have his final resting place as Reading Crematorium. So he might have died of wounds or illness.

Clayton Mansfield (1906–45)
USA
Modern pentathlon
1932 Los Angeles

Clayton Mansfield was born on 21 May 1906 in Norristown, Pennsylvania. He graduated from West Point in 1928, becoming a career officer with the cavalry. He was originally posted to Fort Riley, Kansas, and here he began training and showed a flare for the modern pentathlon. In 1932 he was selected to take part in the men's individual modern pentathlon at the Olympics in Los Angeles. He came thirteenth overall, his best positions being sixth in the swimming and seventh in the fencing.

In 1933 he graduated from the cavalry school at Fort Riley and went on to study tank warfare at Fort Knox, Kentucky. When America joined the war Mansfield was put in command of the First Battalion, 36th Armoured Regiment, Fourth Armoured Division, at Pine Camp, New York. He was promoted to colonel and took command of the 92nd Reconnaissance Battalion, 12th Armoured Division, at Camp Campbell, Kentucky. In August 1944 he was posted to Europe, becoming Chief of Staff of the 2nd Armoured (Hell on Wheels) Division. In December 1944 he became commander of the 66th Armoured Regiment. Leading his regiment in the Battle of the Bulge on 9 January 1945 he was hit by enemy fire and seriously wounded. He was presented with the Silver Star for gallantry on the field shortly before he died later the same day.

Edward Manteuffel-Szoege (1908–40)
Polish
Art
1932 Los Angeles

Edward Antoni Manteuffel-Szoege was born on 5 July 1908 in Latvia, son of Leon and Aniela (née Zieliński). He had two brothers, Tadeusz Julius Joseph (1902–70), who became a well-known Polish historian specialising in the Middle Ages, and Leon Edward (1904–73) who became a surgeon.

Edward studied graphics and painting at the Warsaw School of Fine Arts under Professor Karol Tiche, evening drawing under Professor Stanislaw Czajkowski, and the design of solids and planes under Professor Wojciech Jastrzebowski. While there he met and later married Wanda Zawidzka (1906–94). He also studied in Leipzig and Berlin. He then worked on designing covers and magazines and became famous as a brilliant illustrator of books.

In 1932 he was selected to represent Poland in the art competition at the Los Angeles Olympics competing in mixed painting, but he didn't win a medal.

Having had previous military training, he was mobilized in 1939 on the Soviet invasion of Poland and posted to the 9th Armoured Battalion as a second lieutenant. He was taken prisoner by the NKVD and murdered at Starobielsk in April or May 1940. He is commemorated in the Powazki Warsaw Cemetery, section 68-2-14.

Colonel Baron Takeichi Nishi (1902–45)
Japanese
Equestrianism
1932 Los Angeles (Gold)
1936 Berlin

Takeichi Nishi was born on 12 July 1902 in the Azabu district of Tokyo, the third and illegitimate son of Tokujiro Nishi who was a *danshaku* (a baron under the *kazoku* peerage system). He was often in trouble for fighting while at school. On his father's death, despite being illegitimate he came into the family title. Pursuing a military career, he first went to the Hiroshima Army Cadet School and the Imperial Japanese Army Academy. He was then posted to the First Cavalry Regiment based in Setagaya, Tokyo, and was commissioned as a second lieutenant, in 1927 becoming a full lieutenant. He married and had a son.

A keen horseman, he bought *Uranus* while in Italy, who was to remain with him throughout his horse-jumping career. He was selected to take part in the 1932 Los Angeles Olympics where, riding *Uranus*, he won the gold medal in the men's individual jumping event (to date the only medal won by Japan in an equestrian event). While in Los Angeles he became friends with Charlie Chaplin, Mary Pickford and Douglas Fairbanks.

On returning from the Olympics, he was assigned to the 16th Narashino Cavalry Regiment. He became an instructor and was promoted to captain in 1933.

In 1936 he was selected to represent Japan at the Olympics in Berlin. Riding *Uranus* again, he came twentieth in the individual jumping event, sixth in the jumping event team, twelfth in the three-day event individual and, after falling from his horse, failed to be placed in the three-day event team.

On his return to Japan he was promoted to major in March 1939. As cavalry regiments were disbanded and replaced with tank regiments, Nishi was posted as regimental

commander of the 26th Tank Regiment. He was promoted to lieutenant colonel in August 1943. His regiment was posted to the defence of Iwo Jima. However, en route the ship carrying the regiment and its tanks was torpedoed by the USS *Cobia* and all the regiment's twenty-eight tanks were lost. Nishi returned to Tokyo and managed to replace twenty-two of them before returning to Iwo Jima.

After an extensive air and naval bombardment, the US Marine Corps began their amphibious assault. The American forces broadcast daily appeals for Nishi to surrender, stating that the world would regret losing 'Baron Nishi'; Nishi never responded.

Nishi died on 22 March 1945, although the circumstances of his death are disputed. Some say he was killed by machine-gun fire. Others that he committed suicide by shooting. Others that he was burnt to death by flamethrowers as he and his men carried out a final assault. Nishi was posthumously promoted to colonel. His horse *Uranus* died a week after his master and was later commemorated at the War Horse Memorial in the History and Folklore Museum in Honbetsu, Hokkaido.

His son Yasunori later became vice president of the Iwo Jima Association.

Jadwiga Salomea Hładki-Wajwódowa (1904–44)
Polish
Art
1932 Los Angeles

Jadwiga Salomea Hładki-Wajwódowa was born on 14 January 1904 in Warsaw, daughter of Franciszek and Salomea Katarzyna (née Ciechanowicz). A talented painter, sculptor and graphic artist (specialising in woodcuts), she studied at the Municipal School of Decorative Arts and Painting, graduating in 1926. She then studied under Professor Karol Tiche (1871–1939) at the Academy of Fine Arts in Warsaw, later becoming a member of the Association of Polish Graphic Engravers. While studying at the Academy she met and married Antoni Wajwod and became close friends with Edward Manteuffel-Szoege (murdered by the NKVD in 1940). The three of them teamed up and established the Warsaw MEWA Decorative and Advertising Graphic Studio in 1933.

In 1932 she was chosen to represent Poland at the Los Angeles Olympics in the mixed painting event, but although her work was commented upon, she failed to take a medal.

In 1933 she joined the Association of Polish Graphic Artists, and her illustrations for children's books became well known and much admired. Such was her popularity that in 1934 she was commissioned to decorate part of the interior of the first Polish transatlantic liner the MS *Piłsudski*. In 1935, as a member of MEWA, she began designing the covers of the resumed *Skamander* (a literary magazine based in Warsaw published in 1920–28 and then again in 1935–39). She and her husband were associated with the sculptor and art dealer Karol Tchorek's art salon 'Nike'.

Fighting with the Polish Resistance in the Warsaw uprising, both Jadwiga and her husband Antoni were murdered by the Nazis between 6 and 12 August 1944.

1936

Silvano Abbà (1911–42)
Italian
Modern pentathlon
1936 Berlin (Bronze)

Silvano Abbà was born on 3 July 1911 in Rovinj, Croatia. His father was killed in the First World War, leaving his mother to bring him up on her own at no small hardship. However, she managed it and first sent him to the Technical Institute of Rovinj and then the Royal Military Academy at Modena in Italy. He worked hard and eventually became a second lieutenant in the 10th Regiment 'Lancieri di Vittorio Emanuele II'.

A fine all-round athlete, he was selected to represent Italy in the 1936 Berlin Olympics in the modern pentathlon. He came first in the riding event, fifteenth in the fencing, tenth in the shooting, fourteenth in the swimming and fifth in the running. Overall he won the bronze medal.

He fought in the Spanish Civil War, commanding a company and winning the Silver Medal for Military Valour. His citation read: 'Commander of chariot company that first entered Mazaleon, first in Gandesa, first in Tortosa, he instilled, above all by example in his department, the enthusiasm, audacity and daring needed to overcome in a month of action the most arduous and risky situations. In the fight on the Las Fojas altitudes, to fulfil a task made particularly difficult by the roughness of the ground, with contempt for danger and conscious courage, even under violent reaction from opposing fire, he left his chariot to search and indicate to his crews the tracks that they left to hit the enemy positions in the back, only in this way managing to achieve its intent and the task entrusted to it.'

When Italy entered the Second World War on 10 June 1940 he was attached to the 3rd Savoy Cavalleria Regiment. He fought in France then in Yugoslavia.

Also in 1940 he became the Italian modern pentathlon champion and won the Ceccarelli Cup.

Promoted to captain and sent to the Russian front commanding the 4th squadron of his regiment, he was killed together with thirty-two other members of his regiment in the famous charge at Isbuscensky near Stalingrad on 24 August 1942. Fifty-two Italians were also wounded and over a hundred horses killed. The Italians killed over 150 Russians, wounded a further 300 and took 600 prisoners. They also captured 4 cannons, 10 mortars and 50 machine guns. For this action Abbà was awarded the Bronze Medal for Military Honour. His citation read: 'Commander of a squadron, he led the combat department with skill and firmness. Suddenly revealed an enemy machine gun, which slowed down the advance, he wielded a weapon and with precise shots neutralized the opponent's position. Already distinguished by boldness and contempt for danger. Leimonowka bridge (Russian front), 24 October 1941.'

At the end of the war Abbà was also awarded the gold medal for Military Valour. A street in Rome was named after him, as well as a military stadium and a military school. His sabre and hat are kept in the Cavalry School at Voghera.

Virgilius Altmann (1913–43)
Austrian
Cycling
1936 Berlin

Virgilius Altmann was born on 9 February 1913 in Vienna. A good athlete and keen cyclist he competed for the Mentor Wein Club. In the 1936 Berlin Olympics he competed in the men's individual road race coming sixteenth, with a time of 2-33-08. France took both gold and silver and Switzerland the bronze. He also took part in the team road race and came fifth, in a time of 7-39-22. France took the gold, Switzerland the silver and Belgium the bronze.

He was killed in action on 17 October 1943 in Kozerogi, Homel, Belarus.

Altmann can be seen centre with the future dictator Adolf Hitler to the right.

Alick Bevan (1915–45)
British
Cycling
1936 Berlin

Alick Bevan was born on 27 March 1915 to Percy and Rose Anne in Wandsworth, London. Becoming a fine cyclist, he competed for the Fountain Cycling Club. He was selected to represent Great Britain in the 1936 Olympics in Berlin and took part in the men's road race, individual and team. He had never ridden in a massed start race on public roads before, the governing body of British cycling having banned such races since 1890. He failed to finish in the individual race, being involved in a mass pile-up 100 metres before the end of the race. He was also unplaced in the team race.

In the war he first joined the East Surrey Regiment, before being commissioned into the 7th Battalion Hampshire Regiment. In January 1945 he was involved in operations to capture Putt and Walderath in western Germany. He was mortally wounded by a land mine in this operation. He is buried in the Brunssum War Cemetery, Limburg, Netherlands, grave VI. 282. The Alick Bevan Plate Meeting at the Crystal Palace circuit in London is contested in his honour.

Heinz Brandt (1907–44)
German
Equestrianism
1936 Berlin (Gold)

Heinz Brandt was born on 11 March 1907 in Charlottenburg, son of General Georg Brandt. In 1925 he enlisted in the Reichswehr. He was posted to Hanover in 1927 to attend the cavalry school there. He left a year later and was commissioned as a lieutenant.

One of Germany's finest riders, he became German show jumping champion in 1932. In 1936 he was selected as part of the equestrian team to go to the Olympics in Berlin. Riding *Alchemist* in the show jumping individual event he came joint sixteenth. The gold was taken by Brandt's team-mate Kurt Hasse (see page 191). He did considerably better in the team event, taking the gold medal together with Kurt Hasse (d.1944) and Marten von Barnekow (d.1967).

On the outbreak of war he was promoted to Hauptmann and posted to the general staff of the Oberkommando der Wehrmacht (high command of the armed forces) as an aide to General Heusinger, head of the operations unit of the general staff. He was promoted to Major in January 1941, Oberstleutnant in April 1942, and Oberst (colonel) in May 1943.

On 13 March 1943 he was an unwitting participant in an attempt on Hitler's life. Losing a bet, he was ordered to carry a package, which he was told contained Cointreau, onto Hitler's aircraft for delivery to Oberst Helmuth Stieff. It was in fact a bomb. He got it onto the plane but it failed to detonate.

On 20 July 1944 he was seriously wounded in another attempt to assassinate Hitler. On this occasion he unwittingly saved Hitler's life. On 20 July Brandt arrived at the Wolf's Lair headquarters in Rastenburg, East Prussia, for a situation conference attended by Hitler. Major Stauffenberg left a briefcase in the conference room containing a powerful bomb as close to Hitler as he could before making his excuses and leaving. Brandt, wanting to get a better look at the campaign map, found the briefcase was in his way, and moved it. Seven minutes later the bomb exploded, blowing off Brandt's leg. He was rushed to hospital and operated on but died the following day after surgery. Hitler posthumously promoted him to Generalmajor. It was later established that Brandt's moving the bomb behind a strong table leg saved Hitler's life.

John Cherry (1914–43)
British
Rowing
1936 Berlin

John Conrad 'Con' Hazlehurst Cherry was born on 7 September 1943 in Paddington. He was educated at Westminster School and Brasenose, Oxford. He matriculated in 1933 as the Heath Harrison Minor Exhibitioner. While at Brasenose he rowed for the first eight and was selected to row in the Boat Race in 1936; Oxford lost by five lengths. In the same year he was selected to row in the eight for England at the 1936 Olympics in Berlin. The crew came fourth, just missing out on a medal. The USA took the gold, Italy the silver and Germany the bronze.

In 1937 Cherry became president of the OUBC and once again rowed for Oxford against Cambridge. This time Oxford won by three lengths in a time of 22 minutes 39 seconds, securing their first victory since 1923. It was also the slowest winning time and the narrowest margin of victory since 1877. Cherry rowed for Oxford again in 1938 and again was in the winning boat, Oxford winning by two lengths in a time of 20 minutes 30 seconds.

He did well at Henley during this time too. In 1936, rowing for the Leander Club VIII, he came second in the Grand Challenge Cup. In 1937, rowing for the Leander Club IV, he won the Stewards' Challenge Cup. He was also captain of the Leander Club between 1938 and 1943.

In 1940 he married Glory Rowe, sister of his 1937 Oxford crew-mate R.G. Rowe.

He was commissioned into the Royal Navy in the war and was killed on 1 February 1943 while serving as a lieutenant on the cruiser-minelayer HMS *Welshman*. She was torpedoed by U617 (later destroyed by the RAF after she ran aground on 12 September 1943) north-east of Tobruk. Cherry has no known grave and his name is commemorated on the Chatham Naval Memorial 73,3.

Don Collinge (1909–44)
Canadian
Fencing
1936 Berlin

Frank Donald Collinge was born on 14 October 1909 in Toronto. Becoming an enthusiastic fencer, he competed for the Toronto Sword Club, becoming national Canadian foil and sabre champion in 1936.

At the 1936 Berlin Olympics he competed in several of the fencing disciplines but only advanced to the quarter-finals once, in the team épée, but he failed to win a medal.

In 1937 he was runner-up at the Canadian national championships in the sabre division, losing to his Olympic teammate George Tully (d.1986), who also won the foil and épée titles. In 1938 Collinge came second, fourth and fifth, in sabre, épée, and foil respectively, beaten once again by Tully.

Collinge's fencing career was cut short by the war when he joined the Royal Canadian Air Force, becoming a flying officer and navigator. He died in an accident while training at night in a Stirling bomber III LK 594, the aircraft crashing at Saltby, Lincolnshire. Some reports say the aircraft lost control and crashed, others that it was destroyed by friendly fire.

Collinge is buried at Harrogate (Stonefall) CWGC Cemetery, section B. Row F. Grave 1. His parents had the words 'His memory is as dear to-day as in the hour he passed away' inscribed on his gravestone.

Ferenc Csik (1913–45)
Hungarian
Swimming
1936 Berlin (Gold and Bronze)

Ferenc Csik was born on 12 December 1913 in Somogy, the youngest of three brothers. Their father was killed at the beginning of the First World War. He grew up on the shores of Lake Balaton where he learned to swim, taking a dip most days. However it wasn't until he enrolled into the University of Budapest to read medicine that he took up competitive swimming.

He swam under the guiding eye of two of Hungary's finest swimming coaches, István Bárány, who competed in three Olympics taking a silver and two bronzes, and Jazsef Vartesy, who also took part in three Olympics and won a gold and a silver.

Ferenc became the top Hungarian freestyle swimmer of the 1930s. He competed internationally for the first time at the 1933 World University Games where he won silver in the 100 metres freestyle and bronze in the 50 metres. In the 1934 European Championships he won the 100 metres again, and the 4 × 200 metres freestyle. In 1935 at the World University Games he won the 100 metres freestyle, the 4 × 200 metres freestyle relay, and the medley relay.

In 1936 he went to the Berlin Olympics, winning gold in the men's 100 metres freestyle, beating the much-favoured world record holder American Peter Fick who finished a disappointing sixth. He also beat off a strong challenge from the Japanese swimmers Masanori Yusa, who won two golds and a silver in the 1932 and 1936 Olympics, Shigeo Arai (see page 178), who won a gold and bronze at the 1936 Olympics, and Masaharu Taguchi, who won a gold at the 1936 Games. Csik also won bronze in the 4 × 200m freestyle relay.

Ferenc's last international competition was at the 1937 University games, where he won the gold in the 100 metres freestyle, the 200 metres breast stroke, the 4 × 200 metres relay, and the medley relay.

Domestically, Ferenc took nineteen Hungarian swimming titles. He was also part of three Hungarian 4 × 100 metres freestyle relay teams that set world records three times in 1937/8.

He graduated in 1937 with an MD degree and retired from international competition to practice medicine full time. In October 1944 he was mobilized to the army, serving as a medic in Szolnok, Keszthely and Sopron. A few months before the end of the war Sergeant Ferenc Csik was killed in an air raid in Sopron while treating a wounded civilian.

He was inducted into the International Swimming Hall of Fame in 1983.

Krystyna Dabrowska (1906–44)
Polish
Art
1936 Berlin

Krystyna Dąbrowska was born on 26 November 1906 in Warsaw. A highly talented painter and sculptor, she studied at the National Art School in Poznan between 1925 and 1930 before continuing her education at the Academy of Fine Arts in Warsaw between 1933 and 1935, going on to the Royal Academy of Fine Arts in Rome. She became a member of the Polish Association of Artists, The Capitol.

She was selected to represent Poland in 1936 at the Olympics in Berlin. She competed in mixed sculpturing, statues, which was one of the most popular artistic events of the Olympics, with over a hundred entries, but her entry, *Zeglarz*, was unplaced.

In the war she worked in a sugar factory but was secretly a member of the Polish Resistance. She was killed by the Nazis in the Warsaw uprising on 1 September 1944 while working as a nurse. Most of her works were destroyed in the war.

Paweł Dadlez (1904–40)
Polish
Painting
1936 Berlin

Paweł Dadlez was born on 1 February 1904. He became one of Poland's finest artists. He began his artistic studies in 1922 at the Academy of Fine Arts in Krakow, being taught by Władysław Jarocki (1879–1965), Jan Wojnarski (1879–1937) and Ignacy Pieńkowski (1877–1948). On completing his education in Poland in 1927, he travelled to Paris, coming under the guidance of Józef Pankiewicz (1866–1940). In 1929 he found his way to Italy, where he remained for two years before returning to Krakow. In 1938 he became a professor of general drawing and graphics. His style was considered to be realism with elements of Polish colourism.

He was selected to represent Poland in the artistic competition at the 1936 Olympics in Berlin, but he didn't win a medal.

In 1939 he was imprisoned by the Nazis because of his 'anti-German attitude'. Due to his poor health he was released and returned to Krakow by train, but he died on this return journey on 18 May 1940 at Rava Ruska, Ukraine. His works are in the National Museum in Poznan.

Ernst de Jonge (1914–44)
Dutch
Rowing
1936 Berlin

Ernst Willem de Jonge was born on 22 May 1914 in Sinabang, Aceh, Indonesia. He was the youngest of four siblings born to engineer Johan Maurits de Jonge, who worked for the Java Timber Company, and his wife Pauline Clasina Berg. The family returned to Holland in 1925 where Ernst was educated at the Baarnsch Lyceum. A boisterous lad, he was expelled on no less than three occasions. Despite this he managed to complete his education and was then sent to Ede for his national service. He must have impressed because in 1933 he was commissioned and transferred to the artillery in Leiden. Continually in trouble though, any further promotions became unlikely. His brother later said of him, 'He had the reputation of being the most penalized cadet in the history of the armed forces. The stories even reached the top of the army, which led to an angry letter from the higher ups asking why this troublemaker had not yet been sent out of the service. The commanding officer replied, "He's a wild boy, but if the fatherland is ever in the war, he'll be of great value."'

Following his national service he was accepted into the University of Leiden. While there he became interested in rowing and became a member of the rowing association KSRV Njord. He was later elected as their president.

He first competed in coxed fours but finally decided on coxed pairs, rowing with his old friend Karel Hardman. Their cox was Johan Frans van Walsem. They were selected to represent the Netherlands at the 1936 Olympics in Berlin, but they failed to take a medal.

On returning to Leiden, Ernst studied law. He continued to row, taking part in several varsity rowing events. He later also became president of the students' union. Despite his many outside activities, he was bright and qualified early in May 1938.

He went to work with the Bataafse Petroleum Maatschappil at their offices in London. In August 1939 he was called back to Holland and rejoined his old artillery unit. When the Germans invaded on 10 May 1940 he was evacuated to the Dutch Antilles with his company who had requested his return from military service.

Feeling guilty about the occupation of his country he resigned from the company and returned to London. In 1941 he was interviewed by the British Secret Service, and agreed to be parachuted into Holland to spy. Training with section 9, he did well and by 1942 was ready for his first mission. He was to be parachuted into occupied Europe with his radio operator Evert Radema. However this idea was abandoned and they were dropped on the shore by a motor torpedo boat. They were picked up by the Resistance and taken to Leiden. At this point the two men split up, Radema going to Amsterdam and De Jonge to Wassenaar. In Rotterdam he helped set up the 'Kees group' spy ring. After the arrest of another agent making his way to England with microfilm containing De Jonge's name, he was arrested a few days later on 22 May after refusing to go into hiding. He was taken to Kamp Haaren and from there to Assen before being transported to the concentration camp at Rawitsch in Poland. He died there on 3 September 1944. His remains were never found. The Kees group remained active until the end of the war.

In 1970 Erik Hazelhoff Roelfzema published a book about De Jonge and the Kees group under the title *Het Hol van de Ratelslang* (The Rattlesnake Cave), later called *Soldaat van Oranje* (Soldier of Orange). It became an international best seller. Its success led to a feature film made by Paul Verhoeven which was nominated for a Golden Globe in 1980 and won the Los Angeles Film Critics Association for the best foreign film in 1979. A plaque was erected at the Leiden Student Union 'Minerva' commemorating their former president. On the four panels of the plaque are inscribed the following:

Praeses Njord, Olympische Spelen 1936
Praeses Collegii 1937, Commissaris Sociëteit Minerva 1936,
Geheim Agent WO II, verraden en omgebracht, postuum Bronzen Leeuw,
Jhr mr Ernst de Jonge 1914–1944

(President Njord Rowing Club, Olympic Games 1936, Student Body President 1937, President Minerva Society 1936, Secret Agent WWII, betrayed and destroyed, posthumous Bronze Lion, Jhunker Mr. Ernst de Jonge 1914–1944).

Foy Draper (1911–43)
USA
Athletics
1936 Berlin (Gold)

Foy Draper was born on 26 November 1911 in Georgetown, Texas. The family moved to California and Foy attended the Huntington Park High School in Los Angeles, where he first started running. From there he went to the University of California.

A powerful runner and athlete, he won the 220 yards at the 1935 IC4A (Intercollegiate Association of Amateur Athletes of America). He later took the honours in the Far Western AAU (Amateur Athletics Union) in 1934, improving his time in the 220 yards to 20.8. He also achieved a time of 10.3 in the 100 metres when giving his friend Jesse Owens a close finish in the 1935 NCAA (National Collegiate Athletics Association), all the more remarkable because he was only 5 feet 5 inches tall. He also ran for the USC Trojans (the athletics team that represents the University of Southern California).

He was selected to go to the 1936 Olympics in Berlin, where he won gold with the 4 × 100 metre relay. Running the third leg, the team consisted of Jesse Owens, Ralph Metcalfe and Frank Wykoff. They ran it in a record time of 39.8. It was one of the events that incensed Hitler.

In the war Foy volunteered for the American Air Force. He was posted to the Western Desert in Thelepte, Tunisia, where he flew an A-20B 'Havoc' for 97th Bomber Squadron, 47th Bomb Group. He was promoted to captain. On 4 January 1943 he took off to fly to Fonduck, Tunisia, to take part in air support at the Battle of Kasserine Pass. Neither Foy nor his two-man crew who consisted of S/Sgt Kenneth Gasser and S/Sgt Sidney Holland returned from this mission. His death is assumed to have taken place on 4 January 1943 (some records have it as 1 February). His body was recovered and now lies in the North African American Cemetery in Carthage, plot F, row 10, grave 7. He received the Air Medal and the Purple Heart.

Josef Gumpold (1908–42)
German
Skiing
1936 Garmisch-Partenkirchen

Josef Gumpold was born on 3 September 1908 in Böckstein, Badgastein, Austria. Growing up in the Gastein Valley, he took part in a variety of winter sports from an early age. Later he moved to Innsbruck, where he worked at the Sport-Hummel sports shop. In 1931 he doubled for Leni Riefenstahl in the film *The White Rush*, playing all her skiing parts. In 1933 he took sixth place on the Bergisel ski jump at the Nordic World Ski Championships in Innsbruck; he was the first Nordic athlete in the state of Salzburg to achieve a top six place. In 1934 at the Nordic World Ski Championships in Sollefteå, he was arrested and banned from skiing for illegal political activity with the National Socialists. Because of this, he left Austria in 1935 and became a German citizen, living in the ski resort of Garmisch-Partenkirchen.

In 1936, as a member of Partenkirchen Ski Club, he took part in the Olympics in his new hometown and represented Germany. He came thirteenth in the men's individual Nordic combined.

On 6 December 1942 Gumpold, serving in the German army as an acting group leader, was killed on a mission on the Russian Front. He was buried at Salzburg in the Böckstein Soldiers' Cemetery where his cross can still be seen.

Rudolf Harbig (1913–44)
German
Athletics
1936 Berlin (Bronze)

Rudolf Waldemar Harbig was born on 8 November 1913 in Dresden. Keen on sports from an early age, he ran and played handball for a local sports club. After finishing school he was apprenticed as a wheelwright. However, due to the depression he found it difficult to get employment. He travelled throughout Germany looking for work before joining the German army in 1932. It turned out to be a good move. The army encouraged him and gave him the space to train. On 24 June 1934 he won the 800 metres at the Dresdner SC stadium as a result of which he was selected to start training for the 1936 Games to be held in Berlin. He was trained by the former German Olympian Josef Waitzer (1912 Stockholm).

He left the army in 1935 to concentrate on sports. Although he trained as much as he could, he also had to work, which interrupted his schedule. Having won the 800 metres at the German Athletics Championship in July 1936 at Mommsenstadion in Berlin, he was selected to represent Germany in the 800 metres and men's 4 × 400 metres relay at the 1936 Olympics in Berlin. Shortly before the Olympics however he was taken ill and arrived at the games not fully fit and was knocked out in the first heat of the 800 metres. There were concerns about him running in the 4 × 400 metres, but he was eventually allowed to. He ran last and helped win the bronze medal.

On 1 May 1937 Harbig joined the Nazi party, becoming an enthusiastic member, holding the rank of Sturmmann (storm trooper) in the SA. He took part in the Nuremberg rallies and allowed his athletics prowess to be used for propaganda purposes. He also continued racing. In July he won the 800 metres at the German Athletics Championships for the second time, equalling the eleven-year-old German record of the great German runner Otto Pelzer (1900–70, Olympic Games 1928 and 1932). A week later he broke the German record in the 400 metres competing in Berlin. A year after that he won the 400 metres at the ISTAF Berlin, followed by the 800 metres at the German Championships. In 1938 he took gold in the 800 metres and the 4 × 400 metres relay at the European Championships in Paris. In 1939 he broke the world record in the 800 metres, defeating his old rival Mario Lanzi (who broke the Italian record in the same race) with an astonishing sprint in the final 125 metres. His time was 1:46.6. This record wasn't broken again until 1955. In 1939 Harbig also set world records over 400 metres and 500 metres and in 1941 set the world record in the 1,000 metres running in Dresden.

In the Second World War he first joined the regular army before transferring to the Fallschirmjäger (Paratroop regiment) where he became a Feldwebel (sergeant). He was killed fighting with the 2nd Parachute Division, Regiment 6, on the Voronezh Front near Kirovohrad in the Ukraine on 5 March 1944.

After the war he became a sporting legend in both East and West Germany. His wife, Gerda Heinrich, published a book about her late husband in 1955, *Unvergessener Rudolf Harbig. Ein Lebensbild des Weltrekordläufers (Unforgotten Rudolf Harbig; a biography of the world record runner)*. A sporting stadium in Dresden was named after him. In 2008 he was inducted into the German Sports Hall of Fame.

Walter Hasenfus (1916–44)
USA
Canoe
1936 Berlin

Walter Martin Hasenfus was born on 18 March 1916 in Needham, Massachusetts. He was a member of the Needham Canoe Club and was selected to compete in the 1936 Berlin Olympics in the men's Canadian doubles 10,000 metres. His partner was his younger brother Joseph. The pair came fifth.

In the war he served as a sergeant with the 307th Infantry, 77 Division, and was killed in the fighting in Leyte in the Philippines on 8 December 1944.

His sister Olive was a sprinter. She was a reserve in the 1928 US Olympic track and field squad but alas didn't compete.

Josef Hasenöhrl (1915–45)
Austrian
Rowing
1936 Berlin (Silver)

Joseph Hasenöhrl was born on 5 May 1915 in Vienna. A fine rower, he competed for Ruderverein Ellida, Vienna. Selected to compete in the 1936 Berlin Olympics, he won silver in the single sculls, being beaten to the gold by the German rower Gustav Schafer.

In 1937 he won the Diamond Sculls at the Henley Regatta, beating J.F. Coulson into second place.

In the war he served in the German army and was killed in action in Luxembourg on 13 March 1945.

Ted Kara (1916–44)
USA
Boxing
1936 Berlin

Theodore Ernst Kara was born on 2 April 1916 in Cleveland, Ohio. He became a talented featherweight boxer, famous for his quick hands and hard punching. He was described in a local paper as 'the most outstanding college fighter ever to toss leather on the West Coast'.

In 1936 he was selected to represent America at the 1936 Berlin Olympics. Captaining the team, he recorded a first-round knockout of Felipe Gabuco of the Philippines and a second-round decision over Estonia's Evald Seeberg. He fell in a quarterfinal match to eventual silver medallist Charles Catterall (1914–66) of South Africa in a decision. Charles went on to win three NCAA boxing titles for the University of Idaho in 1939–40 and 1941. He married Marion Amirkanian, but they had no children.

During the war he joined the US Army Air Corps becoming a second lieutenant with the 418th Night Fight Squadron as a radio operator. He went missing on a patrol on 14 February 1944 (his official date of death wasn't given until 14 February 1946). He was awarded the Air Medal and the Purple Heart. He is commemorated in the Manila American Cemetery and there is another memorial to him in Manila.

His brother Frank was also an NCAA boxing champion, winning the title in 1941.

Władysław Karas (1893–1942)
Polish
Shooting
1936 Berlin (Bronze)

Władysław Karaś was born on 31 August 1893 in Kielce, son of Szymon and Anna (née Domagałło-Dąbrowska). He was educated at the Ekaterinski Junior High School, the School of Commerce in Kielce, and the Real School in Lviv.

In the First World War he joined the Polish Legions, serving with the First Brigade. In the thick of the fighting he was wounded twice and captured by the Russians twice, spending over a year as a prisoner of war. After escaping he became involved with the Polish intelligence corps. Returning to Poland in 1919 he joined the Polish army as a second lieutenant. In 1925 he joined the General Staff and in 1927 was promoted to captain. In 1930 he was transferred to the Border Protection Corps. He was also made inspector of the southern section of the Shooting Association in Lviv.

A sports shooter, he represented Poland at the 1936 Berlin Olympics. Competing in the men's small-bore rifle prone 50 metres he won the bronze medal. He was the first Polish shooter to win an Olympic medal.

After the Olympics he competed for WKS Legia in Warsaw. In 1937 he took part in the qualifying rounds of the Helsinki World Championships. He also competed in the National Shooting Competition in Vilnius.

In the Second World War he organised underground actions against the Nazi occupiers, involving sabotage, mainly in the Krakow area. Working under the name of Dąbrowski he later became head of the newly-formed Union of Retaliation of ZWZ Kraków-Silesia. He was arrested in April 1940 and spent two months in detention in Krakow. Released, he went to Warsaw where he continued with his underground Resistance work, this time going under the name of Pankracy. On 23 April 1942 he was betrayed, arrested and sent to the prison at Pawiak. On 28 May he was shot in a mass execution in Magdalenka near Warsaw. He was posthumously promoted major and is buried at the Powązki Military Cemetery in Warsaw.

Desmond Kingsford MC (1914–44)
British
Rowing
1936 Berlin

Desmond Glover Kingsford was born on 24 July 1914 in Dublin, son of Douglas and Margaret, who later moved to Canada. He was educated at Uppingham and Pembroke College, Cambridge. A keen college rower, he was bow in the 1934 Boat Race against Oxford. Cambridge won by four and a half lengths in a time of 18 minutes 3 seconds. The next year, with his brother Annesley, he rowed again. Cambridge won again by four and a half lengths, in 19 minutes 48 seconds. In 1936 Cambridge won again, this time by five lengths in 21 minutes 6 seconds. He was in the winning boat in all three races.

He and Annesley were selected to row in the British eight at the Berlin Olympics. They reached the final and finished fourth, the USA taking the gold, Italy the silver and Germany the bronze.

In 1937 he was runner-up in the Henley Regatta Silver Goblets, rowing for the London Rowing Club, together with G.M. Lewis, another Pembroke man who he had raced with in the 1936 Boat Race. In 1938, as a member of the English boat, he won the gold medal at the British Empire Games.

Kingsford joined the Irish Guards in the war. He was attached to the 3rd Battalion and was promoted to captain. He was awarded a Military Cross for his actions on 3 August 1944. His citation read:

'This officer commanded a combat group ordered to seize the crossroads one kilometre East of St Charles De Percy on the evening of 3rd August 1944. The group was held up by intense machine gun and anti tank fire and was unable to make progress in

CAMBRIDGE PRACTISING AT CHISWICK : (FROM LEFT TO RIGHT) DUCKWORTH (COX), LAURIE (STROKE), WILSON (7), BURNFORD (6), LONNON (5), KINGSFORD (4), LEWIS (3), MASON (2), AND CREE (BOW).

daylight, but after three efforts succeeded in gaining their objective. Captain Kingsford organised every attack and regardless of extreme danger from intense Spandau fire kept his men in good spirits and overcame severe opposition. He handled his group with great skill and daring. Had Captain Kingsford not persisted in his efforts to overcome this opposition, great delay would have been imposed in the execution of the Divisional plan.'

Kingsford was killed a week later on 10 October 1944 when a shell struck the tent he was sleeping in. He is buried in the Tilly-Sur-Seulles War Cemetery, memorial reference IX. H. 10.

There is a Pathé News film of the 1936 Boat Race on YouTube. Kingsford is in seat 6 (bow being 1).

Harvey Lacelle (1918–1943)
Canadian
Boxing
1936 Berlin

Joseph Harvey Milton Lacelle was born on 18 January 1918 in Ottawa. He was the son of Joseph and Victoria and had one sister, Nora, and a brother, Tony, who also saw service with the RCAF. His father was an electrical contractor and also joined the RCAF, becoming a warrant officer.

Harvey was educated at Hurdman's Bridge School and the Ottawa Technical School, and then worked for his father's electrical contracting company. He boxed at the Ottawa Boys' Club and won the Canadian Amateur bantamweight title in 1936. He also won a Golden Gloves championship in New York.

In 1936 he was selected to represent Canada in the Berlin Olympics. Unfortunately he was knocked out in the first round by the Mexican boxer Fidel Ortiz (1906–75) who had also competed in the 1928 Olympics. Ortiz went on to take the bronze.

He joined the RCAF in the war. He completed his air gunner's course and was posted to the UK, training further at Rockcliff and Trenton before joining 405 Squadron RCAF flying Halifax bombers out of RAF Pocklington. He wrote to his mother to tell her he had been on 'four raids in a week'.

He was promoted to sergeant then flight sergeant before being commissioned as a pilot officer. His Halifax was shot down by Oberleutnant Rudolf Sigmund of Stab II/NJG2 at 3 am on 28 June 1942, crashing into the North Sea off Julianadorp in Holland as it returned from a raid on Bremen. This was Sigmund's fourth claim; he went on to claim twenty-seven Allied aircraft before being shot down and killed himself on 4 October 1943 together with his crew. All seven members of the Halifax's crew were killed. At first it was hoped he might have bailed out and been taken prisoner, but his body was washed up two days later at Callantsoog. He is buried at Bergen-op-Zoom Canadian War Cemetery, grave reference 29.A.7.

Eugeniusz Lokajski (1908–44)
Polish
Athletics
1936 Berlin

Eugeniusz Zenon Lokajski was born on 14 December 1908 in Warsaw. He grew up to become a multi-talented athlete and a fine gymnast. In 1924 he joined the prestigious KS Warszawianka sports club where he trained in a variety of disciplines, including football, swimming and running.

In 1928 he was conscripted into the Polish army. He graduated from the NCO school at Zambrow and joined the Central Sports Education Centre in Bielany. In 1932 he returned to KS Warszawianka and became one of their most prized members. In 1934 he became Polish javelin champion and two years later he threw a world record distance of 73.27 metres that remained for seventeen years. He was also a national champion at gymnastics in 1934 and 1935.

In 1935 he won a silver medal in the javelin at the World Student Games in Budapest and in 1936 he was selected to compete for Poland in the 1936 Berlin Olympics. Unfortunately while training for the javelin he injured a rotator cuff muscle in his shoulder. As a result he only managed a throw of 66.36 metres and came seventh. It later transpired that the injury was so bad that it ended his sporting career.

In 1939 he was called back to the Polish army to fight against the German invasion. He became a platoon commander with the Polish 35th Infantry Regiment. He was captured by Soviet forces in the Siege of Brest-Litovsk but managed to escape back to Warsaw. He operated a photographic shop during the occupation while at the same time secretly working for the Polish Underground. During this time the German occupiers killed his brother Józef and Eugeniusz took over his underground duties with the Armia Krajowa (the Polish Home Army) supplying munitions and transport.

He took part in the Warsaw Uprising together with his sister, joining the Koszta Company defending the Śródmieście area. During the sixty-three day uprising he took over a thousand photographs.

Lokajski became commanding officer of the 2nd platoon of the Koszta Company. He took part in much heavy fighting in Warsaw's Old Town and at one point captured eighteen German prisoners.

Although his unit was successful, others were not and he was eventually forced to withdraw. Returning to his photographic shop on 25 September 1944 to get material to make false identification papers, he was killed when a shell hit the shop. His body wasn't recovered until 1945. He was buried in the Powazki Cemetery.

Many of his photographs were recovered after the war, hidden in a derelict house. Thanks to the hard work and persistence of his sister Zofia Domańska and the Warsaw Uprising Museum, on 4 February 2008 a collection of his photographs was published.

Luz Long (1913–43)
German
Long jump
1936 Berlin (Silver)

Carl Ludwig Hermann Long was born on 27 April 1913 in Leipzig. He was one of five children born to Carl Hermann, a pharmacist, and Johanna Hesse. His great-great-grandfather was the famous chemist Justus von Liebig (1803–73). Luz studied law at the University of Leipzig before practising in Hamburg.

In 1929 he joined the Leipziger Sports Club. In 1934 he finished third in the long jump at the European Championships with a jump of 7.25 metres. He later went on to hold the European record. He also won the German long jump championship on six occasions, in 1933–9.

In 1936 he was selected to represent Germany in the Berlin Olympics. To compete against the great American long jump record holder Jesse Owens had long been his dream. In the heats Long set the standard early by breaking the Olympic record. Owens on the other hand was struggling: his first two jumps were ruled no-jumps. Owens was worried: he knew he had to clear 7.15 metres to move on to the next stage. Long's son told a reporter in 1964 that his father approached Owens, who was looking dejected, and advised him to jump several inches behind the take-off board. Owens took his advice and in his third and final jump jumped clean and made the distance. The final was an exciting event with the jumpers

Luz Long seen pictured here with Jesse Owens at the 1936 Olympics.

The medal ceremony, where Luz Long collected his silver medal. (*Bundesarchiv, Bild 183-G00630*)

breaking the Olympic record five times. Owens went on to win the gold with a jump of 8.06 metres while Long only managed 7.87, taking the silver. Long was the first to congratulate Owens. They posed for photographs together and left the stadium arm in arm. Owens later remarked, 'It took a lot of courage for him to befriend me in front of Hitler. I would melt down all the medals and cups I have and they wouldn't be a plating on the twenty-four carat friendship that I felt for Luz Long at that moment. Hitler must have gone crazy watching us embrace?' Long received much negative attention from the Nazi press and public after the event. It was later said that Hitler was 'not amused'. The Japanese long jumper Naoto Tajima (d.1990) came third to win bronze. Two days later Long finished 10th in the triple jump. In 1938 he took the bronze in the European Championships with a jump of 7.56.

Long served with the German army in the war. In January 1941 he was a sports instructor to the FDJ (Free German Youth) in Wismar. He was promoted to lance corporal and joined the 10th Paratrooper Flak Regiment 'Hermann Göring' in Sicily. In July 1943 he was in action against Americans around the San Pietro airfield when he was captured. He was later murdered in the Biscari Massacre on 14 July 1943 by American soldiers of the 180th Infantry Regiment. He was buried in the German War Cemetery of Motta Sant'Anastasia where 4,561 German soldiers are buried.

Luz Long wrote to Owens after the 1936 Olympics. In his final letter he asked him to contact his son after the war and tell him 'what times were like when we were not separated by war. I am saying – tell him how things can be between men on this earth.' Owens travelled to Germany after the war to meet Kai, Luz's son. So strong was the relationship that Owens later served as best man at Kai Long's wedding.

René, Baron de Lunden (1902–42)
Belgian
Bobsleigh
1936 Berlin

René Henri Theophile Lunden was born on 2 June 1902 in Brussels. When his father died in 1921 he inherited his title and castle in Humbeek. He graduated in Engineering from Leuven University, but never took up the profession as by now running the castle and estate, which he did with his mother, took up all his time. Later, however, he worked as a diplomat in South America.

In 1925 he was called up for military duty, serving first with the cavalry and later the Belgian air force.

Lunden was a fine all-round sportsman and a noted steeplechaser; however his passion was winter sports, and he excelled at the bobsleigh. In 1936 he was selected to take part in the Winter Olympics in Garmisch-Partenkirchen. He competed in the two-man and the four-man bob, finishing eighth in both. Despite this disappointment he went on to win the gold medal at the 1939 World Championships in St Moritz in the two-man bob with Jean Coops as his brakeman. By achieving this he became the first Belgian to win a world title in the sport.

When the Germans invaded Belgium in 1940, Lunden, together with his regiment, fled to France and then to England. On arrival he joined 23 (Belgian) Squadron RAF. Too old to become a pilot, he trained as a navigator, becoming 87708 Pilot Officer Lunden. On 3 April 1942, when returning from a sortie over France, his Boston Mk III crashed at the airfield in Chichester. Although Lunden was removed from the wreckage and rushed to Chichester Hospital, he died shortly after arrival. He was initially buried near Pirbright, but in 1949 his remains were returned to Belgium.

Frederick Riley (1912–42)
British
Football
1936 Berlin

Frederick Riley was born on 9 January 1912 in Manchester. A fine footballer, he played for Casuals FC with some success: the team won the 1936 FA Amateur Cup and was runner-up in the Isthmian League the same year.

In 1936 he was selected to represent Great Britain at football at the 1936 Berlin Olympics. He was on the bench as a substitute for the game against China which Great Britain won 2–0. He played against Poland in the quarter-final, but Great Britain lost 5–4. Italy took the gold, Austria the silver and Norway the bronze.

They were forced to meet Hitler and shake his hand, but they refused to give the Nazi salute before either the game against China or Poland (which the professional England squad did in 1938 to much controversy), disobeying the instructions given from the very top of the game. Hitler and Nazi diplomats were furious after the first snub, but it made little difference, as they refused again against Poland.

In 1937, Riley was a member of the England squad that toured New Zealand, Australia and Sri Lanka.

In the war he joined the RAF on a short service commission. After completing his training he went to 236 Squadron at Stradishall on 6 November 1939, serving with it throughout the Battle of Britain.

He was killed on 7 December 1942 flying in Spitfire PR VII R6964 of 542 Squadron. He was on a low-level sortie to photograph wireless installations in the Desvres area. He is buried in the Boulogne Eastern Cemetery.

The British Olympic football team in 1936.

Hugh Thompson (1914–42)
Canadian
Athletics
1936 Berlin

Hubert Thompson was born in 1914 in Nanaimo, British Columbia. He was brought up by his aunt and uncle and educated at the John Shaw school. While there he began to show a talent for track and field events, especially the 1,500 metres. Winning the BC mile championship gave him the opportunity to trial to represent Canada in the Olympic Games. Unable to afford the costs, the city of Nanaimo decided to help and collected the $350 necessary to send him to Montreal for the try outs. Keen not to let his hometown down, he qualified, and was selected to run for Canada in the 1936 Berlin Olympics; but unfortunately he finished eighth in his heat in the opening round and was eliminated.

Returning, he found work as an exercise instructor and began to train for the British Empire games to be held in 1938. Bad fortune dogged him however, and after breaking his leg he had to retire from athletics.

In the war he sailed for England and joined the RAF, but was killed in a training accident in 1942. He was inducted into the Nanaimo Sports Hall of Fame in 2008 as a member of the inaugural class of pioneers.

John Thornton (1911–44)
British
Athletics
1936 Berlin

John St Leger Thornton was born on 6 June 1911, the son of the Reverend Claude and Alice May of Oldcoats, Nottinghamshire. He was educated at Charterhouse and Pembroke, Cambridge. He established himself as an athlete while at Charterhouse, specialising in the hurdles. At Cambridge he improved his style and in 1930 ran in the 480 yards against Oxford at Fenner's. He later became captain of the Cambridge Athletics Club and captained the club tour of America. After Cambridge he went to work for ICI.

Thornton finished second to Don Finlay, later Battle of Britain ace, in the AAA 120 yards hurdles three times (1936–38), and was a finalist in 1931/2. He was selected to represent Great Britain in the 110 metres for the 1936 Berlin Olympics where he reached the final, finishing fifth (Don Finlay took the silver).

In 1935 he married Joan Walker-Smith, the daughter of Sir Jonah Smith MP.

Thornton enjoyed his best season in 1937. He won both his international match races, defeating his old rival Finlay, competing against Germany. In the same year he established his career best when he beat the American star Leroy Kirkpatrick in Brussels. The following year he came fourth in the European Championships 110 metres.

In 1939 he joined the Territorial Army before being commissioned into the Seaforth Highlanders. He saw action at El Alamein and in the Sicilian campaign and was mentioned in dispatches. He was promoted to major and killed in action near Lisieux, Normandy, on 18 August 1944. He is buried in Banneville-la-Campagne War Cemetery, grave V.D.21.

Freddie Tomlins (1919–43)
British
Figure skating
1936 Garmisch-Partenkirchen

Frederick William Edwin Tomlins was born on 5 August 1919 in Lambeth, son of Ernest and Grace. A keen skater, he turned his attention to figure skating and was soon winning competitions all over the country. He became British champion before moving on to international events.

In 1936 he was selected to represent Great Britain in the winter Olympics in Garmisch-Partenkirchen. Although he didn't take a medal, he made a creditable tenth in the figure skating singles. He followed this by coming eighth at the European Championships in the same year. In 1937 he came fifth in the World Championships. In 1938 he came sixth in the European Championships and fifth in the World Championships. His greatest year was 1939 when he won the silver medal in both the World Championships and the European Championships.

On three occasions Tomlins was introduced to Hitler, who personally presented him with a gold watch. Much was made in the propaganda of the time that Tomlins used this very same watch while on bombing raids with the RAF over Germany. He said, 'That watch will come in handy one of these days; it is just right for timing the release of bombs.'

In the war he was commissioned as a pilot officer in the RAF and sent to Canada for training. On 20 June 1943 he took off from RAF St Eval in Armstrong Whitworth Whitley VII LA 814, serving with Coastal Command on a daytime submarine sweep over the Bay of Biscay. Together with another Armstrong, flown by Pilot Officer Orr, they spotted the Italian submarine *Barbarigo* on the surface and both planes attacked. Orr narrowly missed with his depth charges but his rear gunner put long bursts into the submarine. Tomlins' aircraft then attacked, also missing with its depth charges, but as it passed over the submarine it was hit by anti-aircraft fire and seen to catch fire. After that the plane seemed out of control and crashed into the sea. The entire crew were killed. Tomlins is commemorated on the Runnymede Memorial, Panel 133. As for the *Barbarigo*, it was never seen again.

Freddie's biography, *Freddie Tomlins – Life on Skates*, was later written by his sister.

Jack Turnbull (1910–44)
USA
Hockey
1936 Berlin

John Inglehart Turnbull was born on 30 June 1910 in Baltimore, Maryland. He was educated at the Baltimore Polytechnic Institute. A fine sportsman, he became captain of the college lacrosse team in 1926, also competing well in football and basketball. In 1928 he reached the playoffs to attend the 1928 Olympics in Amsterdam but unfortunately didn't quite make it. He then went up to John Hopkins University where he was on the lacrosse team. He was also an active member of the Mount Washington Lacrosse Club. He was selected to represent the US at Lacrosse at the 1932 Los Angeles Olympics, but only as part of a demonstration event. He became known as the Babe Ruth of Lacrosse. He graduated from Johns Hopkins with a BA in engineering.

Considered one of the finest lacrosse players in the USA, he was named an All-American in each of his three years on the Johns Hopkins Blue Jays team. He also played ice hockey, which he helped introduce into the university.

In 1936 he was selected to represent the USA in field hockey at the Berlin Olympics. The team came tenth. They lost 3–1 to Hungary, 7–0 to India and 5–0 to Japan. During the games Turnbull was introduced to Hitler. He later said, 'I could have reached over and strangled the sonofabitch then, and we wouldn't be here now.'

Turnbull began working for the American Radiator Company and at the same time joined the Maryland National Guard as an aviation cadet, being commissioned in 1940 into the 104th Observation Squadron. He eventually became a lieutenant colonel.

He was mobilized in February 1941, joining the 492nd Bombardment Group and sent to Europe. They were known within the USAF as the 'hard luck group' because of their heavy losses; after 89 days of combat the 492nd had lost 52 aircraft with 588 men killed or missing.

He was reassigned to the 44th Bomber Group and involved in a mid-air collision flying his B24 bomber in severe weather on 18 October 1944 while returning from a mission. He died from his injuries two days later.

He was first buried not far from his crash site in the Henri-Chappelle Cemetery in Belgium. However on the request of his mother his body was returned home in 1947 and now rests in All Hallows Chapel Cemetery, Davidsonville, Maryland.

In 1965 Turnbull was inducted into the National Lacrosse Hall of Fame and is regarded to this day as one of the best players ever. He also lends his name to the Jack Turnbull Award, given to the nation's best collegiate attackman.

Mini Biographies

Stefan Adamczak (1892–1939), Polish, pole vault, 1924 Paris.
Stefan Adamczak was born on 27 November 1892 in Mansfeld, Germany. He competed in the men's pole vault in the 1924 Paris Olympics. He finished fifteenth. He was killed in action in the defence of Katowice in September 1939.

Herbert Adamski (1910–41), German, rowing, 1936 Berlin (Gold).
Herbert Adamski was born on 30 April 1910 in Berlin. Between 1936 and 1939 he was German champion in the coxed pairs with Gerhard Gustmann and cox Dieter Arend. Selected for the 1936 Olympics in Berlin, he won gold in the coxed pair competition (again with Gustmann and Arend). In 1937 they were European champions and in 1938 runners up. In 1939 he was German champion in the coxed fours. He was killed in action on 11 August 1941 on the Russian front.

Iwao Aizawa (1906–unknown), Japanese, sprint, 1928 Amsterdam.
Iwao Aizawa was born on 29 August 1906. He competed in the 1928 Amsterdam Olympics. He took part in the men's 100 metres coming fourth, the 200 metres and the men's 4 × 100 metres; he failed to reach the final in either event. He was killed in the Philippines in the war.

Abdurahman Ali (1911–unknown), Filipino, swimming, 1932 Los Angeles.
Abdurahman Ali was born on 6 June 1911 in Jolo in the Philippines. He competed in the men's 100 metres freestyle at the 1932 Los Angeles Olympics. He failed to reach the finals. He was killed some time in the Second World War.

Arno Almqvist (1881–1940), Finnish, modern pentathlon, 1912 Stockholm.
Arno Axel Almqvist was born on 23 September 1881 in Pori. He competed for Russia in the modern pentathlon in the 1912 Stockholm Olympics, finishing twentieth. In the First World War he served as a captain at the Kronstadt naval fortress. He was arrested by the Bolsheviks and spent five months as a prisoner before escaping to Finland. He later fought with the White Guard as a commander of artillery and served as a prison warden. He died in the bombing of Mikkeli on 5 March 1940 while working for the Finnish army as a voluntary civilian.

Erich Altosaar (1908–41), Estonian, basketball, 1936 Berlin.
Erich Altosaar was born on 14 August 1908 in Tallinn. He was part of the national team that was placed ninth in the 1936 Berlin Olympics, where he also served as the flag bearer for Estonia. He held national titles in volleyball (1927, 1929, 1931, 1933 and 1935–39), basketball (1927, 1930–1 and 1941) and association football (1930). Altosaar also played in sixteen international basketball matches for Estonia. He was arrested by Stalin's NKVD and died in a gulag in 1941.

Max Amann (1905–45), German, water polo, 1928 Amsterdam (Gold).
Max Amann was born on 19 January 1905 in Magdeburg. He was European water polo champion in 1931, second in 1934 and third in 1926. Together with his team, SC Hellas Magdeburg, Amann earned German national titles in 1924–6, 1928–31 and 1933. He added another title, this time for swimming with the 4 × 100 medley relay, in 1924. He competed in the 1928 Amsterdam Olympics. The German water polo team took the gold medal. He played in all three matches and scored three goals. He was reported missing on the Russian front in 1944 and his death was confirmed in December 1945.

Artur Amon (1916–44), Estonian, basketball, 1936 Berlin.
Artur Amon was born on 17 February 1916 in Tartu. He graduated from Tartu High School in 1933 and attended the Tallinn Technical University. He played for Tartu NMKA (1932–36), Tallinna Kalev (1936–40), and Tallinna Dynamo (1940–41). He also competed in the 1939 European Championships. He was capped twelve times for Estonia. He competed for Estonia in the 1936 Berlin Olympics, finishing ninth. He was killed in action on 3 September 1944 in Tartu.

Jan Geert Ankerman (1906–42), Dutch, field hockey, 1928 Amsterdam (Silver).
Jan Geert Ankerman was born on 2 March 1906 in Wommels. He took part in the Amsterdam Olympics of 1928 as a member of the Dutch field hockey team. He played in all four matches as a halfback, the team going on to win the silver medal. Jan later married Viola von Boronkay and they had four children. He was captured in the Japanese invasion of Burma and died there on 27 December 1942 in a prison camp in Rangoon.

Shigeo Arai (1916–44), Japanese, freestyle swimming, 1936 Berlin (Gold and Bronze).
Shigeo Arai was born on 8 August 1916 in Shizuoka. He took part in the 1936 Olympics in Berlin, winning gold in the 4 × 200m freestyle relay and bronze in the 100 metres freestyle. He also won three national titles in the 100 metres and four in the 200 metres freestyle between 1937 and 1940. He was killed serving with the Imperial Japanese Army in Burma on 9 July 1944.

Álvaro de Arana (1904–37), Spanish, Sailing, 1928 Amsterdam.

Álvaro de Arana Churruca was born on 3 October 1904 in Bilbao. He represented Spain at the 1928 Amsterdam Olympics in the sailing mixed 6 metres. He came thirteenth. I have been unable to find very much about his life or death. He died in Bilbao in the Spanish Civil War on 16 July 1937.

Kalle Arantola (1913–40), Finnish, skiing, 1936 Berlin.

Kalle Reino Arantola was born on 24 September 1913 in Sotkamo. He took part in the 1936 Winter Olympics in Garmisch-Partenkirchen, competing in the military patrol, which was allowed as a demonstration sport. The Finnish team came second but were not awarded medals.

Kalle was killed in action on 12 February 1940 in Kuhmo.

Hikoroku Arimoto (1915–44), Japanese, artistic gymnastics, 1936 Berlin.

Hikoroku Arimoto was born on 11 October 1915. He competed with the Japanese gymnastics team in the 1936 Olympics in Berlin. The team finished ninth. His best individual result was thirty-fifth in the floor exercises. It is believed he was killed in Burma in 1944.

Albert Arnheiter (1890–1945), German, rowing, 1912 Stockholm (Gold).

Albert Stephen Arnheiter was born on 20 July 1890 in Ludwigshafen. He was a fine rower and athlete. He rowed in the 1909 German Championships, his eight coming second. In 1910 in the same event he came third with the coxless fours, and in 1912 came second. He competed in the 1912 Olympics in Stockholm. He was bow in the coxed four which took the gold medal. The others in the crew were Hermann Wilker (d.1941), Rudolf Fickeisen (d.1944), Otto Fickeisen (d.1963) and Otto Maier (d.1957). Albert was killed on 26 April 1945 in Italy.

Jochen Balke (1917–44), German, swimming, 1936 Berlin.

Joachim Balke was born on 12 September 1917 in Dortmund. He was selected to swim for the German team in the 1936 Berlin Olympics. He came sixth in the 200 metres breaststroke. Two years later he became European champion in the same event. Nationally he won the German 200 metres breaststroke titles in 1936, 1938, 1940 and 1941. He set a new world record of 1 minute 9.5 seconds in the 100 metres breaststroke in 1938, although the event was not an official contest at that time. Joining the German army, he was eventually sent to a punishment battalion in 1943 suffering from battle fatigue. He was reported missing in action in Veliky Novgorod in Russia in January 1944, although he wasn't officially declared dead until 17 September 1957.

Ernst Balz (1904–45), German, Art, 1936 Berlin.

Ernst Balz was born on 24 February 1904 in Forchtenberg. He was selected to take part in the art competition at the Berlin Olympics, competing in the mixed sculpturing, but he failed to win a medal. He was married to fellow sculptor Doris Balz (née Gerstel), the daughter of his art teacher.

He was reported missing in action in 1943. His death was assumed by the local court in Berlin-Zehlendorf to have taken place before 31 December 1945. No place of death is recorded.

Franz Barsicke (1905–44), German, long-distance running, 1936 Berlin.
Franz Barsicke was born on 15 May 1915 in Warsaw, Poland. A talented runner, he became the 1936 German marathon champion. In 1935 he ran with the winning marathon team at the national championships. He competed in the marathon in the 1936 Berlin Olympics but was forced to withdraw from the race after nine kilometres having torn a muscle in his leg. Franz was reported missing in 1944 near Stalingrad. His death was later assumed. His brother Richard was also a marathon runner and a member of the 1935 winning German team.

Franz Bartl (1915–41), Austrian, field handball, 1936 Berlin (Silver).
Franz Bartl was born on 7 January 1915 in Vienna. He competed in the field handball event in the 1936 Berlin Olympics. He played in three games as part of the Austrian team, helping them to take the silver medal. He was killed in action on 12 July 1941.

Helmut Barysz (1916–45), Polish, swimming, 1936 Berlin.
Helmut Barysz was born on 31 August 1916 in Poland. He competed in the men's 4 × 200 freestyle swimming relay in the 1936 Berlin Olympics, coming fifth. He was reported as missing in action in January 1945, and finally declared dead in 1952.

Julije Bauer (1908–45), Yugoslav, sprint, 1936 Berlin.
Julije Bauer was born on 9 October 1908 in Serbia. After coming fourth in the European Championships in Turin in 1934, he was selected to run in the Olympics. He competed in the men's 100 metres at the 1936 Berlin Games, narrowly missing a medal, coming fifth. He was killed in action on 15 March 1945.

Adi Baumgarten (1915–42), German, boxing, 1936 Berlin.
Adolf Baumgarten was born on 3 May 1915 in Hamburg. He took part in the 1936 Berlin Olympics. Fighting as a middleweight, he was beaten in the quarter-finals by the Norwegian Henry Tiller (who went on to win the silver medal). In the 1942 unofficial European Amateur Boxing Championships Adi won silver. He was killed in action on 2 October 1942 in the siege of Leningrad (St Petersburg). His colleagues buried him by the roadside as they advanced on Vitebsk.

Artur Bäumle (1906–42), German, long jump, 1936 Berlin.
Albert Artur Bäumle was born on 4 September 1906 in Lorrach. A good all-round athlete, he specialised in the long jump. He competed for his club, MSV Wünsdorf. Bäumle took part in the 1936 Berlin Olympics. He was placed ninth. He was reported as missing in action on 6 January 1943 in the battle for Stalingrad. The district court at Heilbronn declared him deceased in 1953, giving a date of 31 December 1945 for his death. Today he is commemorated on a memorial at Rososhka in the Ukraine.

Karl Bechler (1886–1945), German, running, 1908 London.

Karl Bechler was born on 15 February 1886 in Poland. He was a Doctor of Philosophy at the Royal Catholic Gymnasium in Konitz, Prussia. He published both theatre and literary reviews and was considered a good draftsman. Serving with the German army in the First World War, he was twice wounded and was awarded the Iron Cross 2nd class. In 1908 he set the world record for the indoor 60 metres, recording a time of 7.2 seconds. In the same year he took part in the London Olympics. He was eliminated in the heats of the 100 metres. He also took part in the javelin, again failing to qualify for the finals. Bechler died from shrapnel wounds on 29 March 1945 in the cellar of his house in Gdańsk.

Martin Beckmann (1885–1944), German, running, 1906 Athens.

Martin Beckmann was born on 17 March 1885 in Leipzig. A fine runner who ran for his club VfB Leipzig, in 1905 he became German champion in the 400 metres. Due mostly to his speed, he was also a fine footballer, competing as a semi-professional. So keen was he to take part in the Olympics, he travelled to the 1906 Games, the 'Second International Olympic Games in Athens', at his own expense. He ran in both the 100 and 400 metres, failing to progress to the finals in either event. In 1913 he was awarded the 'Deutsches Sportabzeichen' (German Sports Badge) in recognition of his sporting achievements. He was one of the first athletes to receive this honour. He was reported missing in action in 1944; his body was never discovered.

Heinrich Bender (1902–43), German, rowing, 1928 Amsterdam.

Heinrich Bender was born on 2 December 1902 in Lohrbach, Germany. He became a high school teacher. Rowing in the eights for the Mannheimer Ruderverein Amicitia, he became German champion in 1931. A fine all-round sportsman, he also played rugby with Heidelberger RK 1872. He competed in the men's eights, rowing in the 1932 Olympics in Los Angeles. The team were knocked out in the heats. He had been selected for the 1928 Games in Amsterdam, but remained a reserve and did not take part in the games. He was killed in action on 10 July 1943 in the Gulf of Corinth aged 40.

Emil Benecke (1898–1945), German, water polo, 1928 Amsterdam (Gold), 1932 Los Angeles (Silver).

Emil Benecke was born on 4 October 1898 in Magdeburg. He earned his living as a merchant. A fine water polo player, he took part in two consecutive summer Olympics, 1928 Amsterdam and 1932 Los Angeles. In Amsterdam he was part of the German team that won the gold medal. He played in all three matches and scored three goals. He remained with the team that played in the 1932 Los Angeles Games, playing in four matches, this time taking silver. In 1931 he took silver and bronze at the European Championships in Paris and in 1926 in Budapest, respectively. Benecke was also an excellent swimmer, being German champion in the 500 metres freestyle in 1917–18, the 100 metres sidestroke in 1917–19, and the 400 metres freestyle in 1921–22. Captured in the Russian Campaign, he died on 12 August 1945 aged 46 in a Russian prisoner of war camp in Riga.

Franz Berghammer (1913–44), Austrian, field handball, 1936 Berlin (Silver).

Franz Berghammer was born on 20 November 1913 in Vienna. He competed in the 1936 Berlin Olympics. He was part of the Austrian field handball team, and although he only played in one match he helped the team win a silver medal. Germany took gold and Switzerland the bronze. He was killed in action on 7 July 1944 near Babruysk in Belarus.

Michelangelo Bernasconi (also known as Piastrella) (1901–43), Italian, rowing, 1928 Amsterdam.

Michelangelo Bernasconi was born on 27 January 1901 in Como. He competed in the men's single sculls at the 1928 Games in Amsterdam. He was eliminated from the competition in the second round. He was killed on 21 March 1943 in the fighting in Tunisia.

Hans Bernhardt (1906–40), German, cycling, 1928 Amsterdam (Bronze).

Hans Bernhardt was born on 28 January 1906 in Leipzig. He took part in the 1928 Amsterdam Olympics. He won bronze in the men's tandem 2,000 metres sprint together with his team-mate Karl Kather. He also managed fourth in the men's 1,000 metres sprint. In the same year, Bernhardt won his only national title, taking the German 1,000 metres time-trial. He was killed in action on 29 November 1940 in Amsterdam, coincidentally the place of his greatest cycling success. He was buried in the German war Cemetery at Ysselsteyn in Holland.

Herberts Bertulsons (1903–42), Latvian, alpine skiing, 1936 Garmisch-Partenkirchen.

Herberts Bērtulsons was born on 14 September 1903 in Riga. He competed in the men's combined event in the 1936 Winter Olympics in Garmisch-Partenkirchen, a combination of downhill skiing and slalom. He failed to win a medal. Taken prisoner by the Russians in the war, he was interned in a Soviet prison camp before being executed around February 1942 (the order for his execution was signed on 14 February 1942).

Karlis Bone (1899–1941), Latvian, football, 1924 Paris.

Kārlis Bone was born on 19 February 1899 in Riga. A well-established Latvian footballer, he competed in the 1924 Paris Olympics. The Latvian team was knocked out in the preliminary matches, being beaten by France 7–0. The gold was taken by Uruguay (who had knocked out France). He was taken prisoner by the Soviets and died or was executed in a Soviet prison camp on 13 November 1941.

Helmut Bonnet (1910–44), German, athletics, 1936 Berlin.

Helmut Bonnet was born on 17 July 1910 in Berlin. A fine all-round athlete, he joined the German police and in 1934 was German Police champion in both the high jump and pole vault. In 1936 he became German national champion in the decathlon. In the same year he took part in the Olympics, competing in the men's decathlon. He was placed eighth. In the war he became a captain and instructor with an air force unit based in Carcassonne. He was shot in the head and seriously wounded while fighting against the Allies. Despite being evacuated to a hospital, he succumbed to his wounds on 27 September 1944. He was later laid to rest in Berlin-Spandau war Cemetery 'In den Kisseln'.

Werner Böttcher (1909–44), German, running, 1936 Berlin.

Werner Böttcher was born on 4 September 1909 in Berlin. He took part in the German Championships in 1936 becoming champion in the 4 × 1,500 metres relay and runner-up in the 1,500 metres (he was also placed third in the same event in 1941). In the same year, he took part in the Olympics, competing in the men's 1,500 metres, coming twelfth. He was reported missing in action on 10 November 1944 (later presumed killed) at the *Różan* bridgehead in Poland. He is buried in the Mława war Cemetery in Poland.

Béchir Bouazzat (1908–44), French, modern pentathlon, 1936 Berlin.

Béchir Bouazzat was born on 5 October 1908 in Gammarth, Tunisia. He competed in the 1936 Berlin Olympics. He didn't perform well and came twenty-eighth, Germany taking the gold. He had the distinction of being a pioneer for his sport in Tunisia. Travelling to France in 1935 he won the free wrestling (light heavyweight) championship of France, as well as the Greco-Roman wrestling (middleweight). In the same year he attended the European wrestling championship, winning a bronze in the 79 kg. He was killed in action on 12 April 1944 in the Val-de-Marne, a victim of 'friendly' fire by an American soldier.

Roger Bureau (1905–45), Belgian, speed skating and ice hockey, 1928 St Moritz, 1936 Garmisch-Partenkirchen.

Roger Eugène Bureau was born on 11 February 1905 in Antwerp. He finished seventh in the speed skating event in the 1926 European Championships. The following year, he won a silver medal at the Ice Hockey European Championships. He played ice hockey at the 1928 Winter Olympics in St Moritz, finishing fifth. Eight years later, in 1936, he was back at the Olympics, this time in Garmisch-Partenkirchen. Playing ice hockey, he finished thirteenth. Serving with the Belgium army in the war, he was arrested by the Nazis on 21 April 1944 near the French-Spanish border. He was sent to a prisoner-of-war camp where he was killed on 11 April 1945.

José Canals (1914–37), Spanish, Cross-country skiing, 1936 Garmisch-Partenkirchen.

José Oriole Canals was born on 10 October 1914 in Barcelona. Becoming a fine cross-country skier, he was selected to represent Spain at the 1936 winter Olympics in Garmisch-Partenkirchen. He competed in the men's 18 kilometres but failed to win a medal, coming 65th. He was killed in action fighting for the Nationalists on the Asturias front in the Spanish Civil War on 5 August 1937.

Giuseppe Castelli (1907–42), Italian, athletics, 1928 Amsterdam, 1932 Los Angeles (Bronze).

Giuseppe Castelli was born on 5 October 1907 in Frugarolo. He became mainly a sprinter. Castelli won two Italian relay championships in 1930: the 200 metres and the medley relay.

He took part in the 1928 Olympics in Amsterdam, competing in the 200 metres and the 4 × 100 metres relay. He was eliminated in the heats in both events. In 1932 he was selected to take part in the Los Angeles Olympics. Again he competed in the 4 × 100 metres relay, taking the bronze medal together with Ruggero Maregatti (1905–63), Edgardo Toetti (1910–68) and Gabriele Salviati (1910–1987). He was killed in action on 19 December 1942 on the Russian front.

Ugo Ceccarelli (1911–40), Italian, modern pentathlon, 1936 Berlin.

Ugo Ceccarelli was born on 11 March 1911. He competed in the 1936 Berlin Olympics, coming fifteenth in the modern pentathlon. Ugo was killed in 1940 in Milan. Some mystery surrounds his death. He was killed near his sports club Canottieri (rowing club) Milano. Some say he was killed by partisans who believed he was Fascist, other reports say he was murdered as a result of a private argument.

Sulo Cederström (1903–44), Finnish, sports shooting, 1936 Berlin.

Sulo Cederström was born on 11 February 1903 in Kouvola. He competed in the men's rapid-fire 25-metre pistol event in the 1936 Olympics, finishing twenty-sixth. He was killed on the Karelian Isthmus in the Winter War against Russia on 26 June 1944, probably in the Vyborg offensive.

Antoni Cejzik (1900–39), Polish, Decathlon, 1928 Amsterdam.

Antoni Cejzik was born on 15 May 1900 in Jelets, Lipetsk, Russia. An outstanding all-round athlete, he first represented Poland in 1924 at the Paris Olympics, taking part in the decathlon and finishing 12th. He was selected again for the 1928 Games in Amsterdam. This time he came 18th. He met his wife, the Polish Olympian Genowefa Kobielska, at the 1928 Olympics. She was taking part in the discus.

Antoni Cejzik was killed in action serving with the Modlin army near Zaborów, Warsaw, on 12 September 1939. Genowefa died in 1993.

Chen Zhenhe (1906–41), Chinese, football, 1936 Berlin.

Chen Zhenhe was born on 15 March 1906 in Jakarta. He studied business administration at the Shanghai Jinan National University in 1926. While there he played football, playing mid-field for the JNU and winning eight college championships in nine years with them. His talent was quickly noticed and he was selected to play for the Loh Hwa team. He toured Australia and South East Asia with them. He transferred to the You-You team, going on to be part of the team that won the football tournament in the Far Eastern Games in 1930. In 1936 he was selected to be a member of the Chinese football team that attended the Berlin Olympics (one of the few players who did not come from Hong Kong teams). They failed to win a medal, coming ninth. He continued to play football internationally as well as for various Shanghai teams. In 1932 Chen joined the Central Aviation School, later becoming a squadron leader in the Chinese Air Force. When the Japanese invaded in 1937, he was stationed in Hangzhou. The Chinese Air Force were using outdated aircraft which were no match for the Japanese Zeros. Although these were later replaced, it was too late for Chen, who on 28 January 1941 crashed and was killed on his first flight, from Xinjiang to Chengdu.

Charles Courtin (1902–44), French, long jump, 1920 Antwerp.

Charles Courtin was born in 1902. He competed in the long jump in the 1920 Antwerp Olympics, finishing seventeenth. He was killed in action in August 1944.

Heinz-Rudolf 'Rudi' Cranz (1918–41), German, alpine skiing, 1936 Garmisch-Partenkirchen.

Heinz-Rudolf Cranz was born on 2 September 1918 in Uccle in Belgium, his parents fleeing to Reutlingen in the First World War. His older sister was Christl Cranz (1914–2004), who dominated international skiing competitions in the 1930s winning twelve World Championships between 1934 and 1939. Rudi was selected to take part in the 1936 Winter Olympics in Garmisch-Partenkirchen. He came sixth in the men's alpine skiing combined event. He went on to win four national titles, alpine combination 1937–41 and the slalom 1939–41. He took part in the World Championships on two occasions in 1937, finishing fourth in the slalom and fifth in the combination. Then in 1939 he finished fourth in both events. Rudi was killed in action on 22 June 1941 on the first day of the German offensive against the Russians (operation Barbarossa) serving as a corporal with the Alpine Division in Różaniec, Poland. On hearing of her brother's death, Christl retired from competition.

Jacinto 'Jumping Jack' Ciria Cruz (?-1944), Filipino, basketball.

Jacinto Ciria Cruz was born in Manila. He first played basketball for the University of Santo Tomas, becoming a regular member of the university team. His natural talent quickly came to notice and he was selected to play for the Philippines in the 1936 Berlin Olympics. The team put up a good show, coming fifth; the USA took the gold, Canada and Mexico took silver and bronze. After the Olympics Cruz became a coach, becoming involved with various collegiate teams. When the Japanese invaded the Philippines, Cruz hid in the jungle and became a guerrilla fighter, attacking the Japanese army where and when he and his group could. Unfortunately he was captured by the Japanese army and beheaded on 25 December 1944.

Czesław Cyraniak (1914–39), Polish, boxing, 1936 Berlin.

Czesław Cyraniak was born on 1 June 1914 in Poznań. He took part in the 1936 Berlin Olympics, boxing as a lightweight. Despite defeating the French champion François Aupetit in the first round, he was eliminated in the second round by Philippine boxer Jose Padilla. Cyraniak started boxing at 14 for the Warta Sports Club. As students were forbidden from joining clubs he fought under the pseudonym of 'Kajnar'. He was soon boxing for the Warta team as a lightweight. He came to notice by defeating the Olympic gold medallist Istvan Enekes. He represented Poland on ten occasions between 1934 and 1936 defeating several famous opponents including the European champion German Otto Kastner, as well as the Belgian champion Van den Casteera. He became Polish lightweight champion in 1935. Persistent injuries however slowed his career. At the outbreak of the Second World War he was commissioned as a lieutenant with the 57th Reserve, part of the 14th Army Division 'Poznań'. While fighting in the battle of Bzura on 11 September 1939 against the 1st German Panzer Division, he was killed. He was buried at the parish Cemetery in Mąkolice.

Georg Dascher (1911–44), German, field handball, 1936 Berlin (Gold).

Georg Dascher was born on 27 June 1911 in Hessen. A brilliant handball player, he won the German Championship in 1934 with his home club Polizeisportverein Darmstadt. He was selected to compete in the 1936 Berlin Olympics as part of the German field handball team. They beat Hungary 22–0, America 29–0 and Austria 10–6. He played in two matches, helping his team to take the gold medal. A police officer by profession, in the Second World War he served as a lieutenant in the army. He was killed in action on the Western Front on 25 November 1944. He is buried in the German War Cemetery in Lommel, Belgium.

Simplicio de Castro (1914–40), Filipino, boxing, 1936 Berlin.

Simplicio de Castro was born on 13 January 1914 in the Philippines. He competed in the 1936 Berlin Olympics. He fought well but was eliminated in the quarter-finals of the welterweight class by Roger Tritz. He was killed in action in 1940.

Nemesio de Guzman (1916–44), Filipino, sprint, 1936 Berlin.

Nemesio de Guzman was born on 8 December 1916 in the Philippines. He competed in the 100 and 200 metres in the 1936 summer Olympics aged 19, but failed to win a medal in either event. He was killed in action in 1944.

Eugen Deutsch (1907–45), German, weightlifting, 1936 Berlin (Silver).

Eugen Deutsch was born on 9 November 1907 in Ludwigshafen. He took part in the 1936 Berlin Olympics in the light-heavyweight category, being beaten to the gold by defending champion Louis Hostin. Interestingly Deutsch was disqualified for missing three snatches at first. However he appealed and was given one snatch back. He was successful and went on to claim the silver medal. The other competitors were furious, saying it was a fix and he only got the decision because he was a German competitor in Germany. Deutsch had previously set the light heavyweight world record in 1934 while a member of his club, SC Augusta Augsburg. In 1935 he won the silver medal at the European Championships in the same weight. Between 1934 and 1936 he also took three national titles. He was killed in action on the Western Front on 8 February 1945 in Großsteinhausen, Rheinland-Pfalz.

Émilien Devic (1888–1944), French, football, 1912 Stockholm.
Émilien Devic was born on 16 November 1888 in Romaunville. He grew up to play football both in defence and in the midfield. He played for CA Paris before joining Racing Club de France, followed by Red Star and CASG Paris with whom he won the French Football Cup in the 1918/19 season. He made his first international appearance for France in 1911, and then nine more until 1921. During this time he scored two goals. He also played in the final of the Allied Games in 1919 against Czechoslovakia, France losing 2–1. He was selected to represent France at the 1912 Stockholm Olympics, but shortly before the Games began France withdrew from the football competition.

In the war Devic joined the Resistance. He was arrested and shot on 21 August 1944.

Tivadar Dienes-Ohm (1907–44), Hungary, polo, 1936 Berlin.
Tivadar Dienes-Ohm was born on 20 October 1907 in Hungary. He was educated at a military school and from there went into the Hussar riding school (1932–3). He later joined the 4th Hussars in Budapest. As well as his military career, Tivadar followed a second sporting career as a horseman and fine polo player. He played several times for the national team and was a well-respected member. He was selected to play polo for Hungary at the 1936 summer Olympics. He played in all three matches and was unlucky not to get a medal, the team coming fourth. In the Second World War he commanded the Nyiregyhazaer 'Hadidik' Hussars and was killed in action with them on 28 October 1944.

Diego Díez (1896–1936), Spanish, Fencing, 1924 Paris, 1928 Amsterdam.
Diego Díez de Rivera y Figueroa was born on 15 December 1896 in Madrid. Becoming one of Spain's finest fencers, he took part in the 1924 Olympics competing in the men's individual foil and men's team épée, though he failed to win a medal in either. He was selected once again to compete at the 1928 Olympics in Amsterdam this time competing only in the team events, but again he failed to win a medal. He was killed in action in the Spanish Civil War in September 1936.

Herbert Gerhard Dill (1908–44), German, race walking, 1936 Berlin.
Herbert Dill was born on 31 December 1908 in Hannover. He was a first-class athlete and a keen race walker. He took part in the men's 50 kilometres walk in the 1936 Berlin Olympics, coming sixteenth. Two years later he won a silver medal in the European Championships and later that year became German champion. He was killed in action on 19 December 1944, serving as a lieutenant near Nothum, Luxembourg, in the Battle of the Bulge. He was laid to rest in the military Cemetery at Sandweiler, Luxembourg, in a so-called 'comrades grave'.

Viktor Flessl (1898–1943), Austrian, rowing, 1928 Amsterdam (Bronze).
Viktor Flessl was born on 6 November 1898 in Breza, Bosnia/Herzegovina. He took part in the double sculls in the 1928 Amsterdam Olympics. Together with his partner Leo Losert he took the bronze medal. He was killed in action on 18 December 1943.

Hans Freese (1918–41), German, swimming, 1936 Berlin.
Hans Freese was born on 17 February 1918 in Bremen. He was selected to swim for Germany in the 400 and the 1,500 metres freestyle at the 1936 Berlin Olympics, but was eliminated in the semi-finals in both events. In 1938 he became European champion in the 4 × 200 metres relay; it was to be his greatest success. Freese was seriously wounded outside Leningrad in the Russian campaign. He was evacuated to Germany, being hospitalized in Bremen, but succumbed to his wounds on 8 July 1941.

Mauricio Galvao (1890–1945), German, hockey, 1908 London.
Mauricio Luis Juan Galvao was born on 21 January 1890 in Buenos Aires. He played hockey for his club, Uhlenhorster HC, mostly midfield. He was selected as part of the German team for the 1908 London Olympics. His brother Raulino (d.1960) was also part of the team. They were beaten 4–0 by Scotland in the first round before beating France 1–0 to take fifth place. Galvao was killed in action in Castelnuovo, Italy, on 6 March 1945.

Peter Hunter Gaskell (1915–44), British, rowing, 1936 Berlin.
Peter Hunter Gaskell was born on 10 May 1915 in Greenwich, the son of Vice-admiral Sir Arthur Gaskell, honorary surgeon to the King. Peter was educated at Charterhouse and Trinity, Cambridge. Although he became a member of the First Trinity Boat Club, he failed to take part in the Oxford and Cambridge Boat Race. After university he became a barrister at the Inner Temple.

He was selected as first reserve for the British eight at the 1936 Berlin Olympics, but he never rowed. Great Britain missed a medal, but came fourth. The USA took the gold, Italy the silver and Germany the bronze.

He did however have success at Henley, winning the Stewards' Cup for coxless fours with the Leander crew.

In the war Gaskell was commissioned as a second lieutenant into the Royal Fusiliers. Later he transferred to the 3rd Reconnaissance Corps, 8th Battalion, Royal Northumberland Fusiliers, Royal Armoured Corps, 3rd Infantry Division. He reached the rank of major. He was killed in action in Normandy on 15 August 1944. He is buried at St Charles de Percy War Cemetery, grave III.A.8.

Günther Gehmert (1913–1940), German, athletics, 1936 Berlin.
Günther Gehmert was born on 9 February 1913 in Berlin. He was selected to take part in the 1936 Berlin Olympics, competing in the high jump. He managed to come tenth with a jump of 1.90 metres. He became German champion in 1939 with a jump of 1.95 metres and went on to win nine international caps. He served with the German army in the Second World War and was seriously wounded. He was transferred to the German field hospital in Montaigu in the Vendée in France where he died on 13 June 1940. He was buried at the Fort-de-Malmaison German War Cemetery in the Aisne.

Josef Genschieder (1915–43), Austrian, cycling, 1936 Berlin.
Josef Genschieder was born on 9 February 1913 in Berlin. He cycled for the Neubauer Radler club of Vienna. He was selected for the men's 4,000 metres cycle team in the 1936 Berlin Olympics. The team were eventually placed tenth. He was killed in action on 3 April 1943 in Beketovka, Volgograd, in the Russian Campaign.

František Getreuer (1906–45), Czechoslovak, water polo, 1928 Amsterdam.

František Getreuer was born into a Jewish family on 18 December 1906. He played water polo for Czechoslovakia at the 1928 summer Olympics but the team did not win a medal. He was arrested by the Nazis in Prague and deported to Dachau concentration camp where he was murdered on 6 February 1945.

Wolfgang Goedecke (1906–42), German, rowing, 1928 Amsterdam.

Wolfgang Goedecke was born on 23 July 1906 in Dubna, Moscow Oblast. In 1927 he was second in the coxed fours in the German championships and third in 1928. He competed for Germany in the men's coxless four in the 1928 Amsterdam Olympics. The team was eliminated in the quarter finals. Goedecke was killed in action serving as a lieutenant on 15 August 1942 in the Russian Campaign.

Otoniel Gonzaga (1913–unknown), Filipino, sports shooting, 1936 Berlin.

Otoniel Gonzaga was born on 30 September 1913 in the Philippines. Selected to represent the Philippines in the 1936 Olympics in Berlin, he competed in three events: men's rapid-fire pistol 25 metres, men's free pistol 50 metres, and men's small-bore rifle, prone, 50 metres. He failed to win a medal in any of the events. Little seems to be known about Gonzaga other than he died in the Second World War.

Jan Górny (1907–45), Polish, boxing, 1928 Amsterdam.

Jan Górny was born on 14 August 1907 in Gliwice, Poland. He boxed for Boxing Clubu Królewska Huta and was selected to box for Poland in the 1928 Amsterdam Olympics. Fighting featherweight, he was beaten in the quarter-finals by Lucian Biquet (who went on to finish fourth) and eliminated from the competition. Forced to join the German army, he was seriously wounded on the Western Front. He was evacuated to the American military hospital in Orglandes where he died from his wounds on 7 May 1945.

Alfred Graaf (1917–42), German, boxing, 1936 Berlin.

Little seems to be known about Alfred. He was born on 18 October 1917 in Dortmund. He boxed flyweight and was selected for the German boxing team at the 1936 Olympics, but for some reason he did not compete. He was killed fighting with the German army in Karljanskoie, Russia, on 9 March 1942.

Generalmajor Gustav Grachegg (1882–1945), Austrian, equestrianism, 1928 Amsterdam.

Gustav Grachegg was born on 17 November 1882 in Graz. He was selected to take part in the 1928 Olympics in Amsterdam. He took part in the men's dressage individual in which he came twenty-first and the men's dressage team in which he came sixth. In the Second World War Gustav became a major general. He was kidnapped by the Soviets on 13 May 1945 and was never seen again. It is believed he was murdered by the NKVD.

Félix Grimonprez (1910–40), French, field hockey, 1928 Amsterdam, 1936 Berlin.

Félix Grimonprez was born on 30 June 1910 in Lille. He played for the Lille Hockey Club, who were the men's grass champions in 1927–28 and 1936. Felix played for France on fifty-two occasions and remains to this day one of the best hockey players France ever produced. At 17, Felix was selected to take part in the 1928 Amsterdam Olympics as part of the French hockey team. The team was eliminated in the group stages. Felix played in all three games and scored one goal. Missing the 1932 Games in Los Angeles, he was selected once again to take part in the 1936 Berlin Olympics. This time the team were a little unlucky not to get a medal when they finished fourth. Felix played as a fullback in all five matches. He was killed in action on 26 May 1940. The Grimonprez-Jooris stadium in Lille is named after him.

Francesco Del Grosso (1899–1938), Italian, Cycling, 1924 Paris.

Francesco Del Grosso was born on 28 September 1899 in San Secondo Parmense. Becoming a fine cyclist, he was selected to represent Italy in the 1924 Paris Olympics. He took part in the men's sprint and the 50 kilometres but failed to take a medal in either event. He was killed in action on 22 July 1938 in Barracas, Castellon, Spain, fighting for the Nationalists in the Spanish Civil War.

Martinš Grundmanis (1913–44), Latvian, basketball, 1936 Berlin.

Mârtiņš Grundmanis was born on 18 November 1913 in Riga. He first played basketball for JKS (Latvian Christian Youth) team before playing for his university team in Tartu. He graduated from the university with a degree in physical education. He went on to play for the military team, Rigas ASK, and was the Latvian champion in 1939 and 1940. He won a gold medal at the 1935 EuroBasket (European basketball championship), becoming the first European champion. He was selected to play for Latvia in the 1936 Berlin Olympics. Latvia failed to win a medal. He played basketball for Latvia on twenty occasions. He also played in the 1937 EuroBasket. In the Second World War he fought with the Latvian Legion and was taken prisoner by the Soviet Red Army. He committed suicide on 20 November 1944 at the Sarkandaugava PoW camp in Riga.

Emil Hagelberg (1895–1941), Finnish, modern pentathlon, 1920 Antwerp, 1924 Paris.

Emil Alfons Hagelberg was born on 25 August 1895. In the 1920 Antwerp Olympics, where he was Finnish flag bearer, he came seventh. In the 1924 Paris Olympics he finished twenty-fifth. A career military officer, he fought in the First and the Second World Wars. Taking part in the Winter War, he commanded the 22nd Regiment (later the 9th) and later became the 13th Brigade Commander. He was killed in action in the Continuation War (fought by Finland and the Nazis against the Soviet Union between 1941 and 1944) in a Soviet air raid on 12 August 1941. He was buried in the Hietaniemi Hero Grave in Helsinki.

Saul Hallap (1897–1941), Estonia, weightlifting, 1924 Paris.

Saul Hallap was born on 10 December 1897 in Erastvere, Estonia. He won the world middleweight weightlifting title in 1922. In 1924 he was selected to compete for Estonia in the Paris Olympics. He finished ninth. Shortly after the Olympics Saul retired from competitive weightlifting and began to work as a strongman with the circus, and also as a masseur. He was murdered by the Soviets on 18 July 1941 near Põltsamaa together with his partner the acrobat Alma Kaal. Since 2002 a weightlifting tournament has been held in Tartu in his memory.

Helmut Hamann (1912–41), German, athletics, 1936 Berlin (Bronze).

Helmut Hamann was born on 31 August 1912 in Berlin. A 400-metre specialist, he ran for Sportverein Allianz Berlin. He competed in the 4 × 400 metre relay in the 1934 European Championships taking the gold medal. In 1935, 1936 and 1939 Hamann won the German Championship in the 400 metres. He was selected to run in the 4 × 400 metres in the 1936 Berlin Olympics. The team ran well and took the bronze medal. Great Britain took the gold and the USA the silver. His team consisted of Friedrich von Stulpnagel (1913–96), Harry Voigt (1913–86) and Rudolf Harbig (1913–44 KIA). Hamann was killed in action on 22 June 1941 near Siedliszcze in Poland.

Hermann 'Hannes' Hansen (1912–44), German, field handball, 1936 Berlin (Gold).

Hermann Hansen was born on 31 October 1912 in Schleswig-Holstein. Interestingly, field handball has only taken place in the Olympics once, and that was in the 1936 Berlin Games. Hansen, who played for SV Polizei Hamburg, was selected to play for the German National team in the 1936 Berlin Olympics. The Germans beat Hungary 22–0 and the USA 29–1 in the preliminary matches before defeating Austria in the final 10–6 to win the gold. Hannes played in two of these matches. In 1938 he became World Champion, earning in total eleven international caps for Germany. Joining the Luftwaffe in the Second World War, he failed to return from a flight on 28 June 1944 and was later assumed to have died on that date.

Franz Haslberger (1914–39), German, ski jump, 1936 Garmisch-Partenkirchen.

Franz Haslberger was born on 3 December 1914 in Bavaria. At the 1936 winter Olympics he came seventeenth in the normal hill, individual. In 1938 he came twentieth in the World Cup in Lahti, Finland. In the same year he became German ski jumping champion. In 1937/8 he was the German ski jumping coach. In 1938 he came fourth on the Holmenkollen in Oslo. Franz was killed in action on 17 September 1939 in the battle of Lvov, which was then in Poland (now Ukraine). His hometown of Reit im Winkl named a ski jump in his memory.

Kurt Hasse (1907–44), German, show jumper, 1936 Berlin (two Golds).

Kurt Hasse was born on 7 February 1907 in Mainz. He was the second son of General der Infanterie Ernst Hasse. Kurt followed the family tradition and studied at the Hannover Cavalry School. The entire family were keen horsemen, his younger brother wining 195 races as an amateur jockey. Kurt was selected for the German show jumping team at the 1936 Berlin Olympics. Despite being one of the youngest members of the team, he won gold in the men's individual jumping and then another gold in the men's team, riding his horse *Tora* on both occasions. Again following in the family tradition he became a military officer. Rising to the rank of major, Hasse was killed in action on the Eastern Front on 9 January 1944.

Hermann Heibel (1912–41), German, swimming, 1936 Berlin.

Hermann Heibel was born on 21 July 1912 in Rheinland-Pfalz. He was selected for the German swimming team in the 1936 Berlin Olympics. He competed in two events, the men's 100 metres freestyle and the 4 × 200 metre freestyle relay. He was knocked out of the 100 metres freestyle in the heats and came fifth in the relay. He was seriously wounded on the Eastern Front and evacuated to the military hospital at Valovo in Russia where he died on 19 August 1941.

Albert Heijnneman (1896–1944), Dutch, sprint, 1920 Antwerp.

Albert Heijnneman was born on 28 October 1896 in Penang, Malaysia. Although he specialized in the sprint, he was also a fine long jumper. He became Dutch champion in both the 100 and 200 metres sprint in 1919. Between 1917 and 1919 he was also three times national champion in the long jump. In the 1920 Antwerp Olympics he took part in the men's 100 metres but was eliminated in the heats. In the 200 metres he was eliminated in the quarter final. The men's 4 × 100 metres relay team was eliminated in the second round. Heijnneman became a member of the Dutch Resistance in the Second World War but he was betrayed. He was arrested by the SS in 1944 and tortured to death in Scheveningen prison on 20 February 1944.

Friedrich 'Fritz' Hendrix (1911–41), German, athletics, 1932 Los Angeles (Silver).

Friedrich Hendrix was born on 6 January 1911 in Aachen. In the 1932 Los Angeles Olympics he ran in both the 200 metres and the 4 × 100 metres relay. He was eliminated in the second round of the 200 metres but won the silver medal in the 4 × 100 metres with his teammates Helmut Kornig (d.1973), Erich Borchmeyer (d.2000) and Arthur Jonath (d.1963). He ran a world record in 1932 and was also German sprint relay champion in 1933/4. He married another German athlete, Marie Dollinger (1910–94). In 1937 they had a daughter, Brunhilde (1938–95), who won a silver medal in the 4 × 100 metres relay at the 1960 Rome Olympics. Fritz was killed in action in Operation Barbarossa in Proletarskaya near St Petersburg (Leningrad) on 30 August 1941. He was promoted to corporal the next day.

Eduard Hiiop (1889–1941), Estonian, figure skating and athletics, 1928 St Moritz, 1936 Garmisch-Partenkirchen.

Eduard Hiiop was born on 19 December 1889. He became interested in skating, gymnastics, athletics and cycling while living in Tartu in 1908. In 1912 he moved to Tallinn to focus on figure skating, tennis and athletics. He went on to win many Estonian titles in all these disciplines. He also competed successfully against the Russians in the Estonia Russian championships. In the 1928 Olympics in St Moritz in February 1928 he was selected as the Estonian team's flag-bearer, although he didn't take part in the games themselves. In the 1936 winter Olympics in Garmisch-Partenkirchen he took part in the figure skating competition with his partner Helene Michelson. They came 18th in the mixed pairs. After retiring from competition he moved to Helsinki, becoming a coach for several years. He then moved back to Tallinn to coach the national team. In August 1941 he was arrested by the NKVD and deported to a camp in the Soviet Union, being murdered on 24 August 1941.

Gunnar Höckert (1910–40), Finnish, running. 1936 Berlin (Gold).

Gunnar Mikael Höckert was born on 12 February 1910 in Helsinki. Although a fine runner, he only really had one successful season, 1936. He was selected to take part in the 5,000 metres in the August 1936 Berlin Olympics. The Olympic champion and fellow Finnish runner Lauri Lehtinen (1908–73) was the favourite to win the race. However, Hockert overtook Lehtinen on the last lap to take the gold medal. In the following month, September 1936, Hockert beat the world record in the 3,000 metres in Stockholm. The next week, again in Stockholm, he beat the world record in the two miles. The week after that he equalled Jules Ladoumègue's (1906–73) world record in the 2,000 metres in Malmö. Hampered by illness he achieved little after his 1936 successes. Hockert, who had done his national service in 1932/3, served as a lieutenant with JR10 in the Winter War and was killed by a grenade in Karelia on 11 February 1940.

Heiner Hoffmann (1915–45), German, cycling, 1936 Berlin.

Heiner Hoffmann was born on 29 April 1915 in Klein-Steinheim, Hessen. A keen cyclist he competed for RC Hessen Offenbach and showed great promise, especially in the men's 4,000 metres team pursuit. He was selected to compete in the 1936 Berlin Olympics and just missed out on a medal, coming fourth in the men's 4,000 metres pursuit. Joining the German army in the war, he was killed in Berlin on 27 April 1945.

Christian Holzenberg (1910–42), German, sprint canoe, 1936 Berlin.

Christian Holzenberg was born on 2 January 1910 in Hamburg. A flat-water sprint canoeist, he took part in the Berlin Olympics in 1936 with his partner Walter Schuur (b. 1910) over 10 kilometres. Getting through to the final, they just missed out on a medal, finishing fourth. He later took bronze in the two-man canoe (same partner) in the 1938 ICF canoe sprint World Championship in Vaxholm. The pair had previously won the German championship in the 1,000 metres in 1935 and the 10 kilometres for three years in a row in 1935–7. Holzenberg was killed fighting in Chudovo on the Russian front on 27 February 1942.

Xaver Hörmann, German, sprint canoe, 1936 Berlin (Bronze).

Xaver Hörmann was born on 21 February 1910 in Bubenhausen in Bavaria. He worked for Schäfer ski makers of Esslingen while training as a canoeist. He was selected to represent Germany in the 1936 Olympic Games in the men's folding kayak singles, 10 km. Getting through to the finals, he led for much of the race, however in the final kilometre the favourite, Austrian Gregor Hradetzky (1909–84), caught up with him and took the gold. The Frenchman Henri Eberhardt (1913–76) took silver, but Hormann managed to hang on and take the bronze. In the Second World War he was taken prisoner on the Eastern Front. He died a prisoner in the Ukraine on 23 February 1943.

'Gösta' Horn, Swedish, diving, 1928 Amsterdam.

Lars Gustaf Horn was born on 24 January 1907 in Torshalla. A fine diver, he competed for the Eskilstuna SS club. He was selected to compete in the 1928 Amsterdam Olympics in the men's platform, but he failed to reach the finals. He was killed on 10 December 1943 when his aircraft crashed into the sea on the northern tip of Öland. The cause of the crash remains unknown.

Václav Hošek (1909–43), Czechoslovak, Athletics, 1936 Berlin.

Václav Hošek was born on 18 August 1909 in Czechoslovakia to a Jewish family. Becoming a fine runner, he competed for his athletics club, SK Kladno and was considered one of the country's best athletes.

He was selected to compete in the 1936 Olympics in Berlin and took part in the men's 3,000 metre steeplechase, but was knocked out in the heats. He was captured by the Gestapo in the war and later shot dead while trying to escape from a concentration camp in Bayreuth in June 1943.

Olavi 'Olli' Huttunen (1915–40), Finnish, military patrol, 1936 Garmisch-Partenkirchen.

Olavi Huttunen was born on 10 September 1915 in Iisalmi. He was selected to compete in the military patrol at the 1936 Winter Olympics in Garmisch-Partenkirchen. The International Olympic Committee would not accept this sport into the Olympic programme at first, but after an intervention by Hitler they changed their minds and agreed to make it a demonstration sport. Huttunen and the Finnish team came second, winning the silver medal. He was killed in action on 19 February 1940 (of the four members of the Finnish team that took part in the 1936 Olympics, three were killed in the war).

Arvids Immermanis (1912–47), Latvian, cycling, 1936 Berlin.

Arvīds Immermanis was born on 9 September 1912 in Siberia. A talented cyclist he worked at the G. Erenpreis Bicycle Factory. He picked up four gold medals in the Latvian cycling championships between 1934 and 1937. He also took three golds in the Latvian national cycling competition. In the 1936 Berlin Olympics he took part in both the men's road race team and the men's road race individual. He failed to pick up a medal in either event. He was arrested by the NKVD in the war and died in a Soviet prison camp in July 1947.

Dr Milutin Ivković (1906–43), Serbian, football, 1928 Amsterdam.

Milutin Ivković was born on 3 March 1906 in Belgrade. He became a medical doctor (graduating in 1934) but was far more famous for his exploits on the football field, being one of the finest defenders Yugoslavia has ever produced. He played right back for his club, SK Jugoslavija, turning out for them 235 times between 1922 and 1929. He later went on to play for Belgrade Club BASK playing for them on forty-two occasions. He played for the Yugoslav national team on no fewer than thirty-nine occasions between 1925 and 1934. In 1928 he represented

Yugoslavia in the Amsterdam Olympics. They were knocked out in the early rounds by Portugal 2–1. Uruguay took the gold, Argentina the silver and Italy the bronze. In 1930 he took part in the first FIFA World Cup in Montevideo, being remembered mostly for his brilliant performance against Brazil when Yugoslavia beat them 2–1. He played his final football match in May 1943. A member of the progressive movement, he became a leading light in the campaign to boycott the 1936 Olympic Games in Berlin. In 1938 he became editor of the *Mladost* and helped form the Communist Youth League. When Germany invaded he joined the National Liberation Movement. He was arrested by the Nazis on 22 May 1943 and shot the following day. He was later honoured by two memorial plaques in 1951, one outside the FK Partizan Stadium and one in a street next to the Red Star Stadium (formerly the SK Jugoslavija ground). A bust of him was sculpted near the stadium of SK Jugoslavija in 1970. It was stolen in 2012 but replaced in 2013.

Mozes Jacobs (1905–43), Dutch, Gymnastics, 1928 Amsterdam.

Mozes Jacobs was born in Amsterdam on 26 November 1905 into a Jewish family. A keen gymnast, he represented the BATO, Amsterdam. He also became a gymnastics teacher. In 1928 he was selected to compete in the Amsterdam Olympics and took part in the men's individual all-around, the team all-around, the vault, the parallel bars, the horizontal bar, the rings and the pommelled horse, but he failed to win a medal in any event.

Jacobs married and had three children. After the Nazis invaded he joined the Resistance. He attacked the Nazi occupiers whenever he and his group could, as well as hiding Jews and others from the evil of the Nazi regime and deportation. Betrayed, he was arrested on 1 April 1943 in Vierhouten. He was then deported to the death camp at Sobibor where he was murdered on 9 July 1943.

Adolf Jäger (1889–1944), German, football, 1912 Stockholm.

Adolf Jäger was born on 31 March 1889 in Altona, Hamburg. After playing football in his youth he joined Altonaer FC in 1907, which was part of the North German Football Association. He won several regional championships with his club, also winning the North German championship twice. He played fifty-one times for North Germany. He played eighteen international matches, ten as captain, between 1908 and 1914. In the 1912 Olympics in Stockholm he was selected for the German football squad. They were knocked out by Austria 5–1, Jäger scoring Germany's only goal. By the time of his retirement Jäger had played over 700 games and scored more than 2,000 goals. In 1927 he was honoured with the Eagle Badge, the highest award in German sport. The famous coach Otto Nerz called Jäger 'one of the greatest geniuses of German football and the creator of the modern combination game'. Jäger married and had one son and ran a cigar shop in Hamburg. He was killed by accident on 21 November 1944 while disposing of ordnance on the banks of the Elbe. He is buried in Altona main Cemetery.

Kalle Jalkanen (1907–41), Finnish, cross-country skiing, 1936 Garmisch-Partenkirchen (Gold).

Kalle Jalkanen was born on 10 May 1907 in Suonenjoki. He was a very successful cross-country skier, becoming famous for his sporting achievements in the 1930s. He skied for Iisveden Vesa (TUL), Iisveden Kiri, Helsinki Skiers and Lappeenranta Sports Men. He took part in the 1936 winter Olympics in Garmisch-Partenkirchen, taking the gold medal in the 4 × 10 km together with Sulo Nurmela, Klaes Karppinen and Matti Lähde. His next achievements came at the Nordic skiing World Championships in which he won four medals: one gold (50 km, 1938), two silvers (18 km and 4 × 10 km, both 1937) and one bronze (18 km, 1938). Oddly, he never won the Finnish title. He later ran a café and became a bookkeeper. He was killed by a land mine while on an intelligence gathering mission in Lempaala Ingeria (now Lembolovo) on 5 September 1941.

Edmund Jankowski (1903–39), Polish, rowing, 1928 Amsterdam (Bronze).

Edmund Bernard Jankowski was born on 28 August 1903 in Wrocki, Golub-Dobrzyń. He won a bronze medal at the 1928 Amsterdam Olympics in the coxed fours. Italy took the gold and Switzerland the silver. Jankowski was executed in the 'Valley of Death' in Bydgoszcz on 1 November 1939; between 1,200 and 1,400 Poles and Jews were murdered there in October and November 1939 as part of 'Operation Tannenberg', the aim of which was to destroy Poland's elite.

Akilles 'Aki' Järvinen (1905–43), Finnish, decathlon, 1928 Amsterdam (two Silver), 1932 Los Angeles (Silver), 1936 Berlin.

Akilles Eero Johannes Järvinen was born on 19 September 1905 in Jyväskylä. He was considered one of the most versatile Finnish athletes of the 1920s and 30s. He served as the Finnish flag bearer at the three Olympics he attended and won three silver medals. He also won a European silver medal in the 400 metres hurdles in 1934. He wasn't the only Olympic champion in his family. His younger brother Matti won gold in the javelin in the 1932 Los Angeles Olympics, going on to take the world championship ten times. His elder brother Kalle took part in the shot put in the 1932 Olympics coming ninth (he was later killed in action on 25 August 1941). And their father Verner won gold in the discus in the 1906 Athens Olympics and two bronze medals again in the discus in London in 1908. Aki died on 7 March 1943 when his VL Pyry trainer aircraft crashed on a test flight.

Kalle Järvinen (1903–41), Finnish, shot put, 1932 Los Angeles

Kalle Järvinen was born on 27 March 1903. He competed in the men's shot put in the Los Angeles Olympics of 1932, coming ninth. His brother Akilles (see above) and father Verner were Olympic medal winners too, and his brother Matti an Olympic javelin thrower. Kalle was killed on the Karelian Isthmus in the Winter War on 25 August 1941.

Józef Jaworski (1903–39), Polish, running, 1924 Paris, 1928 Amsterdam.

Józef Jaworski was born on 19 October 1903. A fine middle-distance runner he was selected to run for Poland in the 1924 Paris Olympics. He took part in the 800 metres but was knocked out in heat three. In the 1928 Amsterdam Olympics he took part in the 1,500 metres. This time he was knocked out in round one. He was killed in action serving as a lieutenant with the Polish artillery on 1 September 1939, the first day of the Second World War, in the battle of Oksywie, near Gdynia, while manning a coastal defence gun against the invading Germans.

Jerzy Jełowicki (1899–1939), Polish, art, 1936 Berlin.

Jerzy Jełowicki was born on 11 August 1899 in Rożniatówka. He was educated at the Warsaw University of Life Science. Although he became an agricultural engineer, living between Stadniki and Warsaw, his passion was art, in particular painting, and he studied at the Warsaw Academy of Fine Arts. He painted in the post-impressionistic style, specialising in historical events with horses.

He was selected to represent Poland in the painting event at the 1936 Olympics in Berlin but failed to win a medal.

After becoming a second lieutenant in the cavalry reserve he was killed fighting Russians near Lomianki on 22 September 1939.

Max Johansson (1910–40), Finnish, canoe, 1936 Berlin.

Max Birger Johansson was born on 20 September 1910. In the 1936 Olympics in Berlin he finished seventh in the K-1 1,000 metres. He was killed in action serving with the Finnish army on 4 January 1940 in the second phase of the battle of Summa (now Soldatskoye) in the Winter War against the Soviet Union.

Jānis Jordāns (1899–1944), Latvian, discus, 1928 Amsterdam.

Jānis Jordāns was born in 1899. He was a member of Sports Association Mars. He was a fine Greco-Roman wrestler and weight lifter, but the sport he excelled at was discus. In the 1928 Amsterdam Olympics he competed well but failed to win a medal. In the Second World War he was arrested by the NKVD and died in a Soviet prisoner of war camp on 25 February 1944.

Emil Juracka (1912–44), Austrian, field handball, 1936 Berlin (Silver).

Emil was born on 11 June 1912. He took part in the field handball competition in the 1936 Berlin Olympics, winning the silver medal. He played in three matches including the final, losing to Germany. He was killed in action on 21 February 1944.

Captain Enrique Jurado (1911–44), Philippines, wrestling, 1936 Berlin.

Enrique L. Jurado was born on 15 July 1911 in Lucena, Quezon, one of three sons born to Severo and Peregrina. He graduated from the US Naval Academy in 1934 as a Foreign Midshipman. He returned to the Philippines and taught at the Philippine Military Academy. Despite playing soccer to a high standard, it was wrestling at which he excelled. He took part in the 1936 Berlin Olympics, taking part in the freestyle bantamweight class. He failed to reach the finals. In the Second World War he served on offshore patrols. He commanded a three-boat squadron in the defence of Bataan and only just managed to avoid being captured by the Japanese. He later joined a guerrilla group in Panay. He was sent to Mindoro to try to consolidate the guerrillas there to fight against the Japanese occupation forces. However, he was ambushed and killed by a rival guerrilla group on 14 October 1944. The Philippine Military Academy dedicated their gymnasium at Fort General Gregorio del Pilar in Baguio City to him – 'Jurado Hall'.

Harald Kaarma (1901–42), Estonian, football, 1924 Paris.

Harald Kaarma was born on 12 December 1901 in Paide. A fine footballer he turned out regularly for JK Tallinna Kaley. Between 1921 and 1926 he made seventeen appearances for the Estonian national team, and became Estonian champion twice, in 1923 and 1926. In 1924 he was selected to play with the Estonian football squad at the Paris Olympics. The Estonian side were beaten in the first round by the USA 1–0, a penalty in the fifteenth minute. The USA were beaten in the second round by Uruguay 3–0. Uruguay went on to take the gold medal, beating Switzerland 3–0. In the Second World War Harald served as a police officer and as such was arrested by Stalin's NKVD in 1941. He was deported to the labour camp at Sverdlovsk Oblast where he was executed on 19 August 1942.

Josef Kahl (1913–42), Czechoslovak, ski jump, 1936 Garmisch-Partenkirchen.

Josef Kahl was born on 31 March 1913 in Harrachov. He took part in the 1936 winter Olympics. There were forty-eight competitors in the individual men's normal hill, and Kahl came twenty-ninth. He was killed in action on 23 February 1942.

Eddy Kahn (1906–44), Dutch, equestrianism, 1936 Berlin.

Eddy Kahn was born on 11 December 1906 in The Hague. Before the war he was a successful dressage rider, taking part in the 1936 Berlin Olympics. He eventually finished thirteenth riding 'Espoir'. Kahn ran a fashion shop in The Hague until September 1940, after which he set himself up in Amsterdam. He married an American girl from Pittsburgh in 1931 and they had one child.

As a result of this he was able to flee to America in 1941. He later decided to do his bit and was commissioned as a lieutenant in the British army, joining the 6th Royal Welch, Parachute Battalion. He became involved in Operation Dragoon, the Allied invasion of Southern France on 15 August 1944, and was killed a few days later on 19 August 1944. He is buried in the British plot of the Banneville-la-Campagne war Cemetery, along with over 2,000 other Allied troops.

Kalle Kainuvaara (1891–1943), Finnish, diving, 1912 Stockholm, 1920 Antwerp.

Kalle Kainuvaara was born on 19 March 1891 in Kuopio. A fine athlete, he was Finnish champion in the floor jump in 1920, 1923, 1926 and 1927, and was Finnish jumping champion in 1926. In the 1912 Olympic Games he competed in the men's 10 metre platform (in this event the divers executed one plain running dive and one backwards somersault dive from 5 metres, one plain running dive and one plain standing dive from 10 metres, and three optional dives from 10 metres; the optional dives were to be selected from a table of thirteen allowable dives). The men's plain high events (the plain high diving event consisted of one running dive and one standing dive from 5 metres and one standing dive and two running dives from 10 metres. All the dives were selected from a table of 13 allowable dives). He failed to take a medal in either event. Eight years later, in 1920, he was back, this time taking part not only in the 10 metres platform and the plain high, but also the modern pentathlon. Again he failed to win a medal. Interestingly, he took a bear with him to the games hoping to make some money. However, the authorities were unhappy about this and the bear was eventually handed over to a local zoo. While serving as a major he was seriously wounded in action and died of cardiac paralysis in a field hospital in Sound City on 21 October 1943.

Martin Karl (1911–42), German, rowing, 1936 Berlin (Gold).

Martin Karl was born on 3 June 1911 in Würzburg. He rowed in the eights for the Würzburger Ruderverein 1875, winning the German championship with the club in 1933 and 1934. He also won the European coxless fours championships in 1934. In 1936 he rowed with the coxless fours in the Berlin Olympics, taking the gold medal. His crew was made up of Rudolf Eckstein (1915–93), Anton Rom (1909–94) and Wilhelm Menne (1910–45). Great Britain came second and Switzerland third. Karl was killed in action on the Russian front on 1 March 1942.

Joachim Karsch (1897–1945), German, art, 1932 Los Angeles (Bronze).

Joachim Karsch was born on 20 June 1897 in Wrocław. He was a post-expressionist, specialising in sculpting and graphic art. He studied at the School of Applied Arts in 1911 and 1914. In 1917 he won the prize of the Karl Haase Foundation for his sculpture 'Standing Woman'. In 1920 he won the Prussian State Prize for the figurative group 'Job and his friends'; this was combined with a scholarship at the Villa Massimo. In 1934 he won first prize in the 'Folkwang Competition' for wood sculpture. In 1932 he took part in the Olympic Games in Los Angeles in the category of paintings, graphic works. Coming third he won the bronze medal with his drawing 'Stabwechsel' (Changeover). In 1942 Karsch received a commission from the city of Godingen, which did much to help his financial situation, but in 1943 his studio was destroyed by bombing. When the Russian army occupied Berlin, they destroyed many of his works and put both Karsch and his wife on a deportation list. They committed suicide to avoid being shipped east on 11 February 1945. They are buried together in the Park Cemetery, Berlin-Lichterfelde.

Karl Kaschka (1904–41), Austrian, fencing, 1936 Berlin.

Karl Konrad Kaschka was born on 8 January 1904 in Vienna. He competed in the 1936 Berlin Olympics, specialising in the sabre. The team just missed out on a medal, coming fifth. In the war Kaschka served with the Luftwaffe. He became a major and commander of III./ZG 26. On 4 December 1941 at Al-Marj, Libya, Kaschka's BF110 was shot down by a Hurricane of 274 Squadron flown by Flight Sergeant James Dodds. Kaschka and his gunner were both killed. He is buried in the German War Cemetery in Tobruk.

Tatsugo Kawaishi (1911–45), Japanese, swimming, 1932 Los Angeles (Silver).

Tatsugo Kawaishi was born on 10 December 1911 in Ogaki. He was educated at the Keio University where he studied law. It was here that he also began to swim competitively. His talent came to notice and he was selected to swim for Japan in the 1932 Olympics in Los Angeles. He won a silver medal in the 100 metres freestyle (his team-mate Yasuji Miyazaki took gold in the same event and broke the world record). On returning to Japan he became an instructor in the Japanese Naval Academy in 1933–35. He later joined the 11th Infantry Regiment. Promoted to first lieutenant, he was sent to China to take part in the Second Sino-Japanese War. Returning to civilian life he re-enlisted in June 1944 and was sent to join the garrison at Iwo Jima where he was killed in action on 17 March 1945. He was posthumously promoted to captain.

Robert Keres (1907–46), Estonian, basketball, 1936 Berlin.

Robert Keres was born on 14 August 1907 in Urvaste. He attended the Tartu Training College and Tartu University where he began to play basketball. He played for Tartu Kalev between 1924 and 1930. He was selected to play basketball for the Estonian team in the 1936 Berlin Olympics. Twenty-two teams took part. Unfortunately the Estonian team were knocked out in the first round by the Philippines 39–22. Keres, a popular figure, was the captain of the Estonian basketball team at the 1937 European Championships, playing forward. He earned a total of fourteen caps. Seriously wounded in the war, he died on 29 October 1946.

Reinhold Kesküll (1900–42), Estonian, sprint, 1924 Paris.

Reinhold Kesküll was born on 26 November 1900 in Kingisepp in Russia. He took part in the 1924 Paris Olympics, running in the 100, 200, and 400 metre events but failed to win a medal. He was arrested by the NKVD and died in a Soviet prison camp sometime in 1942.

Lauri Kettunen (1905–41), Finnish, fencing/modern pentathlon, 1928 Amsterdam, 1936 Berlin.

Lauri Kettunen was born on 12 February 1905 in Kamennogorsk in Russia. Specialising in the modern pentathlon, he first appeared in the Amsterdam Olympics in 1928 where he took part in the men's individual modern pentathlon, coming thirteenth, and men's fencing, taking part in the individual épée and being knocked out in the heats. He next took part in the Berlin Olympics in 1936, this time only taking part in the men's individual modern pentathlon. He finished fourteenth. Serving as a major in the Continuation War, he was killed in action while fighting with the Finnish III corps in Kiestinki on 15 August 1941.

Ferdinand Kiefler (1913–45), Austrian, handball, 1936 Berlin (Silver).

Ferdinand Kiefler was born in Vienna on 4 August 1913. He was part of the Austrian handball team that went to the 1936 Berlin Olympics. It was the first time handball had been an Olympic sport. Six teams participated in the 1936 tournament. Austria defeated Romania 18–3, Switzerland 14–3, Switzerland (again) 11–6, and Hungary 11–7. They finally lost to the Germans 6–10 and took the silver medal. Kiefler played in four of the five matches. He was killed in action on 13 January 1945 in Liblar in North Rhine-Westphalia.

Alfred Kienzle (1913–40), German, water polo, 1936 Berlin (Silver).

Alfred Kienzle was born on 1 May 1913 in Stuttgart. In the 1936 Berlin Olympics he competed with the German water polo team which took the silver medal, beaten by Hungary in the final. He played in one match. He was also a member of the team that took the silver medal in the 1938 European Championships, once again beaten by Hungary in the final. He represented his country on twenty occasions during his career. He was killed in action on 4 September 1940 at Reims.

Juhan 'Jaan' Kikkas (1892–1944), Estonian, weightlifting, 1924 Paris (Bronze).

Juhan Kikkas was born on 5 June 1892 in Valga. He didn't start out as a weightlifter but as a cyclist. He converted to weightlifting (middleweight) in 1921, coming fourth in the World Championships. In 1923 he won silver at the Baltic Championships. In 1924 he was selected to represent Estonia in the Paris Olympic Games. He did well, taking the bronze medal in the snatch, and set a personal best in clean and jerk. In 1925 he won the national weightlifting title; it was to be his only national title. Retiring from competition he ran a metal workshop in Tallinn. He was killed in a Soviet air raid on 9 March 1944.

Michael Kirchmann (1914–42), German, military patrol, 1936 Berlin.

Michael Kirchmann was born on 14 August 1914 in Oberstaufen. He was selected to represent Germany in the military patrol at the winter Olympics in Garmisch-Partenkirchen in 1936; he finished fifth.

Although it was only a demonstration sport at the time, thirty-six skiers from nine countries competed. Italy won, the first time they had ever won a Nordic skiing event. Each member of the team received 30,000 lira as a reward. Finland came second and Sweden third.

Michael Kirchmann was killed in action with the German army on 15 November 1942 near Volkhov at the Siege of Leningrad.

Aaro Kiviperä (1912–44), Finnish, modern pentathlon, 1936 Berlin.

Aaro Kullervo Kiviperä was born on 6 February 1912 in Seinäjoki. He competed for Finland in the modern pentathlon in the 1936 Berlin Olympics, finishing twentieth overall, his best position being eighth in the swimming event. He was killed in an air crash on 11 July 1944 over the Karelian Isthmus.

Kārlis Kļava (1907–41), Latvian, shooting, 1936 Berlin.

Kārlis Kļava was born on 9 March 1907 in Sigulda. Deciding on a career in the military, he graduated from the Latvian Higher Military School in 1931. Between 1932 and 1940 he was a lieutenant in the Riga Infantry Regiment. In 1938 he was awarded the Order of Viesturs, V class. He represented Latvia in the men's rapid-fire pistol, 25 metres, in the 1936 Berlin Olympics and finished twenty-third. In the 1937 World Championships he won gold with an automatic gun and became an unofficial world champion shooting the parabellum. He was the first Latvian athlete to become a world champion in any sport. In the Second World War he served as a lieutenant of the Riga Infantry Regiment. He was arrested by the NKVD, deported to a Soviet prison camp and shot in 1941.

Josef Klein (1916–41), Czechoslovak, athletics, 1936 Berlin.

Josef Klein was born on 12 November 1916. A fine all-round athlete, he represented Czechoslovakia in the 1936 Berlin Olympics, taking part in the men's javelin and men's decathlon. He was knocked out in the heats in the javelin and finished sixteenth in the decathlon. A member of the Czech Resistance, he was captured and died as a result of torture after being released from captivity in 1941.

Arthur Knautz (1911–43), German, handball, 1936 Berlin (Gold).

Arthur Knautz was born on 20 March 1911 in Daaden. A carpenter by trade, he played football (goalkeeper) for Daaden gymnastics club. He began to take an interest in handball and won the national championship with Westphalia in the 1930s. He was selected to captain the German Olympic handball team in the Berlin Games of 1936. The team went on to win the gold medal defeating Austria 10–6 in the final. Knautz was also a fine long-jumper, high-jumper, and javelin and discus thrower. He served on the Russian front in the Second World War and was reported missing in action on 6 August 1943 in Belgorod. There is a sports hall named after him in Daaden, the Arthur-Knautz-Halle.

František Kobzík (1914–44), Czechoslovak, rowing, 1936 Berlin.

František Kobzík was born on 22 March 1914 in Břeclav, one of four brothers and three sisters. He was educated at a general and burghers' school in Břeclav before becoming a locksmith like his father. On 1 October 1936 he joined the army, becoming an NCO the following year and being posted to the 10th Infantry Regiment. A keen rower, he was part of the eight in the Berlin Olympics in 1936. The team failed to win a medal. In the same year he became Czechoslovakian champion in the eights. When German forces occupied Czechoslovakia, he first escaped to Poland and then joined the French Foreign Legion before being evacuated to England. He joined the Czechoslovak army in exile and underwent training in parachuting, sabotage and shooting. After completing these courses he was attached to the SOE and was parachuted into Vacenovice with his fellow SOE member Josef Vanc. They managed to reach the village of Rudice, where they were discovered hiding in a barn. The local police surrounded the building and called on the two agents to surrender. They refused and instead committed suicide on 7 May 1944. His name is on the memorial plaque of the fallen citizens of the city at the Břeclav town hall.

Erland Koch (1867–1945), German, shooting, 1912 Stockholm (Bronze).

Erland Koch was born on 3 January 1867 in Saxony. He was a well-known sports shooter and took part in the 1912 Stockholm Olympics winning a bronze medal in the men's trap team. He came twelfth in the individual men's trap, seventeenth in the men's running target, double shot team, and thirteenth in the men's single running shot. He was killed on 29 April 1945 in Berlin at the age of 78, one day before Hitler's suicide.

Karl Koch (1910–44), German, cycling, 1928 Amsterdam.

Karl Koch was born on 30 June 1910 in Hessen. He trained as a baker and pastry maker. His passion however was cycling. In the 1928 Amsterdam Olympics Koch was part of the

German road cycling team which failed to finish the race (he was the only member of the team to actually cross the finish line). He was, however, classified 45th in the individual race. The same year he became German road champion. In 1930 he participated in the Tour of Germany, and in 1931 came 15th in the Paris-Roubaix Classic. He was killed in action serving with the German army on 28 June 1944.

Yasuhiko Kojima (1918–45), Japanese, swimming, 1936 Berlin.

Yasuhiko Kojima was born on 1 September 1918 in Hiroshima. He represented Japan in the 100 metres backstroke in the 1936 Olympics. Despite being only 17, he reached the final and finished sixth. He was killed in action on Okinawa on 12 June 1945. It is estimated that 110,000 Japanese soldiers and Okinawan civilians were killed in the battle, which lasted from 1 April to 22 June 1945.

August Kop (1904–45), Dutch, hockey, 1928 Amsterdam (Silver).

August Johannes Kop was born on 5 May 1904 in Purmerend. A fine hockey player, he competed for the Netherlands in the 1928 Olympic Games. As a member of the Dutch field-hockey team he reached the final with a surprising 2–1 win over Germany. They were beaten in the final by India 3–0, taking the silver medal. August played all four matches as a forward. Captured by the Japanese in the war, he was interned in the concentration camp at Pakan Baroe and forced to labour on the Sumatra Railway. He died on 20 April 1945.

'Dora' Köring (1880–1945), German, tennis, 1912 Stockholm (Gold and Silver).

Dorothea Köring was born on 11 July 1880 in Saxony. She was Germany's finest female tennis player. In the 1912 Olympics she took the gold medal in the mixed doubles (only the second Olympic gold medal won by a German woman) with her partner Heinrich Schomburgk, going on to take silver in the ladies' singles, losing to Marguerite Broquedis (1893–1983). Köring was winning the match when Broquedis left the court to change her shoes. This tactic disturbed Köring's rhythm which she never regained, and as a result she lost the match. Köring also took the 1912–13 German women's singles championship. She was killed on 13 February 1945 in the RAF's bombing of Dresden.

Elmar Korko (1908–41), Estonian, rowing, 1936 Berlin.

Elmar Korko was born on 8 February 1908 in Tartu. He began his sporting life with the Tartu Kalev in 1922 where he began to row and play iceberger (a team game similar to ice hockey). He graduated from the Hugo Treffner Gymnasium in 1928 and later worked as a writer and police officer. In 1936 he rowed in the single sculls at the 1936 Olympics but failed to win a medal. He later began to judge sporting competitions such as boxing, swimming and wrestling. Korko was murdered together with his wife by the former boxer and national traitor Evald Lukkin in the summer war on 10 July 1941.

Kurt Körner (1912–45), German, ski jump, 1936 Garmisch-Partenkirchen.

Kurt Körner was born on 13 May 1912 in Klingenthal. A talented skier, he won his first competition at Oberwiesenthal in 1930. In 1931 he came fifth in the second Olympiad in Mürzzuschlag. In 1934 he won the Silesian Championship in Krummhübel. In 1936 he was selected for the German team to take part in the winter Olympics. He came twelfth with jumps of 66 and 65.5 metres (he might have done better had he not crashed in the first round). In 1937 he finished fifteenth in the Nordic World Ski Championship in Chamonix. In 1940 he won the Vogtland Championship in Mühlleithen and later the Sachsenmeisterschaft in Oberwiesenthal. Körner married and had a son and a daughter. He disappeared in the Second World War and was declared dead in 1945.

'Heinz' Körvers (1915–42), German, field handball, 1936 Berlin (Gold).

Heinrich Körvers was born on 3 July 1915 in Alpen, Nordrhein-Westfalen. He represented Germany in the handball competition in the 1936 Berlin Olympics. It was the first time the sport had appeared in the Olympics. Germany defeated Hungary 22–0, followed by the USA 29–1. They finally beat Austria in the final 2–1 to take the gold medal. He played in one match as goalkeeper. He played for MSV Hindenburg Minden, becoming German champion with them. He played for his country on five occasions. He also won the master title in 1939 and 1940. He was killed in action at the battle of Stalingrad on 29 December 1942 (although he wasn't officially declared dead until 1945).

Lauri Koskela (1907–44), Finnish, wrestling, 1932 Los Angeles (Bronze), 1936 Berlin (Gold).

Lauri Koskela was born on 16 May 1907 in Leningrad. A Greco-Roman wrestler, Koskela began his career as a featherweight. He represented Finland in the 1932 Olympics in LA, coming third and taking the bronze medal. He then went on to win the 1935 European Championship and won seven Finnish domestic championships between 1932 and 1943. Switching to lightweight he took part in the 1936 Berlin Olympics, this time taking gold. He then won the European Championship again in 1937 and 1938 and came third in 1939. Koskela joined the Finnish army becoming a corporal and was killed in action in the Continuation War near Baryshevo, Leningrad Oblast, then part of Finland, on 3 August 1944.

Karl Kotratschek (1914–41), Austrian, triple jump, 1936 Berlin.

Karl Kotratschek was born on 24 October 1914 in Vienna. He won the Austrian Championship in 1935–38. His Austrian record of 15.28 metres, which he jumped in 1936, was only beaten in 1974. He represented Austria in the triple jump in the Berlin Olympics of 1936 but failed to win a medal. After the Anschluss, Karl was forced to represent Germany. As a result, when he came third in the European Championships in 1938 he won bronze as a German, not an Austrian. He was killed in action it is believed in Libya on 4 July 1941.

Marian Kozłowski (1915–43), Polish, sprint canoe, 1936 Berlin.

Marian Kozłowski was born on the 6 June 1915 in Poznań. He competed in the sprint canoe for Poland in the 1936 Berlin Olympics coming eleventh in the K-2 1,000 metres. In the war he was shipped to Germany as forced labour after the Nazi invasion of Poland. He was killed in an Allied air raid in 1943.

Paul Krauß (1917–42), German, ski jump, 1936 Garmisch-Partenkirchen.

Paul Krauß was born on 18 October 1917 in Johanngeorgenstadt. In the 1936 winter Olympics he came eighteenth in the men's individual normal hill. In 1937 he finished sixth in the Nordic World Championships. The following year, 1938, he finished seventh at Holmenkollen, the best placed German competitor. In 1939 he finished eighth. In 1941 he set a new world record at Planica with a 112 metre jump. He was killed in action on 20 February 1942 near Borvik in Russia.

Hans-Helmuth Krause (1905–44), German, running, 1928 Amsterdam.

Hans-Helmuth Krause was born in 1905 in Berlin. He became a country parson in Silesia and was apparently very popular. He had a passion for running and was chosen to run for Germany in the 1,500 metres at the Amsterdam Olympics in 1928. He ran well but failed to take a medal, finishing seventh. At the World University Games in the same year he won gold. He also took the German 4 × 1,500 metre title in 1928, followed by the German 15,000 metre titles in 1930 and 1931. He was killed in action serving as a lieutenant and battalion commander on 26 February 1944 while fighting partisans.

Leonhard Kukk (1906–44), Estonian, weightlifting, 1928 Amsterdam.

Leonhard Kukk was born on 12 August 1906 in Pangodi. He competed as a middleweight weightlifter in the Amsterdam Olympics of 1928 but failed to reach the finals. He was murdered as a civilian by Stalin's NKVD in Tallinn sometime in 1944.

Ernst Künz (1912–44), Austrian, football, 1936 Berlin (Silver).

Ernst Künz was born on 23 February 1912 in Santakai. A fine footballer he played for FC Lustenau. Selected to play as a defender for the Austrian team in the 1936 Berlin Olympics, he played in four matches helping the team to come second and take the silver medal. They played Italy in the final, losing 1–0 in extra time (Italy were the reigning world champions). He was killed in action on 21 August 1944.

Willi Kürten (1908–44), German, hurdles, 1936 Berlin.

Willi Kürten was born on 4 April 1908 in Düsseldorf. He competed for the athletics club DSD Düsseldorf and in the 400 metre hurdles in the 1936 Berlin Olympics. He was eliminated in the semi-finals. Although he never won the German title, he did take silver in 1931–32 and 1936. He was killed in action on the Russian front on 18 July 1944.

Stanisław Kuryłłowicz (1909–45), Polish, rowing, 1936 Berlin.
Stanisław Kuryłłowicz was born on 6 June 1909 in Wierdubje, Belarus. He grew up to row for the KW04 Poznań Polish rowing club. Selected for the Polish Olympic team he rowed in the coxed fours in the 1936 Berlin Olympics. The team was eliminated in the semi-finals. Kuryłłowicz enlisted in the Polish army after the German invasion in 1939. He was killed in action on 2 February 1945 in the fighting on the Poznań citadel against the Red Army.

Albert Kusnets (1902–42), Estonian, wrestling, 1924 Paris, 1928 Amsterdam (Bronze).
Albert Eduard Kusnets was born on 12 August 1902 in Suure-Kambja. Wrestling for his club Kalev Tallinn/Sport Tallinn, he took part in the Greco-Roman wrestling competition in two Olympic Games. Despite winning five matches he just missed out on a medal, coming fourth, beaten into third place by the Finnish wrestler Källe Westerlund. Four years later he was selected for the Amsterdam Olympics. This time he managed to take the bronze medal, a remarkable achievement considering he had broken his leg earlier in the year. He had already won the silver medal in the European Championships of 1927. He won silver again in the 1931 European Championships and the bronze in 1933. He won the Estonian championships as a featherweight in 1921, as a lightweight in 1922 and 1924, and as a middleweight in 1926 and 1927. In 1930–32 and 1933 he won again, this time as a welterweight. He then worked as a wrestling coach preparing the next generation of wrestlers for the Olympics. In the war he was arrested by the NKVD and deported to a labour camp, Verkhnyaya Toyma, where he starved to death in the winter of 1942.

Aksel Kuuse (1913–42), Estonian, high jump, 1936 Berlin.
Aksel Kuuse was born on 18 September 1913 in Sipa. He became a member of the EASK Tartu athletics club and was selected to compete in the 1936 Berlin Olympics. He failed to take a medal, America taking the gold, silver and bronze. He was arrested by Stalin's NKVD and deported to a work camp in the Soviet Union where he starved to death, dying on 27 April 1942.

Johann Lahr (1913–42), Czechoslovak German, ski jump/Nordic combined, 1936 Garmisch-Partenkirchen.
Johann Hans Lahr was born on 21 January 1913 in Friesovy Boudy. He took part in the Nordic World Ski Championship in 1935 in the High Tatras. He finished 5th in Nordic combination (ski jumping and cross-country skiing) and 25th in ski jumping. He took part in the winter Olympics in 1936, representing Germany. He finished thirty-second in the ski jumping and ninth in the Nordic combined. On 2 March 1941 he made a world record jump of 111 metres in Planica (alas his record was beaten the same day!). He was killed in action in the Russian Campaign on 24 February 1942.

Frederik 'Frits' Lamp (1905–45), Dutch, sprint, 1924 Paris.

Frederik Joseph Lamp was born on 6 September 1905 in Haarlem. He was selected to run in the men's 100 metres for the Netherlands in the 1924 Paris Olympics. He was eliminated in the heats and failed to win a medal. In 1927 he moved to the Dutch East Indies. Captured by the Japanese in the Second World War his health broke down while working on the Pakan Baru railway in Sumatra. He died on 27 May 1945.

'Fritz' Landertinger (1914–43), Austrian, canoe, 1936 Berlin (Silver).

Friedrich Landertinger was born on 26 February 1914 in Krems an der Donau. He grew up to row for the Steiner rowing club of 1876. He competed in the 1936 Berlin Olympics, taking part in the men's kayak singles 10,000 metres and winning the silver medal, Ernest Krebs for Germany taking the gold and Ernie Riedel for the USA taking the bronze. He was killed in action on the Russian front on 18 January 1943. Two Danube promenades, in Stein and Krems, were named after him and his fellow club member Gregor Hradetzky (d.1984).

Johann Langmayr (1910–43), Austrian, hurdles, 1936 Berlin.

Johann Langmayr was born on 29 August 1910 in Volgograd, Russia. He hurdled for his club, Oe. J. K. Wien. He was Austrian champion in the 110 metre hurdles on four occasions, 1931, 32, 34 and 39. He was selected to take part in the 110 metre hurdles in the 1936 Berlin Olympics, but was eliminated in the heats and failed to win a medal. He was reported missing in action in 1943 outside Stalingrad. His death was officially confirmed in 1945.

Martti Lappalainen (1902–41) Finnish, cross-country skiing, biathlon, 1924 Chamonix (Silver), 1928 St Moritz, 1932 Lake Placid.

Martti Eemil Lappalainen was born on 11 April 1902 in Liperi. He took the silver medal in the 1924 Winter Olympics in Chamonix in the military patrol, which consisted of 25 kilometres of cross-country skiing and rifle shooting, each patrol being a team of four, with rules very similar to modern biathlon. He went on to compete in the 1928 Olympics finishing seventh in the 18 km and ninth in the 50 km competition. In 1932 in Lake Placid he took part in the 50 km cross-country event but failed to finish. In the 1934 FIS Nordic World Skiing Championship in Sollefteå he won a gold in the 4 × 10 km and a bronze in the 19 km, a fine end to a fine career. He was killed in action on the banks of the Svir River, Mantysova, East Karelia, in the Continuation War on 6 October 1941.

Karl Leban (1908–41), Austrian, speed skating and modern pentathlon, 1936 Berlin and Garmisch-Partenkirchen.

Karl Leban was born on 27 November 1908. He trained with the sporting club EVW Klagenfurt and Heeressportverband Wien. Leban was one of Austria's finest all-round athletes. He competed in the Olympics of 1936 in Berlin in the modern pentathlon in which he came twenty-sixth, and in the winter Olympics in the same year in Garmisch-Partenkirchen in the speed skating 500 and 1,500 metres. He came sixth in the 500 metres and twelfth in the 1,500 metres. Leban also finished fourth in the 1932 European Speed Skating Championships. He won Austrian athletics titles in the 5,000 metres in 1930 and 1934 and in the 4 × 1,500 metre relay in 1932 and 1937. In 1936 he took part in the Speed Skating World Championships, coming thirty-sixth. After the Anschluss, Leban claimed three third places at the German 1940 Speed Skating Championships. He was killed in a plane crash near Zagnitkiv on the Russian front on 28 July 1941. He was buried in Kamenka near Zagnitkiv.

Wilhelm Leichum (1911–41), German, athletics, 1936 Berlin (Bronze).

Wilhelm Leichum was born on 12 May 1911 in Hessen. In the 1936 Berlin Olympics he competed in the long jump and the 4 × 100 metres relay. He won bronze in the 4 × 100 metres (running first), and narrowly missed a medal in the long jump, coming fourth by one centimetre behind the Japanese jumper Naoto Tajima. He also jumped in the European Championships of 1934 and 1938. He served as a lieutenant with the German army in the Second World War and was killed in action on the Russian front on 19 July 1941 at Nizhny Novgorod. He was buried in the war Cemetery in Gorki. He was posthumously promoted to captain in 1943 so that his wife and three small children received a better pension.

Albert Leidmann (1908–45), German, boxing, 1928 Amsterdam.

Albert Leidmann was born on 23 February 1908 in Munich. He was selected to box middleweight for Germany in the 1928 Amsterdam Olympics. He was eliminated in the second round after losing to the eventual bronze medallist Leonard Steyaert. Leidmann came second in the 1930 European Championships fighting as a light-heavyweight. He turned professional in 1930, finally retiring in 1935. He was reported missing in action on 1 February 1945.

Ludwig Leinberger (1903–43), German, football, 1928 Amsterdam.

Ludwig Leinberger was born on 21 May 1903 in Bavaria. He started playing football at the age of 18 for TV 1846 Nuremberg. He went on to play for several German clubs, winning many championships, including the North Bavarian and the South German. He also won twenty-four international caps (eleven times as captain) for Germany in the interwar years. He was part of the German football squad that took part in the 1928 Amsterdam Olympics. They were beaten by Uruguay in the heats (Uruguay going on to take the gold). After retiring, Leinberger first became a merchant and then a sports coach. Between 1933 and 1938 he was the regional coach of Bavaria, Hessia and Saxony, and from 1938–41 with FC Schweinfurt 05. While serving with the German army he was taken ill and died of appendicitis in a military hospital on 3 March 1943.

Hermann Lemp (1914–43), German, modern pentathlon, 1936 Berlin.

Hermann Lemp was born on 20 July 1914 in Rosenheim. He represented Germany in the modern pentathlon in the 1936 Berlin Olympics. He finished sixth. He was killed in action serving with the German army on 9 November 1943 in Somaki, Vitebsk, in the Russian Campaign.

Herbert Leupold (1908–42), German, cross-country skiing and biathlon, 1936 Garmisch-Partenkirchen.

Herbert Leupold was born on 20 June 1908 in Wüstewaltersdorf. A career soldier he took part in 1934 in the 4 × 10 km event in the FIS Nordic World Skiing Championship in Sollefteå, winning the silver medal. He then took part in the 1936 winter Olympics while at the same time serving as a lieutenant in the army. He was a member of the German relay team which finished sixth in the 4 × 10 km relay competition. He also participated in the demonstration event, military patrol (biathlon). The German team finished fifth. Leupold was also German 50 km cross-country skiing champion in 1936, 1937 and 1939. He was wounded at Navaginskaya, Krasnodar, in the Russian Campaign, and died in a military hospital on 22 December 1942.

Emil Lohbeck (1905–44), German, basketball, 1936 Berlin.

Emil Lohbeck was born 15 September 1905 in Hiddinghausen. He was a career soldier but played basketball for Heeressportschule Wansdorf. He won his first unoffical championship with them in 1938. He took part in the 1936 Berlin Olympics. It was the first time basketball had been allowed at the Olympics. Germany lost to Switzerland (25–18), Italy (58–16) and Czechoslovakia (20–9) and were eliminated. Lohbeck was killed in action on 29 July 1944.

Leszek Lubicz-Nycz (1899–1939), Polish, fencing, 1932 Los Angeles (Bronze).

Leszek Lubicz-Nycz was born on 20 August 1899 in Brzesko. Deciding on a career in the army he was decorated for his bravery against the Bolsheviks. In the 1932 Olympics he competed in the individual sabre and team sabre. Although he failed to win a medal in the individual event, he took a bronze medal in the team event. He had already won bronze in the unofficial World Championships with the team sabre in 1930. In 1931 and 1934 he was Polish champion in the individual sabre. Retiring from the army he became a fencing (international) and ski instructor at the Central Institute of Physical Education in Warsaw. He also wrote a book on fencing. He was killed in action on 22 September 1939 on the first day of the German invasion near Warsaw. He was posthumously promoted to the rank of lieutenant colonel.

Jaakko Luoma (1897–1940), Finnish, running, 1924 Paris.

Jaakko Luoma was born on 9 July 1897 in the USA. He represented Finland in the 1924 Paris Olympics. He competed in the men's 1,500 metres coming twelfth. He was killed in action on 12 March 1940 in Uomaa in Karelia.

Gustav Mader (1899–1945), Austrian, bobsleigh, 1928 St Moritz.

Gustav Mader was born on 28 March 1899 in Vienna. He competed in the four-man bobsleigh event in the 1928 winter Olympics in St Moritz, representing Austria. He was killed in action on 18 April 1945 in Rijeka, Croatia.

Hans Maier (1909–43), German, rowing, 1928 Amsterdam, 1932 Los Angeles (Silver), 1936 Berlin (Gold).

Johann Adolf Friedrich Maier was born on 13 June 1909 in Mannheim. One of Germany's finest rowers, he rowed in the German eight at the Amsterdam Olympics in 1928 (Gustav, his older brother, rowed with the same eight). The team were knocked out by Great Britain (who went on to win silver) in the third heat. The American crew took the gold, beating Great Britain by two seconds. He next appeared in the Los Angeles Games in 1932 in both the coxed fours and coxed eights. On this occasion the coxed fours took the silver medal, beaten to the gold by Great Britain. In the eights, the German team were knocked out in the heats. Maier appeared in the Games for a third time in 1936. This time he took the gold medal in the men's coxed fours with Switzerland taking the silver and France the bronze. Maier was German champion in 1928–31 in the eights, 1929–1931 and 1933 in the coxless fours, and 1936 in the coxed fours, all achieved with the Mannheim rowing club Amicitia 1876. He was killed in action in Tunisia on 6 March 1943 trying to hold the Mareth line against a British offensive. His body was never discovered and it wasn't until 9 December 1952 that he was finally pronounced dead.

Jarl Malmgren (1908–42), Finnish, football, 1936 Berlin.

Jarl Edvard Malmgren was born on 12 September 1908 in Karjaa. He was a trained surveyor and was also a well-known footballer. He played for eight seasons with the football club IFK Helsinki, winning the Finnish championship on four occasions: 1930, 31, 33 and 37. He was also capped thirty-two times. He captained the Finnish team in the 1936 Berlin Olympics, playing in the mid-field. They were eliminated in the heats and failed to win a medal. Malmgren was also a talented bandy player (a sort-of cross between ice hockey and field hockey played on ice) winning the Finnish championship in 1934–35 and 1938 with the club HIFK. He was commissioned into the German army in the war, becoming a lieutenant. He was killed in action on 5 June 1942 in Pogost village near Olonets in Russian Karelia, in the Finnish Continuation War. He is buried in Hietaniemi Cemetery in Helsinki.

Charles Marion (1887–1944), French, equestrian, 1928 Amsterdam (Silver), 1932 Los Angeles (Silver and Gold).

Marion was born on 14 January 1887 in Saint-Germain-en-Laye. He became an outstanding horseman. In Amsterdam in 1928 he won the silver medal in the men's dressage individual on his horse *Linon*. Germany took the gold and Sweden the bronze. He also appeared in the men's dressage team, coming fourth. Four years later, in 1932, Marion and *Linon* were back at the Olympics again. This time they had to travel to Los Angeles. He won the silver medal in the men's dressage individual, and the gold medal in the men's dressage team. Charles came from an aristocratic background and was the 5th Baron Marion. Most of his ancestors had been French military officers. In the Second World War he was promoted to general and served with the French Vichy government as a prefect. At the end of the war he was arrested, imprisoned, tried and sentenced to death by a military court martial. Before he could be executed however, he was kidnapped by the French Resistance group FTP and murdered by them on 16 November 1944.

Mini Biographies

François Marits (1884–1945), Dutch, shooting, 1924 Paris.

François Marits was born on 25 November 1884 in Kapelle. He competed in the 25 metre rapid fire pistol event in the 1924 Paris Olympics. He failed to win a medal, coming twenty-fifth overall. He was deported to a German prisoner-of-war camp in the war, dying in the camp on 2 April 1945.

Hans Marr (1914–42), German, ski jump, 1936 Garmisch-Partenkirchen.

Hans Marr was born on 7 October 1914 in Oberhof. A shoemaker by trade, his passion was skiing. In 1930 he won the Thuringia Championship. At the Nordic World Championships he was placed 18th in 1938 and 13th in 1939. He took part in the winter Olympics in 1936 in Garmisch-Partenkirchen, coming tenth in the men's normal hill. He served as an Unteroffizier (NCO) in the war, and was killed on 20 March 1942 near Minsk in Belarus when he skied into a minefield. After the war, a ski jumping competition in Oberhof was named the Hans Marr Cup in his memory.

Martti Marttelin (1897–1940), Finnish, running, 1928 Amsterdam (Bronze).

Martti Bertil Marttelin was born on 18 June 1897 in Nummi. He ran the marathon in the 1928 Amsterdam Olympics coming third and taking the bronze medal. He was killed in action on 1 March 1940 on the Russian front in Burnaya River, Leningrad, in the battle of Taipaleenjoki.

Antoni Maszewski (1908–44), Polish, sprint, 1936 Berlin.

Antoni Maszewski was born on 5 May 1908 in Kamiensk and went to Bolesław the Brave High School in Piotrków Trybunalski. A good sprinter, he was selected to run in the 4 × 400 metres relay in the Berlin Olympics in 1936. The team were eliminated in the heats. He was national champion at a number of distances, winning eight gold medals in the 400 metre hurdles. He was also the Polish record holder in the 500 metres and the 4 × 400 metres relay. In the war he served as an officer in the Independent Carpathian Rifle Brigade, taking part in the September Campaign and the battles of Kutno and Kock. He also saw action in the battle of Tobruk, becoming a commander in the 6th Battalion 3rd Carpathian Infantry Division. He took part in the battle of Monte Cassino and became a commander in the 4th Battalion of the 3rd Carpathian Infantry Division. He then took part in the battles for Ancona and Roncitelli, was promoted to major, and was killed on 5 August 1944 in the battle of Roncitelli. After his death he was decorated with many awards, including the Cross of Valour and Silver Cross of Merit with swords. Major Maszewski is buried in the Polish War Cemetery in Loreto.

Akira Matsunaga (1914–43), Japanese, football, 1936 Berlin.

Akira Matsunaga was born on 21 September 1914 in Yaizu, Shizuoka. He was educated at the Tokyo Liberal Arts and Science University. While there he was selected to represent Japan in the Berlin Olympics as part of the football team. As a forward Matsunaga was

known for his speed – he was able to run the 100 metres in 10.8 seconds. In his first match against Sweden he scored one goal in Japan's 3–2 victory. The victory was so unexpected that it later became known as the 'Miracle in Berlin'. Reality however hit home in their next match against Italy when they lost 8–0. It was the end of their tournament, Italy going on to take the gold. These two matches were to prove his only international matches. He served in the Japanese 230th Infantry Regiment in the war and was killed in action on 20 January 1943 at the battle of Guadalcanal. The jersey Matsunaga was wearing in the Berlin Olympics is still kept today in the Prince Chichibu Memorial Sports Museum, the oldest one preserved from the Japan national football team.

Aleksander Małecki (1901–39), Polish, fencing, 1928 Amsterdam.

Aleksander Antoni Włodzimierz Małecki was born on the 4 September 1901 in Zarubyntsi in the Ukraine. He took part in the team sabre event in the 1928 Amsterdam Olympics. The team took the bronze medal, beating Germany 9–7 into fourth place. Hungary took the gold, defeating Italy in the final 9–7 (two members of the Hungarian gold medal team, Attila Petschauer and János Garay, would later die in Nazi concentration camps). Małecki served with the Polish army in the September Campaign in1939 near Wielkopolskie in Poland. He was almost certainly killed in the same month, while trying to escape to Hungary.

Ludwig Mayer (1902–45), German, military patrol, 1928 St Moritz.

Ludwig Mayer was born on 16 February 1902. He was selected to represent Germany in the military patrol at the 1928 Winter Olympics; he finished fifth.

In the war he served as a private first class and went missing near Poznan, Poland, and was declared to have been killed in action in 1945.

Johan Meimer (1904–44), Estonian, Javelin and decathlon, 1928 Amsterdam.

Johan Meimer was born on 19 June 1904 in Kehtna, one of four children. While studying at Berlin University he began to train hard in the javelin and the decathlon. His progress was so rapid that he was selected to represent Estonia at the 1928 Amsterdam Olympics. He came thirteenth in the decathlon and eighth in the javelin.

He married Elli Johanna.

In the war he was arrested by NKVD and held in a prison camp. He was shot and killed by Soviet guards on 10 December 1944 trying to escape while being transported to a new prison camp.

Visvaldis Melderis (1915–44), Latvian, basketball, 1936 Berlin.

Visvaldis Melderis was born on 19 January 1915 in Jelgava. He was educated and graduated from the Jelgava 2nd Gymnasium, later joining the army. It was while serving with the Latvian army that he took up basketball, playing for the army team, Rigas ASK. He was twice the Latvian champion while serving with them. In 1939 and 1940 he was team

captain. He became champion again in 1942. He played a total of forty times for his country. A good all-round athlete he also took the bronze in the shot put in the Latvian championships in 1934. In 1935 he took the gold in the EuroBasket becoming the first ever European champion (he also took part in 1937 and 1939). He was selected to take part in the 1936 Berlin Olympics but failed to take a medal. Fighting with the Latvian Legion, he saw action on the Eastern Front fighting with the 19th Waffen Grenadier Division of the SS (2nd Latvian). He was killed in action near Opochka, Pskov, Oblast, in the Russian Campaign on 14 July 1944.

Wilhelm Menne (1910–45), German, rowing, 1936 Berlin (Gold).
Wilhelm Menne was born on 11 August 1910 in Bavaria. He began his rowing career with the Würzburger Ruderverein 1875, winning the German Championship in 1933 in their eight. Moving to the coxed fours, he took part in the 1936 Berlin Olympics. Together with his crew he took the gold medal. His crew were made up of Rudolf Eckstein (1915–93), Toni Rom (1909–94), and Martin Karl (1911–42). He won the national coxless fours titles between 1934 and 1936. He was also European champion in 1934 and 1935. Serving with the German army, he was killed in action in Trenčín, Slovakia, on 27 March 1945.

Toni Merkens (1912–44), German, cycling, 1936 Berlin (Gold).
Nikolaus Anton Merkens was born on 21 June 1912 in Cologne. He initially trained as a bicycle mechanic with Fritz Köthke. He won the German sprint championship in 1933–4 and 1935. In 1934 he also won the British Open Championship and the Grand Prix de Paris, repeating the achievement in 1935. He went on to win the World Championships in Brussels, defeating the Dutch champion Arie van Vliet. He represented Germany in the 1936 Berlin Olympics, taking the gold medal in the men's 1,000 metre sprint. Despite protests from the Dutch team regarding interference (he was fined 100 gold francs but not disqualified) the result stood. Van Vliet (1916–2001) won the silver and the French cyclist Louis Chaillot (1914–98) took the bronze. After the Olympics, Merkens turned professional, going on to win several German championships and becoming German professional champion in 1940. He died of wounds received in action against the Russians on 20 June 1944. A memorial stone was erected in 1948 at the velodrome in Cologne in his memory.

Fritz Messner (1912–45), German, field hockey, 1936 Berlin (Silver).
Fritz Messner was born on 7 November 1912 in Berlin. Playing for the athletics club Berliner SV 92, he won the German championship in 1940. He was selected to play for Germany in the 1936 Olympics and reached the final. They were defeated by India 8–1 and took the silver medal. Messner played in three matches as a forward, against Afghanistan (4–1 victory), Netherlands (3–0 in the semi-final), and against India in the final. Between 1934 and 1942 Messner represented his country on twenty-eight occasions. He was captured by the Russians on the Eastern Front and sent to a PoW camp where he was executed on 7 November 1945.

Konrad Miersch (1907–42), German, modern pentathlon, 1932 Los Angeles.

Konrad Miersch was born on 19 January 1907 in Brandenburg. In the 1932 Los Angeles Olympics he came sixth in the modern pentathlon. He had also been considered for the free shooting event but the event failed to take place. Miersch was a police officer by profession and became an officer in the Waffen SS. He was killed in action on 2 March 1942 in the fighting on the Eastern Front. He was buried in the Sologubovka military Cemetery in Russia. Representing West Germany, his son Ekkehard took part in the 100 metres backstroke in the XVIth Olympiad in 1956 in Australia.

Jovan Mikić ('Spartak') (1914–44), Yugoslavian, athletics, 1936 Berlin.

Jovan Mikić was born on 6 July 1914 in Opovo in Serbia. He studied at the Subotica Law School. He was a fine linguist and enjoyed writing poetry. Between 1932 and 1939 he was one of Yugoslavia's finest athletes, becoming national champion in the pentathlon, decathlon, javelin, long jump, and discus. In the 1936 Olympic Games he came twenty-first in the triple jump. Mikić was a fierce anti-fascist and commanded a partisan group in Hungarian-occupied *Bačka*. He was shot and killed by a Hungarian soldier at the Subotica train station on 10 October 1944. A national hero, the football club FK Spartak Subotica is named after him.

Josef Miner (1914–44), German, boxing, 1936 Berlin (Bronze).

Josef Miner was born on 15 July 1914 in Warsaw, Poland. The family moved to Germany when Miner was young and he began boxing bantamweight. He won his first championship at that weight in 1934, before moving up to featherweight and coming second in the German Championship, losing the gold to Arthur Battner. The following year, however, he became German champion at featherweight and automatically qualified for the Olympic Games, where he managed to pick up a well-deserved bronze medal, defeating the Hungarian fighter Dezso Frigyes (1913–84). He successfully defended his European title in 1937, but the following year lost it to his old rival Battner. He was killed in action in Husi, Romania, serving with the German Army some time in 1944.

Tsutomuko Mitsudome (1914–unknown), Japanese, rowing, 1936 Berlin.

Very little seems to be known about Tsutomuko Mitsudome other than he was born in Japan in 1914. He rowed in the coxless pairs in the 1936 Berlin Olympics, his pair being knocked out in the heats, and was killed in the Second World War.

Aleksander Mitt (1903–42), Estonian, speed skating, 1928 St Moritz, 1936 Garmisch-Partenkirchen.

Aleksander Mitt was born on 8 February 1908 in Tartu. He was educated at the Police Academy, graduating in 1929. He went on to study law at Tartu University. A natural skater, Mitt was national speed skating champion on eleven occasions, winning all four distances, 500, 1,500, 5,000 and 10,000 metres. He finished twentieth in the 1931 World Championships. He was also a fine all-round athlete and won the Estonian Championship in the 5km cycling. He appeared in two Olympic Games as a speed skater. In 1928 in St Moritz he came twenty-second in the 500 metres, twentieth in the 1,500 metres and twenty-first in the 5,000 metres. And in the 1936 winter Olympics in Garmisch-Partenkirchen he took part in the 500, 1,500, 5,000 and 10,000 metres, but he won no medals. In the war he served with the Tartu Police. He was arrested by Stalin's NKVD and shot on 18 April 1942 while in a prison camp in Kirov.

Nicolaas Moerloos (1900–44), Belgian, gymnastics and weightlifting, 1920 Antwerp (Silver), 1924 Paris.

Nicolaas Moerloos was born on 10 August 1900 in Sint-Niklaas. He trained at the 'Strength and Patience' gymnastics club in Sint-Niklaas. In 1920 he represented Belgium in Antwerp with twenty-four of his teammates. The team took the silver medal in the men's team all-round athletics event. This event was composed of five parts: 1. exercises with instruments, 2. horizontal bar, 3. parallel bars, 4. pommelled horse, 5. hurdle exercise. Teams were generally made up of between 16 and 24 athletes. He returned to the Olympic Games in 1924, this time in Paris, competing in featherweight weightlifting. He came twelfth. He was Belgian champion in 1923, 1924, 1925 and 1928. He was killed in action in Belsele, Belgium, on 4 November 1944, fighting as a member of the Belgian Resistance.

Ernst Moltzer (1910–41), Dutch, sailing, 1936 Berlin.

Ernst Octavianus Moltzer was born on 1 May 1910 in Amsterdam. He represented the Netherlands in the Berlin Olympics in 1936, his events taking place in Kiel. Moltzer was a member of the *De Ruyter* team together with Jool Carp (1897–1962), Ansco Dokkum (1904–85), Kees Jonker (1909–87) and Herman Looman (1907–89). The team sailed well, finally finishing eighth, Great Britain taking the gold, Norway the silver and Sweden the bronze. In 1939 while working as a director for Lucas Bols, the distillers, he met and married Countess von Sarnthein of Austria. He was killed on 15 November 1941 when the plane in which he was escaping from the Netherlands crashed into the North Sea.

Michael Murach (1911–41), German, boxing, 1936 Berlin (Silver).

Michael Murach was born on 1 February 1911 in North Rhine-Westphalia. He was employed by the Gelsenkirchen council for most of his working life and boxed as an amateur. He won five German titles between 1937 and 1940 and fought for Germany as a welterweight in twenty-one international matches. In the 1936 Berlin Olympics he was beaten in the final by the Finnish boxer Sten Suvio (1911–88) but walked away with the silver medal. He won the European Championship in 1937 and 1938. He eventually lost the title to the English boxer Robert Thomas in 1939. He served with the German army in the war on the Russian front, being killed in action at the Siege of Leningrad on 16 August 1941.

Eugen Mühlberger (1902–44), German, weightlifting, 1928 Amsterdam.

Eugen Mühlberger was born on 30 August 1902 in Ludwigshafen. He was German featherweight champion in 1925, 1927, 1929 and 1932, and runner up in 1931–34 and 1936. In 1928 he represented Germany in the men's featherweight competition in the 1928

Amsterdam Olympics. He came twelfth. In March 1929 and 1930 he set two world records in the featherweight snatch, lifting 93 kg. In 1930 he won the European Weightlifting Championship (featherweight) coming second in 1931 and 1933 and fifth in 1934. Mühlberger was reported missing in action on the Russian front in August 1944 and his death was assumed to have taken place on that date.

Eiichi Nakamura (1909–45), Japanese, field hockey, 1932 Los Angeles (Silver).

Eiichi Nakamura was born in 1909 in Tokyo. While playing for his club, Kyoto Prefecture, he came to international notice and was selected to play hockey for Japan in the 1932 Olympics in Los Angeles. It was the first occasion that Japan had taken part in the Olympic hockey competition. Much to everyone's surprise, Japan took the silver medal, being defeated by India 11–1 in the final. Nakamura was killed in action on 27 May 1945.

Saburo Nagao (1910–unknown), Japanese, athletics, 1932 Los Angeles.

Saburo Nagao was born on 25 August 1910 in Osaka. Little seems to be known of his life other than he competed for Japan in 1932 Los Angeles Olympics. He competed in the men's javelin, coming tenth. He was killed in the war.

Helmuth Naudé (1904–43), German, modern pentathlon, 1932 Los Angeles.

Helmuth Naudé was born on 30 November 1904 in Gdańsk. He married Margarethe Marie Rose in 1933 and they had three children. He represented Germany in the modern pentathlon in the Olympics in Los Angeles in 1932, coming seventeenth. He was killed in action on 3 February 1943 serving as an Oberst (colonel) with the German army.

Bruno Neumann (1883–1943), German, equestrianism, 1928 Amsterdam (Bronze).

Bruno Neumann was born on 26 April 1883 in Kaliningrad. On finishing his studies, he decided on a career in the army, in which he rose to the rank of major. He was stationed at the Cavalry School in Hannover. A fine horseman, he was selected to take part in the 1928 Olympic Games held in Amsterdam. Riding his horse *Ilja*, he won the bronze medal in the individual eventing competition. He was also part of the German eventing team, but Walter Feyerabend was unable to finish the cross-country section and the team was forced to withdraw from the event.

Neumann went missing on the Russian front on 31 December 1943, his death being assumed in 1944.

Mauri Nyberg-Noroma (1908–39), Finnish, gymnastics, 1928 Amsterdam, 1932 Los Angeles (Bronze), 1936 Berlin (Bronze).

Mauri Nyberg-Noroma was born on 31 January 1908 in Vyborg, Russia. He worked for the railroad at the Elisenvaara Junction, near Vyborg. Noroma has the distinction of being one of the few Olympians to have appeared in three Olympic Games. In Amsterdam in 1928 he competed in the men's individual all-around, coming sixth, and the men's team all-around, coming fifth. In

Los Angeles in 1932 he again competed in the men's single and team all-around events. This time he took a bronze medal in the team event. In Berlin in 1936 he failed to win a medal in the men's individual all-around gymnastics, coming sixteenth. He did, however, win a second bronze medal in the team event. He was killed in action on 23 September 1939 near Muolaa, which at that time was located in Finland, in the Soviet-Finnish war.

Amador Obordo (unknown-1945), Filipino, basketball, 1936 Berlin.

Very little is known about Obordo, other than he competed in the 1936 Berlin Olympics as a basketball player. The team came fifth. The US took the gold, Canada the silver and Mexico the bronze. He was killed in action in 1945 in the Second World War.

Masayoshi Ochiai (1910–unknown), Japanese, athletics, 1932 Los Angeles.

Masayoshi Ochiai was born on 3 June 1910 in Shimane. Once again, very little appears to be known about his life and death, other than he took part in the 1932 Olympics in Los Angeles. Competing in the hammer throw, he came twelfth. He was killed in action some time in the Second World War.

Sueo Ōe (1914–41), Japanese, athletics, 1936 Berlin.

Sueo Ōe was born on 2 August 1914 in Maizuru, Kyoto, and educated at Keio University. He became a well-known Japanese athlete who concentrated on the pole vault. He was selected to represent Japan at the 1936 Olympics in Berlin. He had drawn in the event with his great friend Shuhei Nishida, and they were instructed to take part in a jump-off to see who should take which medal. However, so strong was the friendship that the two refused to compete against each other. In the end Nishida was awarded the silver, on the basis that he had cleared the height in fewer attempts. When the two returned to Japan, they had their medals cut in half and paid a jeweller to splice them together. The medals became known as 'The Medals of friendship'.

In 1937 Ōe set the Japanese pole-vaulting record with a jump of 4 metres 35 centimetres, a record that stood for twenty-one years.

In 1939 Ōe enlisted into the Imperial Japanese Army and was killed at the Battle of Wake Island on 24 December 1941. His medal is now in private hands, but Nishida's is kept on display at Waseda University. Nishida died in 1997.

Kurt Oleska (1914–45), German, basketball, 1936 Berlin.

Kurt Oleska was born on 21 August 1914 in Eisfeld. He was a professional soldier, but still found time to play basketball nationally for Heeressportschule Wünsdorf. He won the first unofficial German championship with them in 1938. He played basketball for Germany in the 1936 Berlin Olympics. It was the first time basketball had been introduced into the Olympic Games. They lost their matches against Switzerland (25–18), Italy (58–16) and Czechoslovakia (20–9) in the first two rounds and were eliminated. He was reported as missing in action on the Russian front on 9 January 1945.

Heinrich Paal (1895–1942), Estonian, football, 1924 Paris.

Heinrich Paal was born on 26 June 1895 in Rakvere. He played for Estonia in the 1924 Paris Olympics. The Estonian team failed to reach the finals. Uruguay took the gold, Switzerland the silver and Sweden the bronze. He was arrested by the NKVD and transferred to a prisoner of war camp where he was executed on 20 September 1942.

Tjiepke 'Tjeerd' Pasma (1904–44), Dutch, modern pentathlon, 1928 Amsterdam.

Tjiepke Pasma was born on 24 June 1904 in Rinsumageast. Deciding on a career in the army, he became a guard-master 1st class (sergeant 1st class). While still serving with the army he was selected to take part in the 1928 Olympics, representing the Netherlands in the modern pentathlon. Normally you had to be an officer to be allowed to take part in the Olympics, but Pasma had been Dutch champion twice in the high jump. He came 35th in the shot put, 13th in the swimming, 34th in the fencing, 5th in the field running and 24th in the high jump. He eventually came 24th in the event. In 1940 and he was given an honourable discharge from the army.

At 7.55 am on 27 December 1944 a V1 rocket crashed prematurely and exploded at the junction of Verlengde Maanderweg and Kamperfoelielaan. It killed fifteen residents. Tjeerd, who lived at number 83, died the following day in hospital. His 13-year-old daughter Gerda was killed instantly. His wife Klazina and their sons Ankie and Tjipke were all seriously injured but survived.

Fritz Pellkofer (1902–43), German, cross-country skiing, 1928 St Moritz.

Fritz Pellkofer was born on 3 August 1902 in Bavaria. In 1922 he founded the Skiclub Bayrischzell together with his friend Gustl Müller. Pellkofer was German champion in the 4 × 10 km relay with the club in 1928. He participated in the 1928 winter Olympics in St Moritz representing Germany and coming in sixteenth in the 50 km cross-country ski. Although he captained the 1936 Olympic team in Berlin, he did not take part in any of the events. He was reported missing in action in Rossosh, Russia, on 23 January 1943 (he was later assumed to have died on that date).

Emil Perška (1896–1945), Croatian, football, 1920 Antwerp, 1924 Paris.

Emil Perška was born on 20 June 1896 in Stara Pazova. He deserted the army in the First World War and escaped to Vienna. A decent footballer, he signed for Gradanski, playing with them for a year before returning to Croatia. He then spent most of his career with Gradanski Zagreb, with whom he won three Yugoslav Championships 1923, 26 and 28. He was selected to play for the Yugoslavian team in the 1920 Antwerp Olympics. The team was knocked out in the heats and failed to take a medal. He was selected again for the Olympics in 1924 in Paris. Again they were knocked out in the heats (Perška did not play in any of the matches). In total he represented his country on fourteen occasions, scoring two international goals. He retired from football in 1929 and became a sports journalist. He was a keen supporter of the Ustaše movement, a Croatian revolutionary fascist movement which was active between1929 and 1945. Its members murdered hundreds of thousands of Serbs, Jews, Roma and political dissidents. He was shot and killed by Yugoslav Partisans in Zagreb on 8 May 1945.

Aarne 'Arvo' Peussa (1900–41), Finnish, running, 1924 Paris.

Aarne Aatami Peussa was born on 25 December 1900 in Primorsk. He competed in the men's 1,500 metres in the 1924 Paris Olympics running for Finland, finishing ninth. He was killed in action on 19 July 1941 near Salmi on the Karelian Isthmus in the Continuation War.

Étienne Piquiral (1901–45), French, rugby, 1924 Paris (Silver).

Étienne Piquiral was born on 15 June 1901 in Perpignan. He studied engineering at the École Polytechnique, later becoming an engineer. Piquiral was a fine rugby lock and back-row forward, playing for CA Périgourdain and then SA Bordeaux in 1919–20, Bordeaux Étudiant Club in 1920–21, Racing Club de France in 1921–26, and finally FC Lyonnaise in 1926–28. He won nineteen French caps. He was selected to play for France in the 1924 Paris Olympics. In front of 40,000 spectators the US beat France 17–3 (they had also defeated France in the 1920 Antwerp Games) with six different players scoring. France took the silver medal. After these Games, rugby would not return to the Olympics until the introduction of rugby sevens in 2016. In the war Piquiral served as a captain in the 248th French Infantry Regiment. Captured by the Germans, he died of illness on 13 March 1945 in the Lübeck prisoner of war camp.

Ernst Pistulla (1906–44), German, boxing, 1928 Amsterdam (Silver).

Ernst Pistulla was born on 28 November 1906 in Goslar. An electrician by trade, he boxed as an amateur light heavyweight. He fought at that weight in the 1928 Olympics in Amsterdam. He reached the final before being beaten by the Argentine champion Victor Avendano (1907–84) on points, taking the silver medal. He was the only German boxer to reach the finals. In the same year he won the European Amateur Championship. He turned professional in the 1930s. He was reported missing in action on the Russian front on 14 September 1944. His death was later assumed to have taken place on that date.

Werner Plath (1918–45), German, swimming, 1936 Berlin.

Werner Plath was born on 27 July 1918 in Berlin. A good swimmer, Plath swam for two Berlin clubs, Wiking and Askania. He took part in the 1936 Berlin Olympics, finishing fifth in the 4 × 200 metres relay. In 1938 he was part of the relay team that won the 4 × 200 metres in the European Championships. He also finished second in the individual 400 metre freestyle. In 1941 he became the 100 metre German freestyle champion. He was the 200 metre champion in 1936 and 1938 and then in 1940 and 1941, and was the 400 metre champion in 1937, 1940 and 1941. He also became the 1,500 metre champion in 1940/1. For reasons I have been unable to discover, he was executed by the SS in 1945.

Wanda Pleszczyńska (1903–43), Polish, art, 1928 Amsterdam.

Wanda Pleszczyńska was born on 25 May 1903 in Lublin, daughter of Stefan and Waleria (née Downar-Zapolska). Although she began studying music, she later switched to art and moved to Warsaw where she studied at the School of Painting and Drawing, and at the private school of Konrad Krzyżanowski, one of the early expressionists centres. Between 1923 and 1930 she studied under the guidance of Władysław Skoczylas (1883–1934) who also took part in the 1928 Olympics winning a bronze medal with his work *Archer*.

At the Olympics Wanda submitted a woodcut called *Football*, but failed to take a medal.

After graduating she became an art teacher in Warsaw. During the German occupation of Warsaw she adopted various pseudonyms and joined the Polish Resistance becoming secretary to the head of the 2nd Division of the Home Army, Lieutenant Colonel Szczekowski (1898–1944).

The Gestapo arrested her in November 1943. She was taken to the infamous Pawiak prison where she was tortured for over a month but refused to betray her comrades. She was finally shot on 17 December 1943.

Otto Pohla (1899–1941), Estonian, wrestling, 1928 Amsterdam.

Otto Pohla was born on 20 March 1899 in Hageri. A plumber by trade, he wrestled Greco-Roman light heavyweight for Sport Tallinn as an amateur and was Estonian champion on numerous occasions. He won the Greco-Roman heavyweight championship in 1924, 1927, and 1929, the light-heavyweight in 1930 and 1934, and the freestyle light-heavyweight in 1925 and 1927. Pohla also competed at the 1926 European Championships. He took part in the 1928 Amsterdam Olympics, coming fifth. He joined the Soviet army in July 1941, and after training in Tallinn was shipped to Leningrad together with hundreds of other new recruits. En route the ship was attacked by a U-boat and sunk with all hands (he was officially declared dead in January 1943).

Siegfried Powolny (1915–44), Austrian, field handball, 1936 Berlin (Silver).

Siegfried Powolny was born on 20 September 1915 in Linz. He played handball for his club, LASK, Linz and was selected to take part in the 1936 Berlin Olympics. The Austrian side reached the final before being defeated by the Germans 10–6. Powolny played in two matches. He was killed in action serving with the German army on 19 July 1944.

Janez 'Ivan' Porenta (1896–1942), Yugoslavian, gymnastics, 1924 Paris, 1928 Amsterdam (Bronze).

Janez Porenta was born on 3 June 1896 in Ljubljana. He was a member of the Slovenian Sokol athletics movement. (The Sokol movement, founded in Prague in 1862, is a gymnastics organisation based on the principle of 'a strong mind in a sound body'.) In the Paris Olympics of 1924 Porenta took part in the men's individual all-around and team all-around events. He took part in the horse vault, the parallel bars, the horizontal bar, the rings, the pommelled horse and rope climbing. He came twentieth in the individual event and fourth in the team event. In 1928 in the Amsterdam Olympics Porenta came third in the all-around team event taking the bronze medal. In the Second World War he became involved with the Liberation Front of the Slovene Nation. He was arrested by the Italians for his involvement in the murder of the banker Avgust Praprotnik and executed on 13 June 1942 at the Gramozna Jama (gravel pits) in Ljubljana.

Siegfried Purner (1915–44), Austrian, field handball, 1936 Berlin (Silver).

Siegfried Purner was born on 16 February 1915 in Innsbruck. He played handball for his club, Innsbruck (AUT). He was selected to take part in the 1936 Berlin Olympics and played in two matches but failed to score. Austria took the silver medal, defeated by the Germans 10–6 in the final. He was killed in action on 10 February 1944.

Richard Rau (1889–1945), German, athletics, 1912 Stockholm.

Richard Rau (he also ran under the name of Richard Einsporn) was born on 26 August 1889 in Berlin. He started his athletics career in 1908, specialising in the sprint and hurdles. He competed for the SC Charlottenburg Club, Berlin. During his career he won a number of national championships and set twenty national records. He was the second German to run 100 metres in 10.5 seconds (1911) and the first to run the 200 metres in under 22 seconds (1912). He was selected for the 1912 Stockholm Olympics. He took part in the 100 metres but was knocked out in the heats, the 200 metres coming fourth, and the 4 × 100 metres when the team was disqualified. On retirement from athletics he became a businessman and ran a sports shop. In 1933 he joined the Nazi Party reaching the rank of SS Hauptsturmbannführer (captain). He was captured by the Americans in 1945 and handed over to Soviet troops. He was shot and seriously wounded in an escape attempt and died from his wounds on 6 November 1945 in the Vyasma PoW camp.

Stasys Razma (1899–1941), Lithuanian, football, 1924 Paris.

Stasys Razma was born in 1944 in Kaunas, growing up to play football for LFLS Kaunas. He was selected to play in Lithuania's first international match against Estonia in 1923, which they lost 0–5 mainly due to them being an inexperienced team. In 1924 he was selected as part of the side to play in Lithuania's first appearance in the Olympic Games. They were beaten 0–9 by Switzerland and were knocked out of the competition. Razma played in three more international matches, including Lithuania's first ever international win again Estonia 2–1. He was killed in action in 1941.

Josef Rehm (1902–44), German, military patrol, 1928 St Moritz.

Josef Rehm was born in 1902. Little seems to be known of him other than that he was a talented German skier. At the 1928 winter Olympics he finished fifth.

The military patrol was the precursor to biathlon and was at the time a demonstration event. It was a team sport in which athletes competed in cross-country skiing, ski mountaineering and rifle shooting. The event was first contested in the Olympics in 1924, then as a demonstration event in

1928, 1936 and 1948. In 1948 the sport was reorganized under the Union Internationale de Pentathlon Moderne et Biathlon and became re-accepted as an Olympic sport in 1955. The first Biathlon World Championship was held in 1958.

Two years later, Rehm competed at the 1930 World Championships and came fifth in the 30 kilometres cross-country skiing for military personnel.

In the Second World War he served with the German army as a private first class and went missing on 1 July 1944 on the Russian Front.

Willi Reinfrank (1903–43), German, weightlifting, 1928 Amsterdam.

Wilhelm Reinfrank was born on 30 May 1903 in Mannheim. He was a trained as a mechanic but later worked as an auctioneer. A lightweight weightlifter, he won the German national lightweight title in 1923–27 and the middleweight title in 1929. He won the European Championship in 1924 and was placed second in 1929. He also set eleven lightweight world records between 1924 and 1927, one in the press, one in the snatch, five in the clean and jerk, and four in the combined. He took part in the 1928 Amsterdam Olympics, coming fifth. He was reported missing in action on 1 January 1943 (later presumed killed) serving with the German army at the battle for Stalingrad.

Toivo Reingoldt (1906–41), Finnish, swimming, 1932 Los Angeles.

Toivo Walfrid Reingoldt was born on 15 March 1906 in Kotka. In 1931 he won the 200 metres European breaststroke. In the same year he achieved world records in the 500 metres breaststroke and the European record in the 200 metres. He also won the Nordic Championship in Helsinki and eight Finnish championships in the 200 metre breaststroke. In 1932 he was selected to represent Finland in the Los Angeles Olympics. Unfortunately he failed to make the finals. He next competed in the Magdeburg European Championships in 1934 finishing fifth. A fine all-round athlete he also represented Finland in the 1926 Ski World Championship. He came seventh in the ski jump and twenty-second in the combined ski. Reingoldt was killed in action on 28 September 1941 in Eastern Karelia when his plane crashed.

Olli Remes (1909–42), Finnish, military patrol, 1936 Garmisch-Partenkirchen.

Olavi Remes was born on 8 September 1909 in Iisalmi, the son of Pekka and Maria. One of the country's finest cross-country skiers, he won a bronze medal at the Nordic World Ski Championships 50 kilometres in 1934.

In 1936 he was selected to represent Finland in the military patrol at the Olympics. The team came second. His team-mates were Eino Kuvaja (d.1975) and Kalle Arantola (d.1940).

He married Eine Mukkala (d.2000). Remes was commissioned as a lieutenant into the Finnish army and fought in the Winter War and later the Continuation War. He was awarded the Mannerheim Cross for his bravery. He was killed in action by a sniper's bullet on 31 December 1942 while fighting in the Krivi, East Karelia, area. He is buried in Vieremä.

Wilhelm Rietschel (1911–41), German, art, 1936 Berlin.

Wilhelm Rietschel was born on 26 January 1911 in Saxony. An artist and a sculptor, he was a pupil of Karl Albiker (a German sculptor and lithographer who studied with Rodin in Paris and was a professor at the Dresden Academy of Fine Arts) and Richard Scheibe (1879–1964). He took part in the 1936 Berlin Olympics in the art competition, mixed sculpturing event. He failed to win a medal. He was killed in action outside Leningrad on 8 December 1941, serving with the 271 Infantry Regiment.

Josef Ritz (1899–1943), Austrian, fencing, 1936 Berlin.

Josef Ritz was born on 14 December 1899 in Vienna. He took part in the men's individual foil in the 1936 Berlin Olympics, but although a good fencer he unfortunately failed to take a medal. He was a soldier with the Wehrmacht in the war and was killed in action on 31 July 1943 outside Kharkov in the Russian Campaign.

Boris Roolaid (1917–1942/3), Estonian, swimming (backstroke), 1936 Berlin.

Boris Roolaid was born Boris Rosenberg on 3 February 1917 in Tallinn. He began swimming in 1932 and won three national swimming titles between 1935 and 1937. He was selected to swim in the 1936 Berlin Olympics and competed in the 100 metres but failed to gain a medal. He swam with his brother Egon. In 1941 both brothers were arrested by Stalin's murderous NKVD and sent to labour camps in the Soviet Union where they died or were murdered sometime between 1942 and 1943.

Egon Roolaid (1918–1942), Estonian, swimming (freestyle), 1936 Berlin.

Egon Roolaid was born Egon Rosenberg on 26 September 1918 in Tallinn. He began his swimming career in 1932 and between 1934 and 1940 won nineteen national titles. Together with his brother Boris he competed in the 100 metres swimming event in the 1936 Berlin Olympics. They both failed to take a medal. Both were arrested by the NKVD and died or were murdered in captivity sometime between 1942 and 1943.

Evžen Rošický (1914–42), Czechoslovakian, athletics, 1936 Berlin.

Evžen Rošický was born on 15 October 1915 in Olomouc. He took part in the 1934 European Championships coming fourth in the second heat of the 800 metres and being eliminated. He ran his personal best of 1:54:6 in Vienna in 1935. Despite being an active member of the boycott movement for the 1936 Berlin Olympics, he was finally persuaded to take part. He ran in the 800 metres and the 4 × 400 metres relay, failing to win a medal in either. Becoming a journalist, he joined the Resistance group 'Captain Nemo', who fought against the Nazi occupation of Czechoslovakia, together with his father Jaroslav. He wrote and distributed many anti-Nazi pamphlets. He and his father were arrested on 18 June 1942 by the Gestapo and tortured. After the assassination of Heydrich, both were sentenced to death and shot on 25 June 1942 at the Kobylisy shooting range in Prague. About 550 Czech patriots were murdered there, mostly between 30 May and 3 July 1942. The bodies were later incinerated in Strašnice crematorium. There is a memorial to them on the site. The Evžena Rošického stadium was named after Evžen.

Petrus 'Piet' Ruimers (1884–1945), Dutch, track and field, 1908 London.

Petrus Adrianus Antonius Ruimers was born on 21 October 1884 in Rotterdam. He took part in the 1908 London Olympics, competing in the 3,500 metre and the ten mile walks. He was eliminated in the first round of both and failed to win a medal. He was executed by the Nazis on the beach on Texel on 6 April 1945 in the Texel uprising. The Georgian Uprising, between 5 April 1945 and 20 May 1945, was a mutiny by the 882nd Infantry Battalion, part

of the Georgian Legion of the German army stationed on the German-occupied Dutch island of Texel. The battalion was made up of 800 Georgians and 400 Germans, with mainly German officers. It was one of the last battles in the European theatre. Approximately 565 Georgians, 120 Texel islanders and 800 Germans were killed in the fighting. Many of the Georgian troops were later handed over to Stalin.

Alfreds Ruks (1890–1941), Latvian, running, 1912 Stockholm, 1924 Paris.

Alfrēds Ruks was born on 10 November 1890 in Sigulda. He competed in the Olympics in 1912 and again, remarkably, twelve years later in 1924. In Stockholm he competed for Russia in the 1,500 metres being knocked out in the heats. In Paris he competed for Latvia in the ten kilometres walk, again being knocked out in the heats. In the war he was arrested by the NKVD and deported to a prison camp in Solikamsk, where he was murdered on 30 November 1941.

Heinrich Sack (1909–41), German, canoe, 1936 Berlin.

Heinrich Sack was born on 10 December 1909 in Hamburg, growing up to represent Canuclub Alsterfreunde Viktoria Hamburg. He took part in the 1936 Berlin Olympics, finishing fourth in the doubles with his rowing partner Hans Wedemann (1912–89) in the men's Canadian doubles 1,000 metres, just missing out on a medal. In 1934 and 1936 they won the German title in the same event. Sack was killed in action on the Russian front just outside Kiev on 13 September 1941. He is buried in a military Cemetery just outside Kiev.

Richard Sahla (1900–42), German, show jumping, 1928 Amsterdam.

Richard Sahla was born on 8 April 1900 in Bückeburg. He was a career officer in the military and a fine equestrian. He took part in the 1928 Amsterdam Olympics, competing in the men's jumping individual, in which he finished fourteenth, and the men's jumping team, in which he came seventh, riding his horse *Correggio*. At the time of the Games, Sahla was a senior lieutenant stationed at the Cavalry School in Hannover. He was killed in action on the Russian front on 6 April 1942 approximately twenty miles south of Chudovo.

Kenkichi Saito (1895–unknown), Japanese, swimming, 1920 Antwerp.

Kenkichi Saito was born on 2 January 1895. Like many of the Japanese Olympians, little seems to be known about him. He competed in the 1920 Olympic Games in Antwerp in the 100 and 400 metres freestyle but didn't win a medal. He was killed in the Second World War.

Heinz Sames (1911–43), German, speed skating, 1936 Garmisch-Partenkirchen.

Heinz Sames was born on 10 July 1911 in Berlin. He skated for the Berliner Schlittschuhclub. Between 1934 and 1938 he competed in the German Championships, finishing third in 1938. He also competed in the 1935 World Championships but wasn't placed. He was selected to skate for Germany in the 1936 winter Olympics in Garmisch-Partenkirchen and participated in all four speed skating events, the 500 metres finishing twenty-eighth, the 1,500 metres finishing twenty-seventh, the 5,000 metres in which he wasn't placed, and the 10,000 metres finishing fifteenth. He was reported missing in action in 1943 near Volgograd in the Russian Campaign.

Felix Scheder-Bieschin (1899–1940), German, sailing, 1936 Berlin (Bronze).

Felix Scheder-Bieschin was born on 22 October 1899 in Kiel. He went on to study law and political economics. In 1934 he became CEO of the Nordseewerke (the North Sea Company) in Emden and from 1937 was chairman of the Howaldtswerke in Kiel. A keen sailor, he belonged to the Kiel Yacht Club and in 1936 competed in the Olympics. His events were all held in Kiel. He took part in the mixed eight metre event for team Germania III. Interestingly the owner of the boat was Alfried von Bohlen und Halbach, sentenced to twelve years for war crimes after the Second World War. The team did well and walked away with a bronze medal under skipper Hans Howaldt. Italy took the gold and Norway the silver. In the Second World War Scheder-Bieschin served with the German navy rising to the rank of corvette captain. He was killed when his ship was torpedoed on 2 September 1940 in the Baltic Sea.

Hans Scheele (1908–41), German, athletics, 1936 Berlin.

Hans Scheele was born on 18 December 1908 in Hamburg. He competed for his athletics club, Hamburger SV. He was in the 1934 European Champions in the 400 metres hurdles and the 4 × 400 metres relay. He took part in the 1936 Berlin Olympics. He was eliminated in the 400 metres hurdles and failed to gain a medal. In 1934 and 1936 Scheele was German champion in the intermediate hurdles. Called up in 1939 he became a master sergeant. He was killed on 23 July 1941 near Buynichi in Belarus in the Russian Campaign.

Adolf Scheffknecht (1914–41), Austrian, gymnastics, 1936 Berlin.

Adolf Scheffknecht was born on 4 October 1914 in Bregena. A gymnast, he competed in the 1936 Berlin Olympics. He took part in the men's individual all-around finishing eighty-seventh, and the men's team all-around finishing eleventh. He was killed in action on 11 September 1941 in Zapadnaya Litsa, Murmansk in the Easter Campaign. He is buried in the war Cemetery in Petschenga, Russia.

Emile de Schepper (1885–1940), Belgian, fencing, 1920 Antwerp.
Emile de Schepper was born on 27 July 1885 in Ghent. He was selected to fence for his country at the 1920 Olympics. He came fifth in the individual foil and sixth in the team foil.

He died in the defence of Namur on 12 May 1940. The 8th Infantry Division and the Chasseurs Ardennais had formed a strong position in the Namur defences, anchoring the southern end of the Dyle line.

However, Namur was outflanked to the south by German forces that had broken the French line at Sedan. VII Corps gave up the fight and pulled out to try to avoid becoming trapped. The forts surrendered between 18 and 23 May 1940. De Schepper was posthumously awarded the Order of Leopold with palms. He is buried in the Westerbegraafplaats in Ghent.

Heinz Schlauch (1915–45), German, swimming, 1936 Berlin.
Heinz Schlauch was born on 13 November 1915 in Gera. He swam for the clubs Neptun Gera and Poseidon Erfurt. He was selected to swim in the 100 metres backstroke in the 1936 Berlin Olympics but was eliminated in the heats. In 1938 he won the European 100 metre backstroke Championship. He was killed in action on 21 February 1945 somewhere in the Niederrhein, Germany.

Helmut Schlöske (1904–44), German, athletics, 1928 Amsterdam.
Helmut Schlöske was born on 27 June 1904 in Grünewald. He ran for his athletics club SC Charlottenburg, Berlin. He was German champion in the sprint relay in 1927. He took part in the long jump in the 1928 Amsterdam Olympics but was eliminated in the heats. Schlöske was killed in action near Potsdam on 15 October 1944. He is buried in the Berlin-Charlottenburg war Cemetery.

Alfred Schmalzer (1912–44), Austrian, handball, 1936 Berlin (Silver).
Alfred Schmalzer was born on 28 October 1912 in Vienna. He represented his club, Ferrowatt, Wien. He was selected to represent Austria in handball in the 1936 Berlin Olympics. They won a silver medal, being beaten by German 10–6 in the final (Switzerland took the bronze). Schmalzer played in three matches, including the final. He was killed in action on 21 January 1944.

Eugen Schnalek (1911–1944/45), Austrian, cycling, 1936 Berlin.
Eugen Schnalek was born on 17 March 1911 in Vienna. He cycled for the club Neubauer Radler, Wein. He took part in the 1936 Berlin Olympics, representing Austria in the individual and men's road race cycle team. Although he was knocked out in the heats in the individual event, he came fifth in the team event. He was killed in action some time in 1944 or 1945.

Hans Schönrath (1902–45), German, boxing, 1928 Amsterdam.
Hans Schönrath was born on 8 November 1902 in Gronau. By profession he was a smelter. He boxed for Boxclub 1920, Krefeld. He represented Germany as a heavyweight boxer in the European Championships in 1927, coming second. In 1925 and 1928 he was

German amateur champion. After turning professional he became German champion in 1930/1. He took part in the 1928 Olympics held in Amsterdam. Boxing heavyweight he was eliminated in the quarter-finals by the Swedish heavyweight Nils Ramm who went on to take the silver medal. Argentina took the gold. In 1935 he became, for a short term anyway, a film star taking part in the film *Knockout*, playing the British boxing champion. He drowned when the hospital ship DS *General von Steuben* was attacked by a Soviet submarine and sunk on 10 February 1945.

Koos Schouwenaar (1902–41), Dutch, rowing, 1928 Amsterdam.

Koos Schouwenaar was born on 9 October 1902 in Alblasserdam. He grew up to represent the rowing club Laga, Delft, and was selected to cox the Dutch eight in the 1928 Olympics. It was eliminated in the heats. The US took the gold, Great Britain the silver and Canada the bronze. Schouwenaar was killed when his plane crashed into the North Sea on 22 June 1941 while he was flying to England.

Jakob Schüller (1905–44), German, sprint, 1928 Amsterdam.

Jakob Schüller was born on 26 June 1905 in Duisburg. A merchant by trade, he ran for the athletics club KTSV Preussen 1855, Krefeld. In 1926 he set the European record in the 100 metres. Going on to specialise in the 200 metres, he became national champion at that distance in 1925 until 1928. In 1928 Schuller also set two world records, in the 100 metres with 10.4, and in the sprint relay with 40.8. He was selected to run for Germany in the 200 metres in the 1928 Amsterdam Olympics where he reached the final, eventually coming sixth. He was reported missing in action on 22 January 1944 and was later assumed to have died on that date.

Franz Schüßler (1911–42), Austrian, ice hockey, 1936 Garmisch-Partenkirchen.

Franz Georg Wilhelm Schüßler was born on 20 January 1911 in Vienna. He became an outstanding ice hockey player, playing mostly in defence. He began his career in 1930 with Pötzleindorfer SC but moved to Wien EKE in 1932. He later played for Vienna City, Zürcher SC in Switzerland, and Hamburg SC in Germany. He was also capped twenty-one times for his country. In 1936 he was selected to play for Austria at the winter Olympics in Garmisch-Partenkirchen. The team failed to win a medal, coming seventh. He retired in the 1938/9 season.

In the war he was captured by the Russians and interned in a prisoner-of-war camp in Yushnevo in the Tver Oblast where he died on 29 August 1942.

Arthur Tell Schwab (1896–1945), Swiss, race walking, 1924 Paris, 1932 Los Angeles, 1936 Berlin (Silver).

Arthur Tell Schwab was born on 4 September 1896 in Bortewitz, Germany. His athletics club was SC Charlottenburg, Berlin. Although Schwab was a Swiss citizen, he was a native of Germany and the German race walking coach. He competed in three Olympic Games for Switzerland. In 1924 in Paris he came fifth in the 10 kilometre walk, in 1932 in Los Angeles he failed to win a medal in the 50 kilometre walk, but in Berlin in 1936 he came second and won a silver medal in the 50 kilometres. He had also won a silver medal in the European Championships in 1934. He set eight world records at various distances. The Nazis tried to convince him to represent Germany, but he refused. He was killed on 27 February 1945 when the Red Cross train on which he was attempting to return to Switzerland was bombed near Heilbronn. His son Fritz won a bronze medal in the 1948 Olympics and silver in the 1952 Olympics, both in the 10 kilometre walk.

Ludwig Schweickert (1915–43), German, wrestling, 1936 Berlin (Silver).

Ludwig Schweickert was born on 26 April 1915 in Bavaria. He went on to represent Germany in the 1936 Berlin Olympics as a middleweight Greco-Roman wrestler. He won the silver medal in these games. He also won silver medals in the 1937 and 1939 European Championships. In 1937–42 he won the national championships in Greco-Roman wrestling and in 1938–1940 and 1941 he was national free style champion. He joined the German army in 1936 and was killed in action on 11 July 1943 defending the town of Oryol against the Soviet army.

Karl Schwitalle (1906–45), German, weightlifting, 1936 Berlin.

Karl Wilhelm Johann Schwitalle was born on 12 April 1906 in Warsaw, Poland. He took part in the weightlifting event in the 1936 Berlin Olympics, just missing out on a medal finishing fourth. Although being born in Poland he represented Germany. In 1938 he won a bronze medal in the World Weightlifting Championship. In 1942 he won his only national competition, having won silver in 1935–37 and later in 1939–41. He was killed in action on 7 February 1945 in Szczecin.

Joseph-Adriaan Seckel (1881–1945), Dutch, art, 1928 Amsterdam, 1932 Los Angeles.

Joseph-Adriaan Abraham Seckel was born on 23 December 1881 in Rotterdam. He was a painter and graphic artist and studied at the Academy of Fine Arts in Rotterdam between 1899 and 1904. He further studied at the Acadamie Colarossi in Paris in 1903. He worked and lived in Amsterdam, Rhenen and The Hague for most of his career. He took part in two Olympics, 1928 in Amsterdam in the mixed painting competition where he failed to win a medal, and 1932 in Los Angeles again in the mixed painting competition where again he failed to win a medal. Seckel was killed with his wife and child on 3 March 1945 in the Bezuidenhout bombardment, when the RAF accidentally bombed the area of The Hague instead of the V2 rocket base.

Katsumi Shibata (1909–40), Japanese, field hockey, 1932 Los Angeles (Silver).

Katsumi Shibata was born in 1909 in Tokyo. Little seems to be known of him, but we know he represented the Japanese field hockey team in the 1932 Olympic Games. The team did well and unexpectedly came second winning the silver medal. He played in two matches as a half back. He was killed in action in 1940.

Erich Siebert (1910–47), German, wrestling, 1936 Berlin (Bronze).

Erich Siebert was born on 7 May 1910. He took the silver medal in the Greco-Roman European Championships in 1934. In the same year and in 1943 he also won the German national titles in Greco-Roman wrestling. In 1936 he won the freestyle wrestling championship and was selected to represent Germany in the Berlin Olympics, competing in the men's lightweight freestyle. He fought well, eventually losing to the Estonian wrestler August Neo 3–0 and taking the bronze medal (August took the silver). A police officer by profession, he joined the SS in the early part of the Nazi regime. He was a guard patrolling the Łódź ghetto, which housed 163,777 Jewish detainees, almost all of whom were transferred to various death camps and murdered. He was later captured by the Russians and deported to Russia, where he died a prisoner sometime in 1947.

Evald Sikk (1910–45), Estonian, wrestling, 1936 Berlin.

Evald Sikk was born on 10 February 1910. He took part in the 1936 Berlin Olympics, competing in the men's Greco- Roman bantamweight wrestling event. He reached the final, coming sixth. He was arrested by the NKVD in the Russian occupation of Estonia and deported to a camp in the Soviet Union. He was murdered there on 8 August 1945.

Tadeusz Sokołowski (1905–43), Polish, equestrianism, 1936 Berlin.

Tadeusz Sokołowski was born on 25 September 1905 in Eememyal, Belarus. As a career officer in the Polish cavalry, he took part in various equestrian events for the army and for Poland. Having won the Polish championship, he was selected to take part in the 1936 Berlin Olympics. He competed in the men's jumping individual and team events but failed to take a medal. He was captured by the Nazis after a parachute landing in Operation Belt, which he commanded, and murdered in Minsk on 6 February 1943. He is commemorated on a plaque in St Jacek Church in Warsaw.

Josip Šolc or Josip Scholz (1898–1945), Croatian, football, 1920 Antwerp.

Josip Šolc was born on 30 January 1898 in Zagreb. A career soldier, he was also a talented footballer who played mid-field for HSK Concordia. He competed with the Yugoslavian football team in the 1920 Antwerp Olympics. The team was knocked out in the heats and failed to win a medal. Like so many athletes, he was good at several sports and also participated in fencing events. In the Second World War he became a member of the Nazi-supported Croatian Home Guard. Šolc was commander of the Zagreb Garrison Command. He was decorated with the Iron Trefoil 4th Class with Oak leaves and then on 22 December 1944 was promoted to general. In May 1945 he was captured by Yugoslav partisans and imprisoned in Belgrade. He was sentenced to death and executed on 19 September 1945.

Werner Spannagel (1909–43), German, boxing, 1932 Los Angeles.

Werner Spannagel was born on 6 October 1909 in Barmen, Wuppertal, Germany. Spannagel, a flyweight, fought for the Sports and Games Association Barmen. Travelling to South Africa, he was one of the main attractions in the first public boxing event that took place in the

Stadthalle Wuppertal in Johannesburg. In 1932 he was German bantamweight champion and in 1933 the flyweight champion. In 1932 he took on the American champion Johnny Balzer in Chicago, scoring an unexpected victory. Fighting flyweight he took part in the 1932 Los Angeles Olympics. He won his first-round match against the Argentine Juan Trillo, however despite being one of the favourites for the gold medal he lost to the US fighter Louis Salica (who went on to win the bronze) in the quarter-final. He was killed in action on the Russian front, his death being reported on 23 December 1943.

Sonny Spencer (1903–43), British, Athletics, 1924 Paris.

Sydney Albert Spencer was born on 18 May 1903 in Mitcham, son of Albert and Ann. Becoming a gifted athlete and runner, he competed for the South London Harriers. He came an impressive third in the 880 yards at the AAA Championships in 1923, and fourth in 1924 and 1925. In 1925 he was placed second in the Kinnaird mile. He was selected to run for Great Britain at the 1924 Paris Olympics where he ran in the 1,500 metres. He reached the finals, finishing eleventh. He married in 1925.

In the war Sonny served as aircrew in the RAFVR and was promoted to sergeant. He was killed in a flying accident on 21 November 1943 near Nigg, Ross and Cromarty, when the Short Sunderland 3 L2168 in which he was flying crashed on a night training accident in the Highlands. He is commemorated on the Runnymede Memorial, Panel 165.

Alfred Steinke (1881–1945), German, ice hockey, 1928 St Moritz.

Alfred Wilhelm Steinke was born on 6 June 1881 in Berlin. He began playing hockey in 1900 for BFC Preussen, later moving to Berliner SC. He began his career as a defender and sometimes forward but finished as a goalkeeper, playing for Germany on a regular basis. He took part in the LIHG Championships organised by the Ligue International de Hockey sur Glace (the present-day IIHF, the International Ice Hockey Federation), winning in 1912 and 1913. He won the European Championships in 1910–11, 1913–14 and 1927. The team came second in 1910, 1911 and 1914 and third in 1913 and 1927. They also won the German Championships in 1912–14, 1920, 1923–26, and 1928–29. He won the Spengler Cup in 1924, 1926 and 1928, and took part in the 1928 winter Olympics in St Moritz representing Germany. He had the distinction of being, at 48, the oldest man to take part in the Olympic ice hockey event. The team failed to win a medal, being knocked out in the heats. On retiring from active participation he became an administrator, a technical director, and a member of the Organizing Committee for the Olympic Games in Garmisch-Partenkirchen. He also refereed, and co-authored the sports magazine *Eishockey im Deutschen Eislauf-Verband*. He was killed in action in May 1945 defending Berlin against the Russians.

Hugo Strauss (1907–41), German, rowing, 1936 Berlin (Gold).

Hugo Strauss was born on 25 June 1907 in Mannheim. He rowed for Mannheimer RC 1875 together with his rowing partner Willi Eichhorn. He came second in the coxless pairs German championship in 1935. The following year they won the event, automatically qualifying for the Olympic Games. In the games they defeated the Danish crew in the final by three seconds to take the gold medal. In 1938 they came second in the German Championship once again. A keen member of the Nazi Party he became a member of the SS Death Head Group 'Thuringia'. He was killed in action on 1 November 1941 on the Russian front.

Ludwig Stubbendorf (1906–41), German, equestrianism, 1936 Berlin (two Golds).

Ludwig Stubbendorf was born on 24 February 1906. Deciding on a career in the military he joined the 2 (Prussian) Artillery Regiment as a volunteer. He also trained at the Cavalry School in Hanover. A talented rider, he was selected to take part in the 1936 Berlin Olympics. Riding his horse *Nurmi* he won one gold medal in the men's three-day event individual and a second in the men's three-day event team. Stubbendorf and *Nurmi* fought with the First Cavalry Brigade in the invasion of Poland. They were killed together in battle on 17 July 1941. His grave is about 12 km north-west of Stary Bychow in Belarus and there is a commemorative stone for him and *Nurmi* at the Verden racecourse near the Nurmi oak tree.

Karl Sudrich (1895–1944), Austrian, fencing, 1936 Berlin.

Karl Sudrich was born on 7 October 1895 in Hodschein. He fenced for the Union Fechtclub, Wien. In the 1936 Berlin Olympics he competed in the men's foil, individual and team, and the sabre, individual and team. The closest he came to a medal was with the men's foil team, coming fourth. He was seriously wounded in action and died in a military hospital in Hungary on 18 September 1944.

Teodors Sukatnieks (1894–1940s), Latvian, athletics, 1924 Paris.

Teodors Sukatnieks was born in 1894 in Yekaterinburg, Russia; however, he represented Latvia in his sporting life. He was selected to take part in the 1924 Paris Olympics and competed in the men's discus, coming twenty-first. Arrested by Stalin's NKVD, he was deported to a Soviet prison camp where he died or was murdered sometime in the 1940s.

Gustav Sule (1910–42), Estonian, javelin, 1936 Berlin.

Gustav Sule was born on 10 September 1910 in Tartu. He showed early promise at the javelin by setting the Estonian High School record in 1928 (he also set the record in the high jump and pole vault in the same year). Sule became national champion in the javelin on no less than six occasions. In 1931 he threw the second longest distance in the world that year: 69.54 metres. He was unable to attend the Los Angeles Games in 1932, where he would have been a favourite for a medal, as the Estonian Olympic committee lacked the finances. In Turin in the International University Games in 1933 Sule took the silver medal. He broke the 70 metre barrier in 1934 and was placed second in the world rankings. At the European Championships in 1934 he took the bronze, going on to be named Estonian sportsman of the year by the Tallinn Sports Press Club. In the 1936 Berlin Olympics he was, unfortunately, clearly off form and finished eleventh. In 1937 he broke the Estonian record twice, being ranked fourth in the world. In 1938 he set a personal record with a throw of 75.935 metres, becoming second in the world rankings. Arrested by Stalin's NKVD, he died of pneumonia on 3 April 1942 while part of a labour column.

Fusashige Suzuki (1914–45), Japanese, marathon, 1936 Berlin.
Fusashige Suzuki was born on 15 February 1914, and on 31 March 1935 set the world marathon record. He was chosen to compete in the 1936 Olympic Games in Berlin. He failed to take part in the marathon due to illness, but he did take part in the 10,000 metres, though he failed to win a medal. He was killed in action on 3 June 1945 in the South China Sea.

Monta Suzuki (1913–39), Japanese, sprint, 1936 Berlin.
Monta Suzuki was born on 1 April 1913 in Saitama. He took part in the 1936 Berlin Olympics, competing in the 100 metres and the 100 metres relay, failing to win a medal in either event. He died in China as a lieutenant with the Imperial Japanese Army on 10 July 1939 in the second Sino-Japanese War.

Hildegard Schwarz-Geschel (1907–44), Latvian, figure skating, 1936 Berlin.
Hildegard Schwarz-Geschel was born on 29 September 1907 in Jelgava. She took part in the figure skating event in the 1936 Berlin Olympics with her partner Eduard Geschel. They came seventeenth. They were national Latvian champions in 1931–33 and in 1940. She also came ninth in the 1934 European Figure Skating Championship. Towards the end of the Second World War she made her way into Germany to avoid the advancing Red Army and was killed in an air-raid in Heilbronn on 4 December 1944.

Józef Szajba (1910–45), Polish, sailing, 1936 Berlin.
Józef Szajba was born on 14 January 1910 in Nowa Osada, Lubelskie. He sailed for the Maritime Club of Gdańsk. Szajba was one of Poland's best known and celebrated sailors in the interwar period. He attended the School of Officers of the Artillery Reserve in Włodzimierz Wołyński between 1931 and 1932. He was selected to represent Poland in the 1936 Berlin Olympics. He competed in the six-metre class, sailing *Danuta*, finally coming eleventh. In 1938 Szajba won the prize of the Senate of the Free City of Gdańsk, one of the most valuable prizes of the Sopot regatta week. It is believed that Szajba was arrested by the Nazis and murdered by them sometime in 1945 in Potulice.

Józef Szawara (1902–44), Polish, rowing, 1924 Paris.
Józef Franciszek Szawara was born in 1902 in Minsk. Becoming an accomplished rower, he represented Club Wisla in Warsaw. In 1924 he was selected to row for Poland at the Paris Olympics in the coxed four. They failed to take a medal, being knocked out in the second heat. Switzerland took the gold, France the silver, and the USA the bronze.
    In the war he took part in the Warsaw uprising and was killed on 5 August 1944 by the ruthless RONA brigade.

András Székely (1909–43), Hungarian, Swimming, 1932 Los Angeles.
András Székely was born into a Jewish family on 5 March 1909 in Tatabánya. He grew up to become a talented swimmer and competed for his club, Ferencvárosi TC, Budapest. In 1932 he won gold in the 4 × 200 metres freestyle relay and silver in the 100 metre freestyle at the European Championships,

and was selected to take part in the Los Angeles Olympics. He swam in the 4 × 200 metres relay freestyle, winning a bronze. He also swam in the 100 metre freestyle event but did not win a medal. As a Jew, he was arrested by the Nazis and transported to the Chernyanka, Belgorod, forced labour camp. He was murdered there on 25 January 1943.

Henryk Szlązak (1913–44), Polish, Greco-Roman wrestling, 1936 Berlin.

Henryk Szlązak was born on 3 March 1913 in Jeziorna, Warsaw. A Greco-Roman wrestler, he fought for Legia Warsaw as a featherweight. He took part in the 1936 Berlin Olympics but was knocked out in the heats. He was killed by an artillery shell in the Warsaw uprising on 30 September 1944 while crossing the Vistula and trying to reach Polish troops situated in Praga.

Kazimierz Szosland (1891–1944), Polish, equestrianism, 1924 Paris, 1928 Amsterdam (Silver)

Kazimierz Szosland was born on 21 February 1891 in Grzymaczew. An army officer and rider, he took part in two Olympics: 1924 in Paris where he competed in jumping individual (32nd), jumping team (6th), the three-day event individual (23rd), and the three-day event team (7th); and 1928 in Amsterdam where he competed in jumping individual (13th) and jumping team, wining a silver medal on his horse *Ali*. He was killed in the forest of Grodzisk Mazowiecki on 20 April 1944.

Georges Tainturier (1890–1943), French, fencing, 1924 Paris (Gold), 1932 Los Angeles (Gold).

Georges Charles Armand Tainturier was born on 20 May 1890. He was to become one of Europe's and the world's finest fencers, specialising in the épée. In the First World War he served as a sergeant before being commissioned as an officer in the French Dragoons. He was wounded in the head while leading an attack on a German machine-gun post. He received the Croix de Guerre for his bravery and was later admitted to the Légion d'Honneur.

In 1923 he became French champion in the épée. The following year he was selected to represent France in the Paris Olympics. The team won the gold medal in the team épée. Although Tainturier missed the 1928 Olympics, he was selected to compete in the 1932 Games in Los Angeles. As in 1924, he won gold with the team épée. Between Games, in 1926, he unofficially won the world title in the individual épée.

In the Second World War Tainturier became a distinguished member of the French Resistance in Compiègne. In 1942 his group was betrayed and on 3 March 1943 he was arrested at his home by the Gestapo, in front of his 15-year-old daughter. He was imprisoned in Fresnes before being deported to Saarbrucken in Germany. He was sentenced to death by the 'people's court' there on 19 October 1943 and beheaded with an axe at Cologne prison on 7 December 1943.

A fencing club is named after him Compiègne.

Teizo Takeuchi (1908–46), Japanese, football, 1936 Berlin.

Teizo Takeuchi was born on 6 November 1908 in Tokyo. He began his footballing career in 1924 at the Fifth Junior High School, going on to represent Urawa Higher School and later the Tokyo Imperial University. Playing either fullback or halfback, he was part of the team that won the Kanto University League title over four consecutive years. In 1932 he graduated from the university's Faculty of Economics, and joined the Tokyo Fire Insurance Company. He was selected to represent Japan as part of their football team in the 1936 Berlin Olympics. He captained the team and they beat Sweden 3–2 in the first round. It was the first time Japan had won a football match in the Olympics. It became known as the 'Miracle in Berlin'. Unfortunately they were beaten 8–0 by Italy in the next round and knocked out of the competition. He was captured by Soviet troops in their campaign in China and sent to a PoW camp in Siberia. He died there on 12 April 1946. In 2006 he was elected to the Japan Football Hall of Fame.

Harald Tammer (1899–1942), Estonian, athlete and weightlifter, 1920 Antwerp, 1924 Paris (Bronze)

Harald Tammer was born on 9 January 1899 in Tallinn. Although better known as a weightlifter he was also a very decent athlete. He first came to notice in the Russian Championships in 1916, winning silver in the shot put and bronze in the discus and hammer throws. Between 1918 and 1926 Tammer won twenty-four Estonian track and field titles in the shot put, hammer throw and discus. He won the world heavyweight title in 1922. He took part in two Olympics: 1920 in Antwerp where he was Olympic flag bearer and competed in the shot put coming sixth, and 1924 in Paris where he competed in the shot put, coming twelfth. He did better in the men's heavyweight weightlifting event, coming third and taking the bronze medal. He was also the Estonian heavyweight champion three times between 1922 and 1924. In 1915 Tammer graduated from Tallinn Commerce School and joined the Sports Association Kaley. He later worked as a journalist, first on the Estonian sports newspaper and then as editor on the Estonian daily newspaper. He was also a member of the Estonian Olympic delegation attending both the 1928 and the 1936 Games. He joined the Estonian army and saw action in the First World War and the Estonian War of Independence, serving with the Estonian Defence League in Tallinn. Later he served in the Estonian Parliament. He was arrested by the NKVD and deported to Russia. He died or was murdered in a Gulag prison camp near Sukhobezvodnoye on 6 June 1942.

Mutsuo Taniguchi (1913–unknown), Japanese, sprint, 1936 Berlin.

Once again not very much seems to be known about this Olympian. Mutsuo Taniguchi was born on 5 May 1913 in Japan. He competed in the 1936 Berlin Olympics in the 200 metres and the 4 × 100 metres relay, failing to get a medal in either event, and was killed in action between 1940 and 1945.

Hans Tatzer (1905–44), Austrian, ice hockey, 1928 St Moritz, 1936 Garmisch-Partenkirchen.

Johann Robert Tatzer was born on 25 May 1905 in Vienna. He worked as a painter and later a postal worker. A fine all-round sportsman, he first played club hockey for the Lehrer

1937 World Championships he won the bronze medal in the slalom and the following year in 1938 was fifth in the downhill and sixth in the combination. He was killed in action on 2 February 1942 near Geilenkirchen in Germany.

Jan Wrzosek (1895–1939), Polish, sports shooting, 1936 Berlin.

Jan Wrzosek was born on 6 March 1895 in Stavropol, Russia. He competed in the small-bore rifle, prone, 50 metres event in the 1936 Berlin Olympics. He failed to win a medal. He was killed in action in the first week of the war on 3 September 1939 in the campaign in Zloty Potok.

Mikhail Yakovlev (1893–1942), Russian, football, 1912 Stockholm.

Mikhail Vasilyevich Yakovlev was born on 12 July 1893 in St Petersburg. He played for Unitas, St. Petersburg FC and was selected to play for Russia in the 1912 Olympic Games in Stockholm. He made his debut on 1 July 1912 against Germany, when Russia was defeated 16–0 and knocked out of the event. He was killed in action in 1942 in the defence of St Petersburg.

Kiichi Yoshida (1919–44), Japanese, swimming, 1936 Berlin.

Kiichi Yoshida was born on 6 March 1919. Specialising in the backstroke, he formed part of the Japanese swimming team in the 1936 Berlin Olympics. In the men's 100 metres backstroke he came fifth. It is believed he was killed in action sometime in 1944.

Janusz Zalewski (1903–44), Polish, sailing, 1936 Berlin.

Janusz Zalewski was born on 15 August 1903 in Zawiecie. In the 1936 Berlin Olympics he competed in the mixed six-metre event in the yacht *Danuta*. He took eleventh place. As a member of the Polish Free Army he participated in the Warsaw Uprising, serving with the Kedyw branch of 'Kolegium A'. Wounded, he was evacuated to the hospital at Wola. He was murdered there by the SS, together with all the patients, doctors and nurses, on 6 August 1944. The massacre had been ordered by Hitler to discourage the Uprising.

Johann 'Hans' Zehetner (1912–42), Austrian, field handball, 1936 Berlin (Silver).

Johann Zehetner was born on 4 September 1912 in Vienna. He played for Ferrowatt, Wein. He was chosen to compete in the 1936 Berlin Olympics. Competing in the handball competition they took the silver medal, being beaten by Germany 10–6 for the gold. Zehetner played in two of the matches. He was killed in action on the Russian front on 29 December 1942.

Stanisław Ziffer (1904–unknown), Polish, running, 1924 Paris.

Stanisław Ziffer was born on 1 August 1904 in Krakow. He was selected to represent Poland in the 1924 Paris Olympics, competing in the 5,000 metres coming fourteenth, the 3,000 metres steeplechase coming fifth, and the 3,000 metres, team, who were eliminated in the heats. His date of death is unknown, but it is believed it was sometime in the September Campaign in the early part of the war.

Branko Ziherl (1916–42), Yugoslavia, diving, 1936 Berlin.

Branko Ziherl was born on 9 September 1916 in Ljubljana. He represented Yugoslavia in the diving competition in the 1936 Berlin Olympics. He came tenth in the men's springboard and twentieth in the men's platform. He was killed in action in Kocevski Rog, Slovenia, in August 1942.

Mario Zorzi (1910–44), Italian, shooting, 1932 Los Angeles, 1936 Berlin.

Mario Zorzi was born on 23 July 1910 in Mattarello. He took part in two Olympic Games. In 1932 in Los Angeles he shot in the small-bore rifle, prone, 50 metres, just missing out on a medal and coming fourth, and in 1936 in Berlin he came joint eighth. He was killed in an Allied bombing raid in Frascati near Rome on 17 February 1944.

Feliks Żuber (1905–40), Polish, sprint, 1928 Amsterdam.

Feliks Żuber was born on 10 October 1905 in Warsaw. Already a well-established sprinter, he competed in the 400 metres in the 1928 Amsterdam Olympics. He was knocked out in the heats and failed to reach the final. He was arrested by the SS in June 1940 and tortured before being murdered in the infamous Palmiry massacre on 21 June 1940. The Palmiry massacres were a series of mass murders executed by the Nazis near the village of Palmiry north-west of Warsaw between December 1939 and July 1941. Over one twenty-four hour period, between 20 and 21 June 1940, 358 members of the Polish political, cultural, and social elite were shot.

Jerzy Łucki (1898–1939), Polish, bobsleigh, 1928 St Moritz.

Jerzy Michał Łucki was born on 24 September 1898 in the Ukraine. He took part in the winter Olympics in St Moritz, competing in the men's four-man bobsleigh. They eventually finished seventeenth. Łucki was an officer in the Polish Legion. He won a bronze medal in the Polish Championship, competing in the shot put twice, once in 1923 and again in 1927. He also won a bronze in the hammer throw in 1923. On 18 September 1939, serving as a major and commanding the 21st Armoured Battalion of light tanks, he was killed evacuating his unit over the border into Romania. For his gallantry and heroism he was awarded the Cross of Independence.

Appendix

Olympic Games Venues 1900–36

SUMMER

PARIS 1900

The 1900 Paris Olympics were officially known as the Games of the II Olympiad. There were no opening or closing ceremonies. Competitions began on 14 May and ended on 28 October. The Games were held as part of the 1900 World's Fair, with 997 competitors participating in 19 different sports. Women took part in the Olympics for the first time and Helène de Pourtales became their first champion in the sailing. She crewed on the Swiss boat *Lérina*, winning the gold medal in the first race of the 2–3 ton class and silver in the second. Most of the winners in 1900 did not receive medals but were given cups or trophies, and in one case 3,000 francs. This was also the only Olympic Games to use live animals, when pigeons were used as targets in the shooting competition. Motorcycle racing, underwater swimming, ballooning, cricket, croquet and Basque pelota were included in the Paris Olympics, but were all removed from later Olympics.

ST LOUIS 1904

The 1904 Olympics, known as the Games of the III Olympiad, took place in St Louis, Missouri. Officially they lasted for four and a half months, again as part of the World's Fair, but in reality they began on 29 August and finished on 3 September. It was the first time that the Olympic Games had been held outside Europe. Of the 651 competitors who took part, only 62 were from outside the USA or Canada and only twelve (some records say fifteen) countries were represented. This was mainly due to a fear of travelling because of the Russo-Japanese War. For the first time, Olympic medals were issued, Gold, Silver and Bronze. Boxing, dumb-bells, freestyle wrestling and the decathlon were introduced to the games for the first time.

One of the most interesting competitors at the 1904 Games was George Eyser, an American gymnast who won six medals despite having a wooden leg. Frank Kugler, the German Olympian, won four medals in the freestyle wrestling, weightlifting and tug of war, making him the only Olympian to win a medal in three different sports at the same Olympic Games.

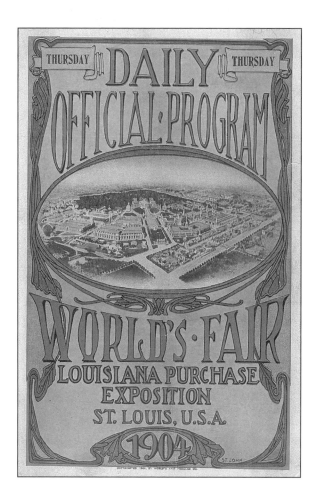

Appendix

ATHENS 1906

There was one Olympic Games outside the usual four-year cycle, Athens in 1906. They were called the Intercalated Games. They were at the time considered to be 'Olympic Games' and were referred to as the 'Second International Olympic Games in Athens' by the international committee. It is strange then that the medals awarded at these games are not officially recognized by the Olympic Committee and are not displayed with the collection of Olympic medals at the Olympic Museum in Lausanne.

LONDON 1908

The 1908 Olympics in London were known as the Games of the IV Olympiad and took place between 27 April and 31 October. They were originally intended to be played in Rome, but due to the eruption of Mount Vesuvius the Italian government was no longer able to afford them. London was chosen to replace Rome and the games took place at the White City Stadium.

The distance for the marathon was decided at these games: 25 miles was altered to 26 so that it could start at Windsor Castle, and then at the request of Queen Mary it was changed again so it would begin beneath the windows of the Royal Nursery; the finish was also changed so that the race would finish in front of the King. The result was a distance of 26 miles and 385 yards, which became the standard from then on.

The 1908 Olympics also saw for the first time the establishment of standard rules for Olympic sports, and judges from different countries were selected rather than just from the host country, making things, it was hoped, fairer.

The most famous incident of the games involved the Italian marathon runner Dorando Pietri, who collapsed only yards from the tape from exhaustion and dehydration; a film of this can still be seen. With the help of some officials, he crossed the line first and took the gold. The American contingent however complained, and he was disqualified. Queen Alexandra took up his cause and presented him with a gilded silver cup the next day to make up for his disappointment.

These games were the first to include winter events; figure skating was included (although the event was held months later). The Swedish Olympian Oscar Swahn became the oldest competitor, at the age of 72 years and 279 days; he took part in the deer shooting. A most unusual sport was duelling, where competitors in protective clothing shot wax bullets at each other. John Taylor became the first African American to win an Olympic gold medal when he was part of the winning medley relay team.

STOCKHOLM 1912

The 1912 Olympics, officially known as the Games of the V Olympiad, were held in Stockholm between 5 May and 22 July. Twenty-eight nations and 2,408 competitors, including 48 women, competed in 102 events in 14 sports. It was the first time that Japan, Egypt, Iceland, Portugal and Serbia took part, and the last time solid gold medals were issued. They were the games in which the decathlon and pentathlon were introduced, as well as the art competition, and women's swimming and diving. Both figure skating and boxing were excluded by the host country. The United States won the most gold medals with twenty-five, and Sweden the most medals with sixty-five. Great Britain won ten golds and forty-one medals overall.

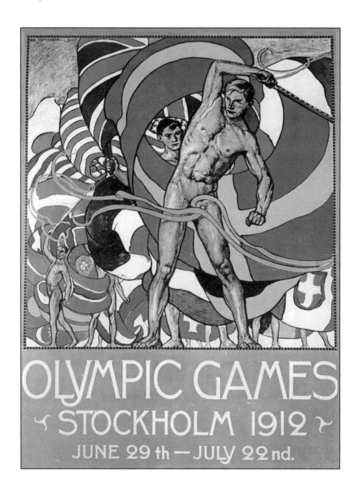

ANTWERP 1920

The 1920 Olympics, officially known as the Games of the VII Olympiad, were held in Antwerp; 336 competitors took part, 326 men and 10 women. They competed in 121 events in 23 sports. It was at these games that the Olympic Oath was read for the first time, doves were released as a symbol of peace, and the Olympic flag was flown for the first time. Ice hockey appeared in the Olympics, and Brazil competed for the first time, winning a gold medal in the shooting event. The USA won 41 gold, 27 silver, and 27 bronze medals, the most won by any of the 29 nations attending.

PARIS 1924

The 1924 Olympics, officially known as the Games of the VIII Olympiad, were held in Paris. Paris had hosted the games once before, in 1900. They took place between 4 May and 27 July. 401 competitors (373 men and 28 women) took part in 128 events in 20 sports. British runners Harold Abrahams and Eric Liddell won the 100 metres and 400 metres respectively. Their stories are depicted in the 1981 movie *Chariots of Fire* (a film that had a profound influence on my life!). The marathon distance was fixed at 26.219 miles, slightly different to the 1908 Games. A standard 50 metre pool was used, with marked lanes. The film star Johnny Weissmuller, famous for portraying Tarzan, won three gold swimming medals and a bronze in the water polo. The Olympic motto, *Citius Altius Fortius*, Faster, Higher, Stronger, was used for the first time. It was borrowed from a speech made by a Dominican priest, Father Henri Didon, to a Paris youth gathering in 1891. Ireland made its first appearance in an Olympic Games as an independent nation. It was also the first games at which the idea of an Olympic village to house the competitors was conceived.

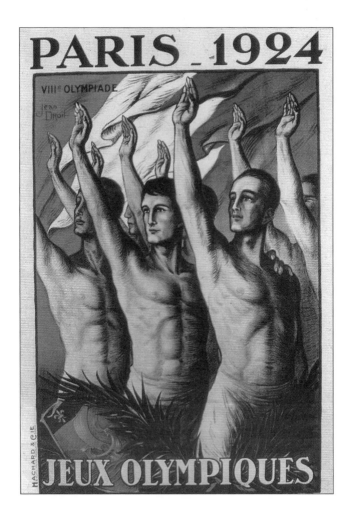

AMSTERDAM 1928

The 1928 Summer Olympics, officially known as the Games of the IX Olympiad, took place between 28 July and 12 August 1928 in Amsterdam. Approximately 3,000 athletes, including around 300 women, representing 46 countries, took part. It was the first time the games were called the 'summer' games to distinguish them from the 'winter' games. It was at these games that the Olympic Flame was lit for the first time; it lasted for the duration of the Olympics, a tradition that continues to this day (the torch relay, however, would not take place until the 1936 Games). The Parade of Nations tradition also began at these games, led for the first time by Greece. For the first time the games were held over sixteen days. Before, it had been somewhat *ad hoc*, with some lasting months. Johnny Weissmuller won two more gold medals, the 100 metres freestyle and the team 4 × 200 metres freestyle relay. India won its first gold medal, in hockey; they were to go on to win five more in consecutive games. Thousands of cars were expected in the city and Amsterdam only had parking for 2,000. To overcome this problem the now famous white P on a blue background parking sign was designed. Coca-Cola made its first appearance in this Olympic Games as a sponsor. Crown Prince Olav, later King of Norway, won a gold medal in the 6-metre sailing event. The newly independent Ireland won its first gold medal when Pat O'Callaghan won the hammer throw. Germany returned to the Olympics, having been banned from the 1920 and 1924 Games because of the war. They finished second in the medal count.

Appendix

LOS ANGELES 1932

The 1932 Olympics, known as the Games of the X Olympiad, were held between 30 July and 14 August in Los Angeles. Because of the worldwide depression several countries were unable to attend. In the end 37 nations competed (46 had attended at the 1928 Games). 1,332 (1,206 men 126 woman) athletes competed in 117 events, in 14 sports (20 disciplines). Oddly, the then president, Herbert Hoover, failed to attend. During these games the victory podium was used for the first time. The female Polish athlete Stanisława Walasiewicz won the gold medal in the women's 100 metres. Four years later she won the silver in the same event. After her death in 1980 it was discovered that she was in fact intersex and would have been ineligible to participate. The Olympic village was built for the first time, but only for the men. The women were booked into the Chapman Park Hotel on Wilshire Boulevard. Kusuo Kitamura, the Japanese swimmer who won the gold medal in the men's 1,500 metres freestyle, was only 14 years 309 days old. He is still the youngest male ever to win an individual gold medal at an Olympic Games. Both American football and lacrosse were demonstrated at these games.

BERLIN 1936

The 1936 Olympics, known as the Games of the XI Olympiad, were held between 1 and 16 August in Berlin. Altogether 3,963 (3,632 men and 331 women) took part in 129 events in 19 sports (25 disciplines). Hitler opened the games. A 100,000 seat stadium had been built specially for them. The games were the first to be televised and broadcast on radio – to forty-one countries. Leni Riefenstahl was commissioned to film the games. The film was named *Olympia*. Hitler used the games to promote his ideas of racial supremacy and anti-Semitism. German Jews were banned or prevented from taking part. Other countries declined to send Jewish athletes to the games for fear of offending Hitler. However under the threat of a boycott Hitler and the Nazis relented up to a point. They eventually allowed black people and Jewish people to participate and added one token participant to the German team – Helene Mayer, who had a Jewish father. They also removed all the anti-Semitic signs and orders from Berlin. As if to cock a snook at Hitler, the American black athlete Jesse Owens took four gold medals in the sprint and long jump. Germany won the most medals however, with 89, the USA coming second with 56. Due to the war these were the last Olympic Games until 1948. The 1936 Games were the first at which the Olympic torch relay was introduced, the idea being to bring the flame from Greece to the Olympic venue. It featured prominently in the film *Olympia*. Five nations made their debut at these games: Afghanistan, Bermuda, Bolivia, Costa Rica and Liechtenstein.

WINTER

CHAMONIX 1924

The 1924 Winter Olympics, known as the I Olympic Winter Games, were held between 25 January and 5 February in Chamonix, Haute-Savoie, France. It was originally called the 'International Winter Sports Week', but this was later changed to the Winter Olympics. They were held in conjunction with the summer Olympics until 1992, after which they happened two years after the summer Olympics. 258 competitors took part in 16 events, over 5 sports and 9 disciplines. The events included bobsleigh, curling, ice hockey, skating, figure skating, speed skating, Nordic skating, military patrol, cross-country skiing, Nordic combined and ski jumping.

ST MORITZ 1928

The 1928 Winter Olympics, officially known as the II Olympic Winter Games, took place in St Moritz, Switzerland, between 11 and 19 February. They were the first true Winter Olympics, held on their own and not in conjunction with the Summer Olympics. They also replaced the Nordic Games.

LAKE PLACID 1932

The 1932 Winter Olympics, officially known as the III Olympic Winter Games, took place in Lake Placid, New York, USA, between 4 and 15 February. Seventeen nations took part, involving 252 athletes (231 men and 21 women), in 14 events in 4 sports over 7 disciplines. The games were opened by Franklin D. Roosevelt. Eddie Eagan became the only Olympian to win gold medals at both the summer and winter games in different sports. He won gold in boxing in Antwerp at the summer Olympics in 1920 and gold in bobsleigh at Lake Placid.

GARMISCH-PARTENKIRCHEN 1936

The 1936 Winter Olympics, known as the IV Olympic Winter Games, took place in Garmisch-Partenkirchen in Bavaria between 6 and 16 February. 646 athletes took part (566 men and 80 women) from 28 countries, in 17 events in 4 sports over 8 disciplines. Adolf Hitler opened the games. The 1936 Games were the last year in which the summer and winter Olympics were held in the same year. Alpine skiing made its first appearance as a combined event for men and women with both downhill and slalom races. Norway won fifteen medals, Germany six and Sweden seven.

Bibliography

Primary Sources

Cook, Theodore Andrea (editor), *The Fourth Olympiad London 1908: Official Report* (London: The British Olympic Association, 1909).

Die Olympischen Spiele in Amsterdam 1928 (Leipzig: German Reich Committee for Physical Exercise, 1928).

Die Olympischen Spiele 1936 in Berlin und Garmisch-Partenkirchen (Altona-Bahrenfeld: Cigaretten-Bilderdienst, 1936).

Olympia 1932 – Die Olympischen Spiele in Los Angeles 1932 (Berlin, Reemtsma Cigarettenfabriken, 1932).

Olympic Games Berlin 1936, Official Daily Programme – various.

The Sphere – An Illustrated Newspaper for the Home

Webster, F.A.M., *British Olympic Association Official Report of the Xth Olympiad Los Angeles 1932* (London, The British Olympic Association, 1932).

Secondary Sources

Ammann, Max E., *Equestrian Sport at the Olympic Games 1912–2008* (Lausanne: FEI, 2012).

Bachrach, Susan D., *The Nazi Olympics: Berlin 1936* (Boston, Little, Brown and Company, 2000).

Baker, Keith, *The 1908 Olympics: The First London Games* (York: SportsBooks, 2008).

Jenkins, Rebecca, *The First London Olympics 1908: The definitive story of London's most sensational Olympics to date* (London: Piatkus, 2012).

Mallon, Bill and Bijkerk, Anthony Th, *The 1920 Olympic Games: Results for All Competitors in All Events, with Commentary* (Jefferson: McFarland & Co, 2009).

Mallon, Bill and Heijmans, Jeroen, *Historical Dictionary of the Olympic Movement* (Washington DC: Scarecrow Press, 2011).

Mallon, Bill and Widlund, Ture, *The 1912 Olympic Games: Results for All Competitors in All Events, with Commentary* (Jefferson: McFarland & Co, 2009).

Paul, Robert and Orr, Jack, *The Olympic Games: The Thrills and Drama From Ancient Greece to the Present Day* (New York: The Lion Press, 1968).

Phillips, Ellen, *VIII Olympiad: Paris 1942, St. Mortiz 1928* (Ontario: Firefly Books, 1996).

Timmers, Margaret, *A Century of Olympic Posters* (London: V&A Publishing, 2012).